THE
CULTURE
CULT

THE CULTURE CULT

Designer Tribalism and Other Essays

ROGER SANDALL

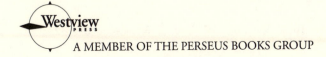

Westview
PRESS

A MEMBER OF THE PERSEUS BOOKS GROUP

Copyright © 2001 by Roger Sandall

A CIP catalog record for this book is available from the Library of Congress.
ISBN 0-8133-3863-8

Published in 2001 in the United States of America by Westview Press,
5500 Central Avenue, Boulder, Colorado 80301–2877,
and in the United Kingdom by Westview Press, 12 Hid's Copse Road,
Cumnor Hill, Oxford OX2 9JJ

Find us on the World Wide Web at www.westviewpress.com

10   9   8   7   6   5   4   3   2

Contents

Introduction

Romantic primitivism has two faces, and its romantic face is by far the prettier. This is the one that gave the world a whole collection of colorful and eccentric Englishmen who liked to dress up as Arabs, jump onto camels, and ride about over the sands of the Middle East. What the camels made of it is anyone's guess—but it was harmless stuff on the whole, and Lawrence of Arabia was only the most famous of his countrymen to enjoy the masquerade.

The primitivist face is more problematic. Not long ago, in 1996, actress and ex-model Lauren Hutton ventured into tourist-anthropology among the Masai in Africa. Taking her two little boys along with her, she visited a witch doctor, tasted his potions, saw a cow slaughtered, and watched red-robed Masai warriors drinking blood from the carcass—the whole episode accompanied by maternal yelps of "wow!"

But there weren't many wows from her boys. In fact they barely cracked a smile, and one of them burst into tears. Watching their reactions it was impossible not to think of the Hans Andersen tale about the emperor who had no clothes. Both of the Hutton children clearly wanted to tell their gushy mum that no matter how hard they looked at those warriors, and no matter how much she enthused about the wonders of Africa, Masai culture "had no clothes"—in other words, it didn't match the romantic idealization she seemed to have fixed in her mind. Despite lots of prompting, they were still not convinced that the life of the Masai was better than the life they knew, or that hot blood straight from the beast tasted better than Coke.

But that was the lesson Ms. Hutton wanted her children to learn. That was the enlightenment their African visit was meant to achieve. The missionary purpose of this Turner Productions show was to convert its audience to the view that Masai culture is just as good as Western civilization, if not better. On top of this, the Culture Cult goes still further. It claims that primitive cultures have a uniqueness which should be seen as sacred, and that to assimilate them to modern ways would be a crime. Indeed, today, for many people of religous temperament, the salvation of primitive cultures has replaced the salvation of souls. There are a number of problems with this new philosophy however.

- The Culture Cult holds that primitive culture is not inferior to modern civilization—just different. All cultures therefore exist on a level plain. But there's a Big Ditch right in the middle of this plain which separates the tribal world from modernity, and attempts to deny its existence can only end in tears. There are political differences between tribalism and Civil Society; there are economic differences between communalism and the way we live now; and there are cognitive differences in the way we think about cause and effect. To pretend that these differences can be "reconciled" merely with enough goodwill is futile. They are not reconcilable, and they are not going to go away.
- The Culture Cult calls for a radical simplification of modern life. It yearns for romantic simplicity, and while going back to the Pleistocene might perhaps be thought extreme, communalism is seen as a practical goal. But there have been thousands of communes, and one way or another they all reinvented the wheel. The complexities they too rashly rejected proved indispensable after all. At the deepest level life itself is about ever-extending complexity, and it is time to stop dreaming about going back to the land or revisiting the social arrangements of the past. They aren't options, and they probably never were.
- Culture cultists take a sour view of modernity—when they can bring themselves to think about it at all. They forget that modern civilization (aka Civil Society) allows changes of government without bloodshed, civil rights, economic benefits, religious toleration, and political and artistic freedom. The alternatives to Civil Society do not. Most traditional cultures feature domestic repression, economic backwardness, endemic

disease, religious fanaticism, and severe artistic constraints. If you want to live a full life and die in your bed, then civilization—not romantic ethnicity—deserves your thoughtful vote.

Romantic primitivism—the idealizing of social simplicity and the world of the "noble savage"—has been around for a long time. You can find it in classical Greece 2,500 years ago: the Cynics and the Stoics are examples. And no doubt you could find it earlier, too. Chances are, even in Nineveh, soon after the invention of the wheel, loud calls were heard for reinstating the holy pedestrianism of the past. In the words of two scholars who looked closely at the subject from its first appearance in classical times, primitivism represents "the unending revolt of the civilized against civilization."[1]

This revolt has one invariable feature. As Jean-Jacques Rousseau himself dramatically demonstrated, those most excited by the idea of "noble savagery" have had no experience at all of true dirt-and-diseases tribal life. What inspires them is an *idée fixe* in the mind. That was pretty clear when Lauren Hutton fronted up to the Masai. Though not all Culture Cultists are as loud in their eager cries of Gee and Wow, the noisiest and most excitable are always media folk or imaginative writers or campus intellectuals who haven't a clue what they're getting into. Romantic primitivism consists of fantasies inside the heads of urban dwellers—delusions of a morally superior, Edenic world beyond the horizon—which are then projected onto primitive peoples themselves.[2]

Against the prevailing trend this book regards everything associated with the Culture Cult as bad news. Part I (and chapter one, in particular) argues that romanticizing the primitive leads to major misunderstandings about tribal minorities—misunderstandings which damage their prospects in the modern world. Chapter two looks at the history of communes. Chapters three and four are about Rousseau on the one hand, and bohemia on the other, and describe the corrupting effect both have had on anthropology.

Part II discusses the contributions of three influential thinkers of our time—Karl Polanyi, Isaiah Berlin, and Karl Popper. Polanyi's obsessive search for an ideal precapitalist culture led him to idealize the bloodstained West African kingdom of Dahomey. Sir Isaiah Berlin, a Latvian immigrant to Britain who had a prestigious academic career, did much to promote the ideals of continental romanticism. Karl

Popper, on the other hand, was very different; his attitude toward the romanticism of the Culture Cult was the opposite of Berlin's. What both he and Ernest Gellner see as a "Big Ditch" separated the "closed societies" of tribalism from the "open societies" of the modern world, and defending the Open Society was the main duty of thinking men and women.

Part III expands the discussion to treat wider issues. Chapter eight considers the factors making for cultural success or failure—matters important at a time when huge cash payments are being made to countries which, in many cases, are institutionally incapable of being helped. Chapter nine examines the history of the terms "culture" and "civilization," and their varied use by Matthew Arnold, T. S. Eliot, and Raymond Williams.

The romantic primitivism of the Culture Cult did not originate among tribal people themselves. Nor is it found among the poor. It is a Western sentimentalism fashionable among spoiled, white, discontented urbanites. But tribal people can easily get caught up in the fantasizing of their media admirers and academic friends, and some of the unhappy results of this are the subject of chapter one, "The New Stone Age."

PART I

ROMANTIC PRIMITIVISM

The Anthropological Connection

1

The New Stone Age

Should American Indians and New Zealand Maoris and Australian Aborigines be urged to preserve their traditional cultures at all cost? Should they be told that assimilation is wrong? And is it wise to leave them entirely to their own devices? Cases vary, but the Australian example suggests that the answers are no, no, and no. The best chance of a good life for indigenes is the same as for you and me: full fluency and literacy in English, as much math as we can handle, and a job. In the year 2000 artificially petrified indigenes are doomed.

Since the folly of locking up native peoples in their old-time cultures is obvious, but it is tasteless to say so, governments have everywhere resorted to the rhetoric of "reconciliation." This pretends that the problem is psychological and moral: rejig the public mind, ask leading political figures to adopt a contrite demeanor and apologize for the sins of history, and all will be well. Underlying this is the assumption that we are all on the same level plain of social development, divided only by misunderstanding.

This is false. The division is deep—there is a Big Ditch between the tribal world and modernity. Until around 1970 governments in the United States, Canada, Australia, and New Zealand accepted this fact, and they saw their duty as helping indigenes to cross the divide. For that reason they concentrated on better health, education, and housing, and let the chips of traditional culture fall where they may. That was how Western civilization had dealt with its own traditions, creatively destroying those that would not change. Creative destruction is the law of historical advance.

But romantic primitivism swept all such progressive policies away. Planning for the future and looking forward was out. Looking backward became the only proper way to look. Transfixed by the Culture Cult, a hyperidealized vision of traditional life was adopted, and the effect on indigenes of romanticizing their past has been devastating.

On the one hand Australian Aborigines found themselves being used as pawns in political games played for high stakes. On the other hand they became the deluded victims of the extravagances of their admirers. If your traditional way of life has no alphabet, no writing, no books, and no libraries, and yet you are continually told that you have a culture which is "rich," "complex," and "sophisticated," how can you realistically see your place in the scheme of things? If all such hyperbole were true, who would need books or writing? Why not hang up a "Gone Fishing" sign and head for the beach? I might do that myself. In Australia, policies inspired by the Culture Cult have brought the illiterization of thousands of Aborigines whose grandparents could read and write.

The New Age Meets the Aborigines

On the desk before me there's an advertisement for an Easter Psychic New Age Festival dedicated to Alternative Schools, Yoga, and Meditation Groups. One hour from Melbourne in an attractive pastoral setting with "heritage accommodation" and vegetarian meals there will be daily fortune readings, workshops, demonstrations, tastings, healing, health products, crystals, spirit drawing, Reiki, natural skincare, and not only numerous stallholders selling the work of artisans but "pundits with the latest New Age skills."

We are also invited to "Experience the Spirit of India" and be escorted on spiritual journeys, to come and see an exhibit of the "Crystals of the World," and to consult Wendy L. Smith, an astrologer with a mobile phone. Does Wendy offer the latest New Age skills? Or does she offer some of the oldest Stone Age beliefs with a digital upgrade? Neither astrology nor spiritual journeys is exactly new.

But that's how things are today. And lots of Native Americans and Australian Aborigines inhabit this modish environment, too. Seamlessly blending into the Stone Age have come New Age beliefs—beliefs which have influenced both American Indian and Aboriginal self-understanding. The result is a synthetic New Stone Age involving bits and pieces from many times and places. And the strange response to all this is one of the more surprising things about *Mutant Message Down Under*, a book by a Kansas City naturopath, Marlo Morgan.

Plainly a work of imaginative fiction, Morgan's narrative tells about her experiences with a group of Aborigines known as the Real People, a tribe created by the loving power of Divine Oneness; how she accompanies the Real People on a "walkabout" across Australia; how the Aborigines refer to all whites as Mutants because they have betrayed the ancient simplicities of True Humanity and introduced poverty, slavery, and disease; how the Real People communicate by telepathy and do not know how to lie; how they practice healing by using lizard and plant oils and by admonishing unruly organs to behave; how after 50,000 years they have destroyed no forests, polluted no water, and endangered no species; how the world is divided into Peaceful Browns and Aggressive Mutant Whites and how the Real People, having had more than enough of the latter, are planning to leave Planet Earth and seek a better world elsewhere.

Standing inside a crystal room as exotic as anything in Coleridge's vision of Xanadu—crystals are very important—and wearing a polished opal on her brow, Morgan learns the ancient Aboriginal art of evanescence, or disappearing into thin air . . . That should be enough to give the flavor of a book in which the lavish use of "incredible" and "amazing" is entirely appropriate.

The anthropologist L. R. Hiatt wrote that nothing remotely like Marlo Morgan's account of Aboriginal life "is to be found anywhere in the reputable literature published since the establishment of the British colony in 1788. If the Real People really exist, they are recent arrivals from outer space pretending to be Aborigines and, for whatever purpose, using Marlo Morgan as their agent. If she really traversed the Australian continent on foot without shoes at an average of twenty miles a day in mid-summer, she may even be one of them."[1] American readers in particular seem to have been delighted to find "the central values and aspirations of the New Age movement enshrined in the world's oldest surviving culture."[2]

But as Hiatt suggests, the Australian response to the book was revealing. Not long after its release an Aboriginal cultural organization tried to get it withdrawn from sale, and the national representative body for Aborigines sent representatives to America to stop any attempt to make a film. Since it consists of the sort of hokum Hollywood would love to get its hands on, that is hardly surprising. But Morgan's absurdities were the last thing Aborigines were worried about. It was not that what she wrote was false (many of them agreed that this was so). What was offensive was that the author had told her story as if she were a fully initiated and paid-up member of the tribe, and was disclosing its secrets to the world at large. About the anthropological untruths in the book they were silent—indeed, they may have rather liked the idea that their ancestors were vegetarian mystics.

You could search a long time before finding anything to equal *Mutant Message*. Literature it is not. But perhaps we should be grateful to Morgan nonetheless, for her book clarified a number of things. It showed how sadly ignorant of their own traditions many Aborigines are today. It showed their willingness to acquiesce in even the grossest mispresentations, providing the aim is to ennoble and glamorize the past. And it showed what their priorities are. In her naïve fashion Morgan pointed to the Big Ditch separating the modern and the tribal worlds.

The Aborigines' objection underlined the point that traditional societies are meant to be *closed* not *open*, *solidary* not *pluralistic*, *aristocratic* not *egalitarian*. For such people the disclosure of secrets is a much worse sin than telling lies. One Aborigine said that for the crime of disclosure, and whether or not what she wrote was true or false or the Real People even existed, Marlo Morgan of Kansas City should be put to death.

Sacralization in California

About eighty years ago an American Indian named Maria Solares told a story to anthropologist John Harrington. She said that Point Conception was once the departure point for the souls of Chumash Indians. Solares herself was a Christian who died in 1923, and the last Indians who might have taken her story about Indian souls seriously had all died long before that. Other Indians denied her version—and there were lots of versions.

But in 1978 her tale took on new significance. Ranchers in the area felt threatened by a plan to build a liquid natural gas plant nearby. They got a public relations firm from Los Angeles to help fight the proposal, and local Indians and environmental groups in the Santa Barbara area joined the cause. Before long the *Santa Barbara News*

Press was able to tell its readers that if the gas plant went ahead, Chumash archaeological sites would be ruined. Protests and demonstrations began and continued. Media reporters said that while the name Point Conception was fine, the old Indian name of the Western Gate made better sound bites on the news, and soon a whole transcontinental complex of exit gates was discovered with souls passing through them en route to the hereafter.

The laws of demand and supply brought into play by the ranchers proved highly creative—and also stimulated the Indians themselves. Most of them knew nothing of their old-time culture, but with the "discovery" of the importance of Point Conception they began to feel they should, and without even knowing what they'd lost they wanted it back. To help them get it came scores of regional scholars, eco-activists, New Age zealots, and free-range political demonstrators hungry for a fight. Most of them had no ethnic credentials whatever. As the American Indian writer Rayna Green remarked, the seemingly fathomless hunger for Indian guruism creates wanna-bes who may be neither genetically nor culturally Indian yet are the most marketable bearers of Indian culture. Through such "substitute impersonation," she said, "Indians . . . are loved to death."[3]

Authors Brian D. Haley and Larry Wilcoxon note the influence of New Age beliefs at Point Conception, and while the results are less fantastical than in Marlo Morgan's epic the motive is much the same. Both American Indians and counterculturalists have used "popular primitivist imagery and fragments of ethnography to create traditions that are very different in form and content from past beliefs and practices . . . either to appropriate beliefs and practices for a New Age . . . or to become Indian Traditionalists themselves." Despite the fact that "the New Age has negative connotations for many Native Americans, [Chumash] Indian Traditionalists and the eclectic New Agers share a conviction of the centrality of nature which is expressly primitivist and countercultural, and there is much syncretic 'mixing and matching' between them."[4]

Beginning around 1978, and for the next two decades, anthropologists helped to spread the Point-Conception-as-Western-Gate story either by silencing their doubts or by repeating the story in their writings. Once it was a public issue, those with reservations about the embroidery and sheer invention they had observed fell silent. Eventually the natural gas installation was canceled.

Why Worry? The Academic View

But why worry about romantic cultural inventions, or muddling New Age fantasies with ethnographic facts? We are expected to all know by now that life is a narrative; words mean only what you want them to mean; embellishment has been with us since the first fisherman told tall tales about his catch; and one man's misinterpretation is another man's liberating myth. Postmodernism calls this wisdom—and who are we to object?

For more than twenty years anthropologists have written about constructing reality as if the world and everything in it were mere artifact, about building identity as if any old self-glamorizing fiction will do, about creating the past as an enterprise more exciting than history, about inventing tradition as if traditions were as changeable as store windows—and about as important, too.

The late Roger Keesing tells us that although fictionalized pasts may be false "their symbolic power and political force are undeniable." And it doesn't matter whether the pasts being recreated are mythical or real as long as they symbolize *resistance* and *revolution*. "Perhaps it matters only whether such political ideologies are used for just causes, whether they are instruments of liberation or of oppression." Here Keesing is saying that the end justifies the means: however false, newly concocted tribal myths are justified so long as the cause is just. Myths of struggle are especially exciting:

> In Australia, idealized representations of the pre-European past are used to proclaim Aboriginal identity and the attachment of indigenous peoples to the land, and are being deployed in environmentalist as well as Aboriginal political struggles. In New Zealand, increasingly powerful and successful Maori political movements incorporate idealized and mythicized versions of a precolonial Golden Age, the mystical wisdom of Aotearoa.[5]

Much the same thing is going on in Hawaii and New Caledonia, wrote the author in 1989, where "the desperate struggle for political power and freedom from colonial oppression" continues night and day.[6] For Keesing, something called liberation was always just over the hill or around the corner, while the unmasking or demystifying of colonial discourse preoccupied his lively mind to the end. Nevertheless, some of what he said was useful because he candidly recognized the romanticism involved. "Maori and Aboriginal Australian ideologues are engaged in reconstructing ancestral pasts characterized by Mystical Wisdom, Oneness with the Land, Ecological Reverence, and Social Harmony," he noted, going on to describe the way "warfare and violence (including Maori cannibalism) are carefully edited out of these reinvented pasts." Warfare and cannibalism were found everywhere in New Zealand, but they clash uncomfortably with the "idealization of the primitive" required among the Maori today.[7]

What Keesing was talking about is a key aspect of romantic primitivism—the moral transfiguration of the tribal world. This projects a benignly Disneyfied way of life, all flowers and contentment, all stress-free smiles and communal harmony. Not surprisingly the tales of Mystical Wisdom and Ecological Reverence described above are eagerly adopted by modern indigenes seeking a more tasteful view of their own past. Keesing was aware of this, and he complained that romantic primitivism recklessly deleted "not simply violence, but domination (of women, the young, commoners) and exploitation. The costs in physical pain and premature death of infectious diseases only crudely addressed by magical means are all too easily edited out as well—particularly nowadays, when the Primitive is assigned a mystical wisdom in matters of holistic health and healing as well as ecology."[8]

It's good to be reminded of the traditional cost in terms of cruelty, pain, and disease. But Keesing might also have paused to notice the huge financial costs his "liberating fictions" have imposed on modern citizens in modern states. When, as a result of imaginative lying, contending parties are hauled into courts of law, and the inevitable collision with reality occurs, millions of dollars are routinely squandered as judicial processes try to disentangle fact from fantasy—if not downright mendacity—while indigenes often find themselves swept up and exploited by powerful political forces beyond their control.

The Hindmarsh Island Affair

They weren't ranchers, and they didn't have dramatic views of the Pacific coast. But the residents of Hindmarsh Island were fond of their sleepy lagoon. They liked their distance from Adelaide, their isolation, their peace, and their water views. And the absence of a bridge joining this secluded refuge to the mainland was an added attraction.

Others however wanted development—two of them with land on the island in particular—and they very much wanted a bridge. Neither environmental law nor Aboriginal interests had been ignored in their proposal, and one inquiry after another had cleared the project. Archaeologists reported that although there had indeed been Aboriginal occupation by members of the Ngarrindjeri tribe long ago, there was nothing more—nothing sacred had happened there, nothing religious, nothing worth a fuss. So in April 1990 the state government authorized the bridge builders to proceed.

Now the challenge was clear. One of the bridge opponents owned "an impressive weekender on the island . . . a modern house that sits high on the bank atop lush lawns that sweep down to a private mooring. From the lawns the view to the south-west takes in a watery foreground and the ferry crossing."[9] The owner of this estate had connections and approached some politicians he knew. As news spread of a growing opposition movement other protestors arrived—among them a union organizer with an iron bar. Said the man with the sweeping lawns to the man with the iron bar, "Let's see if we can get some Aboriginals to help the cause."[10]

No sooner said than done. When asked if there were any sacred places an Aboriginal spokesman said, "not that I know of, but I'm sure if we look around we can find something."[11] This got a laugh. Anthropologists, too, were keen to do their bit. One of them deplored the absence of Aboriginal women's rites ("What a pity about the women's business—it would be nice if there was some women's business"), and soon after these encouraging words had been spread around events moved quickly. Within two weeks a tale was circulating about river mouths, estuarine waters, birth passages, and female fertility in general.

A local Aboriginal activist, Doreen Kartinyeri, now called her people together and laid down the law. To an audience composed of the surprised but credulous on the one hand, and the surprised but doubtful on the other, she claimed inside knowledge not heard of by anyone before. Next a letter was drafted to the federal government which said: "The Ngarrindjeri women are quite adamant about the building of the bridge at Goolwa. They do not want the bridge to be built as the site is incredibly sacred to the women, their culture and spiritual well-being." Further thought and consultation improved this statement to read as follows:

This area represents a crucial part of Ngarrindjeri cultural beliefs about the creation and constant renewal of life along the Lower Murray Lakes. . . . The most serious cultural heritage dilemma concerns the Goolwa channel and its vital cultural heritage significance as part of the Meeting of the Waters. The cultural traditions concerning this "site" and its relationship to the surrounding lakes are highly confidential and only their very general nature is documented in this report.[12]

Bridge construction was then banned by the federal government for twenty-five years.

But now the advantage of having a federal system in Australia became apparent. The national government in Canberra which banned the bridge was Labor. The state government of South Australia was not. Smelling a malodorous infestation of rats the State of South Australia now launched a Royal Commission to enquire into the whole matter, and at the end of it commissioner Iris Stevens reported that in her view "the whole of the 'women's business' was fabricated in order to convince (federal) Minister Robert Tickner to ban the bridge," that the women's rituals described by Doreen Kartinyeri were previously unknown, that the claim that Hindmarsh Island held crucial spiritual significance for the Aborigines was made up, and that some very nasty things had been going on. Right from the start of the commission's work there had been threats of violence—and even death threats—made against witnesses.[13]

Anthropologists had persuaded themselves that tradition was infinitely flexible, and that Kartinyeri's imaginative fabulizing was a worthy effort. The court was not convinced. For the late Roger Keesing and others, Kartinyeri's creative inventiveness should have been an act of liberation born of her struggle against "the hegemonic discourse of colonial oppression." But instead of liberating her people, it dragged many innocent Aborigines through the mud.

Irreconcilable Values:
Solidarity Versus Truth

Few of us would regard the death penalty for Marlo Morgan as warranted. Even if she did disclose something in *Mutant Message* in 1994, how could it deserve taking of life? But that's what you have to expect in "closed societies" of the kind Karl Popper described in his 1945 book *The Open Society and Its Enemies.* In closed societies knowledge tends to be surrounded by high walls and prohibitions, which confine it to elders, or priests, or chiefs, or kings, and these taboos are strictly enforced. Nor is that all. Knowledge itself in such a world is irreconcilable with both what we know and how we think today. And once more a Big Ditch divides the two.

Philosophers sometimes describe knowledge in modern society as *rationally justified true belief.* But in the definition of knowledge used by anthropologists rational justification is irrelevant. Belief of any kind is *culturally justified,* and that suffices. All that is needed is for enough people to believe that X is true, and X is true—even if X asserts that a cow jumped over the moon. What is called tribal "knowledge" usually reflects the needs of group solidarity more than anything else: as such it often represents *culturally justified false belief.*

Trying to get a grip on these matters Ernest Gellner wrote that the illogical role of solidarity in traditional cultures is far from accidental. It is natural enough, and makes sense in its way. One reason a supreme value is placed on solidarity derives from the advantages it offers in warrior societies ruled by force rather than by law, truth, and facts. This led Gellner to propose a universal principle: *Logical coherence and social solidarity are inversely related.* So the more solidarity you have, the less logic you get, and vice versa.[14]

Solidarity is a typical virtue from the world of the past which preceded Civil Society—medieval, Masai, Maori, whatever—where great military risks prevailed. It reflects the defensive psychology of human groups under threat. "All for one and one for all" is the ethic of the ambushed platoon, the encircled army, the besieged nation—of America in 1776, of Britain in 1940, of Russia in 1941. Solidarity of this kind may or may not have logical elements—it often has. But because victory is all-important, solidarity also favors the irrational ways human groups can be made to stick together, whatever lies must be told.

Logical coherence and consistency on the other hand is typical of modern society. It means valuing the way statements and facts rationally hang together, because logical coherence is what leads to truth. For modern societies based on science and on modern law this is essential. The consequence of logical coherence and social solidarity being "inversely related" is that in tribal life facts and truth often get shoved aside—something a specialist in Aboriginal culture has confirmed. Discussing a controversy over a sacred site in northern Australia Dr. Ian Keen tells us that inconsistency and contradiction is exactly what we should expect:

> I think that there is more tolerance in Aboriginal interaction of what white Australians regard as inconsistencies or contradictory statements. Concepts akin to "belief" in the languages of Aboriginal people . . . most closely imply *loyalty to a group* as much as holding a proposition in one's heart as true . . . or commitment to "objective" truth.[15]

Indeed they do. And that's what Gellner was driving at. Solidarity, or what Keen calls "loyalty to a group," outweighs truth. As for the obligatory lying that results from rating loyalty higher than truth, and presents irreconcilable conflicts at law, Keen appears to find no problem for our courts in this. To him there's no Big Ditch at all.

Rousseau in Arnhem Land

The scene is idyllic. A man is wading out into a tropical lagoon, sucking the stem of a water lily as he goes. One or two youngsters are with him and some women too. The sky is reflected in the still surface of the pool, and lilies with big green leaves float on the water. They may be looking for water snakes. No one speaks.

These Aborigines are timeless romantic symbols on a television screen, and if they are mute this is probably deliberate. Human voices might intrude on the pristine image of noble savagery the filmmaker is trying to convey. Anyone who has made documentaries will also notice something else—an unnatural aimlessness about their movements. If they were truly wading in the water, or genuinely gathering eggs or hunting water snakes, their actions would be much more definite. Instead they move with dreamy languor—the "dreamtime" languor of a spiritual people some might say.

But all this has nothing to do with spirituality. It's merely what happens when a film director asks a man to walk into a lagoon without giving him a reason for doing so. On television the whole scene above lasts barely half a minute, though if you added up all the hours it has been used as a picturesque background image by the state-owned television channel, the elapsed time might come to days or weeks. Repeatedly, when news about life on the horrifying outback settlements has been reported—news which in the form of live footage might be very disturbing in urban living rooms—these water lilies have appeared on the screen.

The place where the lily-pond Aborigines live is in the tropical north. Others live in country towns or the countryside nearby, while large numbers live in the cities to the south. It should be clearly understood that the more urbanized southern people have made good progress over the past thirty years. Aborigines have long been a presence in Australian sport—symbolized by the tennis achievements of Evonne Goolagong—and there are now star players in numerous football teams. The runner Cathy Freeman is only one of the many who have been highly successful in athletics. A dance company with a repertoire combining modern and traditional Aboriginal dance styles has been well received. And in each of these fields they have been warmly welcomed into the modern world by their fellow Australians, and won international recognition for their achievements. In other words, they have been successfully assimilated into modern life.

Not so the people who concern us here. These are the Aborigines on the northern settlements, the ones granted a good deal of independence in the past three decades. And these are the people who have suffered the Culture Cult's most vicious effects—the victims of the antiassimilationist policies embraced and promoted by idealistic middle-class whites in the south.

Under the banner of cultural self-determination, lowered standards saw literacy levels fall to almost zero. The lax administration of public health witnessed spreading malnutrition and disease. When controls on alcohol were abolished this was seen as a step toward taking responsibility for one's own well-being. It did not have that effect. One community after another was wiped out as countless millions of dollars in welfare payments were "pissed against a wall," while petrol sniffing became widespread among juveniles. Numerous mutually reinforcing social pathologies have produced a state of affairs so grim that Australians cannot bring themselves to discuss it publicly except in the most guarded manner; few want to discuss it honestly even in private. Nobody any longer believes in a solution, and much of the nation is on the edge of political hysteria—which partly explains the escapism of television's flirtation with Rousseau. But because of the mandatory silence imposed by the Culture Cult, no one dares say a thing.

At a seminar in Sydney in 1999 the effects of bilingual teaching were described. The principal of a Darwin college told how, between 1965 and 1975, Aboriginal students from outlying bush communities arrived with sixth-grade literacy levels. By 1990, after primary education had been handed over to local Aboriginal communities themselves, this had fallen to the third-grade level. Today they arrive at his college completely illiterate, he said, identifying "self-determination," bilingual instruction, and the priority given to preserving Aboriginal traditional culture as the reason.[16]

Thirty years ago their parents and grandparents could read and write, but today, says Bob Collins, a former federal Labor senator who has conducted a review of education, "I often have kids staying in my home who cannot even write their names, let alone read anything. And these kids had grandparents who were able to read books, newspapers—anything they picked up."[17] The problem is widespread and growing. Formerly it was the goal of educational policy to help indigenes across the Big Ditch between the preliterate and the literate worlds, so reading and writing English were emphasized. Not any more. The present Australian Aboriginal leadership is living on the educational capital provided by the teaching policies of thirty to forty years ago, and they now have few literate successors. "Unless this situation is reversed," says Mr. Collins, "self-determination for Aboriginal people is a joke, an absolute joke."[18]

Primitivism Versus Literacy

What is literacy? Why is it important? And why is it that a romantic infatuation with Aboriginal culture in Australia has made it necessary that questions like this should have to be asked? To begin with we might look at John Stuart Mill. At the age of three he was being taught Greek by his father—and paternal encouragement and direction was a vital factor throughout his early years. By the age of eight he had read "the whole of Herodotus, and of Xenophon's *Memorials of Socrates* . . . and the first six dialogues of Plato, from the *Euthyphro* to the *Theaetetus* inclusive." He had also read Hume and Gibbon, had been excited by "the heroic defence of the Knights of Malta against the Turks, and of the revolted provinces of the Netherlands against Spain," and had been required to give his father an account of what he had found in Millar's *Historical View of the English Government*, Mosheim's *Ecclesiastical History*, a life of John Knox, and histories of the Quakers.[19]

His father, James Mill, made a point of putting into his hands "books which exhibited men of energy and resource in unusual circumstances, struggling against difficulties and overcoming them." He particularly remembered an early account of the first settlement of New South Wales. "Two books which I never wearied of reading were *Anson's Voyage*, so delightful to most young persons, and a Collection (Hawkesworth's I believe) of Voyages round the World, in four volumes, beginning with Drake and ending with Cook and Bougainville."[20] Voyages around the world—not just the oceans, but around the whole universe of learning and literature—expand the mind, and this is how one of the best Victorian minds was made.

Another way of seeing the matter is to look at the historic relation between literacy and progress. David Landes has many examples in *The Wealth and Poverty of Nations*. Comparative literacy featured in the contrast between Protestant progress and Catholic backwardness. "Two special characteristics of the Protestants," he writes, were highly significant (and they bear directly on one of the problems in Aboriginal education today—the illiteracy of mothers). "The first was stress on instruction and literacy, for girls as well as boys. This was a by-product of Bible reading. Good Protestants were expected to read the holy scriptures for themselves. (By way of contrast, Catholics were catechized but did not have to read, and they were explicitly discouraged from reading the Bible.) The result: greater literacy and a larger pool of candidates for advanced schooling; also greater assurance of continuity of literacy from generation to generation. *Literate mothers matter*."[21]

But everywhere things have continued to improve. Only in the cultural enclaves of Australia's north have the advances already made now been abandoned, with the illiterization of those whose grandparents could read and write. Only there, under the fateful banner of "my culture, right or wrong," has an environment developed in which education cannot even take place.

A Darwin high school principal said that "education is impossible in the settlement communities because the fabric of life is so disturbed and so broken that real education can't occur . . ." For that phrase about the fabric of life being disturbed read "culture"—the broken sociopathic ruin of Aboriginal settlement culture as it is today, not the picturesque lily-ponds served up with the evening news. Education is impossible in these communities because there is no interest in education on the part of parents—no fathers pushing, no mothers encouraging—and as Landes emphasized, *literate mothers matter*. Literacy will only result, the college principal concluded, when Aboriginal parents themselves want it for their children.

Ernest Gellner once commented on the damaging effects of aggressive ethnic assertiveness in the modern state. In his view romantic primitivism is born of a reaction against industrial modernity, a reaction which tends to freeze or petrify all that is most backward in traditional life. In contrast, "equality of status and a continuous culture seems a precondition for the functioning of a complex, occupationally mobile, technically advanced society. Hence it does not easily tolerate cultural fissures within itself, especially if they correlate with inequality which thereby becomes frozen, aggravated, visible, and offensive."[22]

In northern Australia thirty years of the policy of Aboriginal culture forever, good or bad, healthy or sick, right or wrong, has seen that come about. The Culture Cult has produced frozen, visible, and offensive inequality. Now the Big Ditch is wider than ever. Such is the result of a romantic fixation on tradition—on the idealizing of primitive culture at the expense of every other value and ability needed today. Illiterate, vocationally disabled, unpresentable outside the ethnographic zoos they live in, these tragic people are Australia's contribution to the New Stone Age.

2

Designer Tribalism

Central to the Culture Cult is a belief in the value of tribal collec-tivism—a moral hunger for community felt by numerous people alienated from modern life. These are the men and women who try to draw up new communal institutions from scratch. If you don't have a tribe of your own, invent one—this seems to be the thinking behind their endeavors.

Designer tribalism of this sort goes back a long way, Plato's specu-lative proposals in *The Republic* being the best-known example from the past. More recently, in a typical vision from eighteenth-century France, the Abbé de Mably proposed a community where "all are equal, all are rich, all are poor, all are free, and our first law is that nothing is to be privately owned. We should bring to the public storehouses the fruit of our labours: that would be the Treasury of the State and the inheritance of every citizen. Every year the fathers of families would elect the stewards, whose duty it would be to dis-tribute the goods according to the needs of each individual, and to instruct them as to the work required of them."

Communes being communal, they are also expected to be places where more honest, virtuous, understanding, compassionate, loving, and generous forms of human association are found. Yet they seldom turn out this way. Discipline and authority are always a problem. A prospectus downloaded from "Dreamland" in the United States be-gins with encouraging talk about friendship and harmony, but ends by warning potential recruits that "thieves, liars, users and violent people will be dealt with harshly. I'm not a sucker, and I'm not going to build a charity mission or a soft target for crooks." Strong words. The author doesn't say what he means by "harsh treatment," but the punitive record of communes is not good. Public confession for sins that were never committed has often been a means of control.

Many gifted men and women have formed communes in the past, Robert Owen and John Humphrey Noyes being among them. But whether the communal aims are religious or secular, authoritarian or anarchistic, economic or sexual, communes all tend to reinvent the wheel. Determined to cross the Big Ditch in reverse, turning their backs on institutions they believe dispensable, simplifying arrangements they do not understand, there is hardly a painful lesson in the historical experience of mankind which communes have not defied or ignored—and then been forced to learn all over again.

Dreamland

When I first tried to contact Dreamland I was told "the file does not exist." It was just the kind of message you'd expect, so I didn't pursue the matter and only got through to the site a week or so later. By then the connection had taken on some electronic substance: no longer a late-night hallucination, Dreamland was becoming visible in cyberspace.

And the Web page was worth waiting for. A young man was advertising for like-minded spirits to join him in what he called a dream of a cooperative community. He'd had enough of "normal American life" and wanted a "meaningful existence" instead. Romantic primitivism always comes from a reaction against the ordinary world, and this came through strongly. He knew exactly what he hated: the work ethic, abusive bosses, obnoxious coworkers, invasion of privacy and feelings of fear and inappropriate guilt, along with "blame, accusation, yelling, insults and threats." So he and his wife were going to escape from it all, form a commune, and "get their dream off the ground."

At one time he'd thought of becoming a hermit, but he couldn't bring himself to take the plunge. He was used to home comforts, and solitary life in the woods was just too damn austere. "Call me superficial or materialistic if you want, but I've come to really appreciate things like electric lighting, working toilets, and access to many of the niceties of modern industrial culture like libraries and hardware stores, powered vehicles and medical care when I need it." This, of course, presents a problem. Primitivism demands simplicity. But common sense tells him that radically simple living is no longer possible. He also wants to live without blame, accusation, and yelling. But this goal is likely to be even harder to achieve—or not without a lot more psychological insight into himself and others than this Chief Tribal Designer appears to have.

But he has learned a few things along the way. He knows that both recent history and human nature show clearly that communism doesn't work, that the ideal of economic self-sufficiency was an illusion, and that creating one's own society from scratch is beyond him—the crooked timber of humanity is just too crooked for the task. And, having learned these lessons, he is better prepared for his project than Robert Owen was two hundred years ago.

New Harmony and Robert Owen

By his early forties Robert Owen had successfully managed cotton mills in England and made a fortune. He was famous for influential factory reforms: working hours were reduced, conditions improved, and he banned the employment of children under ten. Then, around 1813, his mind began to fill with much grander plans. After writing a book which set out *A New View of Society*, he urged his countrymen to turn their backs on the Industrial Revolution and return to the land.

This attempt to throw the world into reverse would start in Great Britain, where he called for the setting up of voluntary and independent associations—"villages of unity and mutual cooperation"—which were to become a system of cooperative socialism all over the globe. Each association would be a communal cooperative of 800–1,200 people, and he drew up plans for communal housing where everyone would live amiably together. How his people would actually spend their time was less clear. Owen said vaguely that they would "hold property in common," and do some farming, but he never bothered to spell out the details.

If romantics dream of communities that never were and never will be (something freely admitted by Rousseau), then Owen's case fits this description well. Turning violently against the world he knew, he embraced a vision of rural life—and farming was something he knew nothing about at all. It was as if he had fallen in love with a painting of trees and fields, or a pastoral poem of Arcadian reverie. He seemed to think trudging behind a plow was morally worthy in itself, and so was harvesting with a scythe, and so was churning butter—the aching arms and the sweat on the farmworker's brow were to be seen as signs of virtue. But there was no connection between the old-style rural life he had in his head and the practical problems of personnel and incentives and organization he faced on the ground. This became clear soon after he arrived in America. He announced at the launch of New Harmony on the Wabash River in 1826:

> I am come to this country, to introduce an entire new system of society, to change it from an ignorant, selfish system to an enlightened social system which shall gradually unite all interests into one, and remove all causes for contest between individuals.

He spoke about everyone cultivating the land together. Communal land was to be an essential step away from selfishness. But he had no clear idea what it meant. According to the diary of his son William Owen, he told his associates only four days before signing the purchase papers for the land that "it had occurred to him only this morning, that, perhaps, if he purchased Harmonie (the old Rappite name of the settlement) the community might rent the houses and land from him and cultivate the land in common . . . Mr Clark wished to know what would become of their present property. Mr (Robert) Owen thought if the soil was wet it might be laid down in grass, if dry in cotton or farmed for the private benefit of the individuals of the society."[1]

A. E. Bestor comments that however incredible it may seem, Owen was about to sink his fortune in an experiment without any notion as to whether the recruits who had flocked to New Harmony were to be employees, or almsmen, or partners, or tenants. And whatever they would be, who was going to till the soil? The membership was top-heavy with wordy thinkers who knew a good idea when they heard one, but had never so much as seen a plow. Only after a committee had met, and more than once, were some farming implements put into the fields. But by then Owen had left and gone back to England for five months, leaving control of the "Preliminary Society" in the hands of his twenty-three-year-old son William.

Designer tribalism has limitless faith that the right rules will produce the right results. If the setting is rural, and communal rules are applied, then once private ownership is abolished the remaining problems should look after themselves. That seems to have been Owen's view. In addition to this it is often assumed that as long as people agree on the ultimate goals of an association, communal government can be taken for granted too.

But it can't. Traditional authority needs deeply lived-in institutions and rules, and these don't exist in tribes invented yesterday: the habits of respect are missing. Rational authority needs enough like-minded folk to agree on laws, not an anarchy of opinionated talkers. Charismatic authority demands the ever-present dominating force of an inspiring leader—and time and again this is the primitive solution to problems of authority and governance that communes end up with. It is true that charismatic leadership can hold things together for a while, and perhaps New Harmony might have lasted a bit longer if Owen had stayed. But he didn't. He sailed away to England, and in May 1827, less than two years after it began, the whole enterprise fell in a heap.

John Humphrey Noyes's "inquest on New Harmony," in his book *History of American Socialisms* (1870), is not without a certain disagreeable gloating. But he was right about some of its flaws, and Owen's way of getting recruits was plainly one. In one estimate nine-tenths of the membership was useless; they included "scores of whom the world is quite unworthy—the conceited, the crotchety, the selfish, the headstrong, the pugnacious, the unappreciated, the played-out, the idle, and the good-for-nothing generally."

But could better recruits have saved New Harmony? With so much being handed out free, what motive did anyone have for working? Or was there a much deeper fault than the quality of those involved—a flaw in the communal dream itself? Introducing an "enlightened social system which shall gradually unite all interests into one, and remove all causes for contest between individuals" was easy enough for Owen to say. But once private property had been abolished, who would care for the communal property? What incentives would ensure that work got done?

Aristotle made some useful observations on these matters long ago. Individual ownership, he said, had the advantage that "when the care of things is divided among many, men will not complain of one another, but will rather prosper the more as each attends to his own property." Yet for some reason, he complained, although it was obvious that men who looked after their own property thrived and prospered, alienated Athenian intellectuals couldn't resist the appeal of communal schemes. Day after day they came hurrying up to him in the street, and seized his arm, pressing advertisements for Greek "Dreamlands" and "New Harmonys" upon him—places where private ownership would be abolished and everyone would go around hugging everyone else. Men readily listen to such utopian speculations, he continued,

> and are easily induced to believe that some wonderful love of everybody for everybody will result—especially when someone denounces the evils which now exist as a consequence of the fact that property is not owned in common, for example lawsuits for breach of contract, trials for perjury, and flattery of the rich. But none of these evils are due to the absence of communism. They are due to wickedness, since we see those who jointly own or possess things quarrelling a great deal more than those whose property is separate . . . Justice requires that we state not only any evils from which those under communism will be free, but also those benefits of which they will be deprived; and when this is done life under such a system is seen to be utterly impossible.[2]

John Humphrey Noyes and Oneida

The abolition of private property is usually designer tribalism's number-one priority, and the Abbé de Mably's vision of a world in which "all are equal, all are rich, all are poor, all are free, and our first law is that nothing is to be privately owned" is entirely typical.

But the inspiring hope of new sexual arrangements, usually to benefit men, must run it a close second. Plato long ago proposed that an ideal society would "hold women in common," and the eighteenth-century exploration of Polynesia produced a bright-eyed renewal of interest in more recent times. Bougainville's reports from Tahiti of agile nymphs sportively climbing over the bulwarks, Herman Melville's golden Marquesans in *Typee*, and Margaret Mead's vision of lovers slipping home at dawn "from trysts beneath the palm trees or in the shadow of beached canoes" all helped to keep the vision alive.

In New York State in the 1840s, however, there was a man who needed nothing literary to warm his desires. His drive was urgent, his imagination strong, and his Bible furnished all the text he needed. This was John Humphrey Noyes.

After attending Andover and Yale Divinity Schools, Noyes began, around 1846, with a small group of family members. Their loyalty ensured that there could never be the kind of leadership problems which destroyed New Harmony. His people held him in awe, his domination was absolute, and for more than thirty years the community always knew who was in charge. Noyes took passages from the Bible about the Primitive Church, and, by scriptural interpretation, devised sexual arrangements for his New York community which in some ways resembled those of Australia's Arnhem Land Aborigines, in others appeared modeled on the polyandrous arrangements of Ladakh, while others again bring to mind the customs of polygynous Dahomey.

If someone could have pointed out such comparisons to him, the deeply religious Noyes might have been surprised. But he might just have retorted "So what?" because although the Bible was important as a guide, for all truly charismatic leaders it can never be more than a guide. Much more important is a belief in one's own inspiration, and in the case of Noyes a complete and unblinking certainty as to what was natural and right overruled God's word whenever necessary. As M. L. Carden writes,

He taught that one should follow only the inspired spirit of the Bible, not the letter of the law. For him there were no absolute standards of morality. What is right for one time is wrong for another: it is a higher form of ethics to be responsible to oneself than to an external set of rules. In less specifically religious terms, although not without religious justification, he insisted that life is supposed to be happy. Men, and women too, should cultivate and desire the joys of all experience—including the joys of sexual intercourse. With regard to matters ranging from religion to sex, this nineteenth-century prophet rejected the conventions of his day and often anticipated more than a century of change.[3]

This sounds uplifting. Carden plainly sees Noyes's sexual agenda as heralding good things to come. But though the Oneida Community had undeniable virtues to offset its oddities, it has to be said that for

the most part these were the virtues of God-fearing New England society at large—order, work, thrift, cleanliness, the punctilious paying
of bills. They had nothing to do with polygamy, and belonged in another ethical universe entirely from those governing the sexual
regime of the community's last days in 1879. By then a small number of old men had privileged access to a harem of nubile females
(some as young as ten), one of whom was obliged to service her
creaky elders up to seven times in one week.[4]

Describing Noyes as a tormented spirit is an understatement, but it
suggests the tensions wracking the man. It all began at a revival meeting in 1831. He was twenty. From that point on through the divinity schools of two universities his religious obsession steadily grew
until in 1834 he arrived at "an unshakeable conviction that the Kingdom of God could and would soon literally be realized on earth."[5]

The millennium was nigh—but how nigh, and how could anyone
know? After intensive reading Noyes convinced himself that faith, not
works, was the chief requisite for salvation, and that a man who was
close to "perfect" would probably be saved. Next he claimed to have
achieved this rare condition himself—only to be disowned by his the-
ological mentor, to be ridiculed by those who thought him deranged,
to have his license to preach revoked, and to be driven into the spiritual solitude of "three emotionally devastating weeks in New York
City in May 1834, during which he plumbed the depths of suffering
and came to the brink of mental collapse."[6]

Wandering the streets, day and night, he preached to vagrants and
prostitutes, visited brothels, drank ardent spirits and wildly added
cayenne pepper to his food, and in the midst of this profligacy drew
the reckless conclusion that the entire sexual basis of society had to
be changed. The doctrine he formulated was Perfectionism, and the
chief article of Perfectionism was "communism in love." Noyes's arguments were based on his study of the Early Christian Church, and
were doubtless ingenious. But it is hard to see the main aspects of his
teaching as anything more than the studious rationalizations of a shy
man, intensely religious, disappointed in love and unable to approach
women directly, who showed a remarkable determination to rewrite
the book on sex.[7]

Next he announced a divine commission to implement the Kingdom of God on earth. First the marriage laws had to be revoked:

"The law of marriage 'worketh wrath'" he wrote. "It provokes to secret adultery, actual or of the heart. It ties together unmatched natures. It sunders matched natures. It gives to sexual appetite only a scanty and monotonous allowance, and so produces the natural vices of poverty, contraction of taste and stinginess or jealousy."[8]

The scanty sexual allowance of monogamy would be enlarged by what he called "complex marriage." Under its more generous provisions, monogamy would be replaced by love of the entire community—group marriage, or "multigamy," if you like. Women were expected to change their sexual partners often, and surviving records show that in one case conception could have resulted from any of four different encounters the previous month.[9] A man might approach a woman directly, or through a third party, and she was free to accept or refuse. That was in theory. But what woman would be bold enough to refuse a man representing the Almighty? Noyes himself supervised arrangements for intercourse, and the preferred relationships brought together the more "spiritual" and older residents who had reached a higher level of fellowship with the younger ones who still had a way to go.

What then resulted was an all-too-visible hierarchy. The most perfect Perfectionists comprised a privileged nobility of bearded and rickety old men, whose sexual claims ranked well above a collection of disesteemed minor figures of less perfection, less physical appeal, and less clout.

An unusual feature of Oneida was that reproduction was prohibited. Given that a high level of sexual activity occurred there, what attempt was made at birth control? A procedure was followed which supposedly ensured "male continence" and which one writer has called "celibate intercourse." Technically known as *coitus reservatus*, this involved full penetration without ejaculation. It seems to have worked, however, since very few births were recorded for twenty years. In a discussion of Oneida in his 1981 book, *Religion and Sexuality*, Lawrence Foster says judiciously that "Whatever one's opinion of 'male continence' . . . the practice certainly did require male self-control."[10] Indeed.

But whatever the frustrations of the community's adult membership, children at Oneida grew up much the same as children everywhere. To be sure, boys and girls were raised together in a large communal "children's house" meant to restrict the influence of parents.

But they romped as infants, got into scrapes at a later age, and though the contact of children with their mothers was severely restricted, it is obvious from Pierrepont Noyes's memoir, *My Father's House*, that they were happy and well adjusted on the whole. Nevertheless after thirty years this unusual society did break up. Pierrepont Noyes wrote

> On the 23rd of June 1879, something happened so unthinkable, so perturbing, that the very framework of life seemed falling about me, as the timbers of a house are torn apart and scattered by a cyclone. My father disappeared; departed secretly from Oneida and no one seemed to know whither he had gone. I saw tears in my mother's eyes. She would not discuss with me the cause of this startling event or its probable results, saying only, 'I don't know. We'll not talk about it, Pip, until we know.'[11]

From the author's account his mother may or may not have known—evidently Pierrepont himself did not—that John Humphrey Noyes had fled to Canada to avoid charges of statutory rape.

This ended an instructive sequence of events. Disputes over power and sexual privilege are common in communes. Despite the disapproval of competition for wealth at Oneida, and the community's vaunted egalitarianism, it is obvious that the sexual regime reserved the most delectable pieces of pie for Noyes himself. So-called complex marriage had "disguised what was, in fact, something fairly close to a polygynous system dominated by the leader and a few of the older men who had preferential access to the young more nubile girls, while the young men were encouraged to consort with older postmenopausal women."[12]

The old men enjoyed another privilege too. This was the right to introduce nubile females in the community to complex marriage—to take their virginity at an early age—a right increasingly demanded by Noyes himself. This "right to be first-husband" was nothing more than a primitivistic revival of the medieval *jus primae noctis*, or right of a feudal lord to the first night with his vassal's bride.

It is said of this medieval practice that it was never truly a legitimate right confirmed by law, but occurred when it did as an abuse of power,[13] and blatant abuse of power took place when Noyes tightened control while increasing his privileges. Long interested in selective breeding, he now decided to allow reproduction—on his terms. These laid down rules which overwhelmingly favored the genetic princes of the realm . . . the most perfectly perfect of the Perfectionists themselves. Yet he was shrewd enough not to completely bar commoners from having children. In Pierrepont Noyes's recollection, "My memory, running over the roster of Community members, notes that almost every man had one child, but that, aside from the preferred 'stirps' (or legitimate breeders), they had *only one*."[14] (Emphasis in original.)

Oneida's designer tribe instituted one of the most sensational primitivist projects ever. But the rules Noyes drew up are fully supported by anthropology. The Australian Aborigines were not only polygynous but gerontocratic as well: in Arnhem Land the sexual monopoly of young girls enjoyed by senile elders has been a source of high tension for years. Among small groups like the Bushmen of southern Africa or the Yanomamo of Venezuela, strong leaders might keep up to ten women for their use. Polynesian chiefs traditionally kept up to a hundred women, while—as in the old-time West African kingdom of Dahomey—thousands and even tens of thousands of women were made available to the leaders of ancient empires like Mesopotamia and Egypt, or India and China, not to mention Aztec Mexico or Inca Peru.[15] The main difference between these arrangements, and the primitivism enacted in upper New York State, was that Oneida's resourceful founder had the imagination to quote the Bible in support.

Anyone reading about Oneida will soon notice how indulgently Noyes is treated in most accounts. The attitude is liberal and admiring; the tone is respectful; he is even mentioned as a "Yankee Saint." You will search in vain for any mention of civil rights. So far as I am aware, no book has yet been written from the perspective of a thoroughly intimidated sexually abused ten-year-old girl, unable to escape from the sanctimonious "culture" of Oneida, and having no one to turn to, with a bearded religious fanatic climbing into her bed night after night.

Accommodation in the Kibbutz

Romantic primitivism originates from Western intellectuals dreaming about the tribal world—and one of their more disturbing dreams is a longing to impose communal housing on everyone else. The more alienated such intellectuals are, the more they admire extended families, and the more obsessed they are with building barracks accommodation. It must be hard for anyone who has not read the sociological literature, and especially the attack on the nuclear family for the last 100 years, to understand this preoccupation with jamming people together under one roof.

Research from France has uncovered communal houses dating from the Dark Ages in Western Europe. But it has been Eastern Europe which really fired the imagination. "Learn from the Balkans" was the slogan (and learn from Serbia, especially) as reams of paper were expended on the glories of the *zadruga*, a common household in which fathers and sons, brothers and uncles and nephews, all lived together in unalienated Serbian bliss. Friedrich Engels had launched this with a warm endorsement. "The South-Slavic *Zadruga* provides the best existing example of such a family community," he announced[16]—although he reserved his greatest enthusiasm for the Haida Indians where "some households gather as many as seven hundred members under one roof."[17]

This let everyone know the standard for domestic density tribalism had set, and the writer Rebecca West was one who learned her lesson. It is typical of the romanticizing of something this author herself would find intolerable, that she devotes an admiring paragraph to the *zadruga* in *Black Lamb and Grey Falcon*. There the claustrophobic joys of Serbia are contrasted with the dreariness and solitude of English country life.[18] Arrangements in East European peasant households were usually much more complicated than they seemed, but misty misunderstandings fed socialist imaginings for years—especially in the Israeli kibbutz.

Back-to-the-land designer tribalism was ingrained in kibbutzim from the start. Most immigrants to Israel were patriarchal, capitalistic, and both modern and urban. In contrast the kibbutz was meant to be egalitarian and socialist—a Jewish version of the pastoral dream. For the new men and women of the kibbutz collective living was mandatory, and the communal nature of child care was spelled out as early as 1916: "Child care is not only the responsibility of the mother, but of all the women. The essential thing is to preserve the principle of co-operation in everything; there should be no personal possessions, for private property hinders cooperative work."[19] Collective care also required communal housing:

For several decades most kibbutzim raised their children in age-segregated 'children's houses'. Small groups of eight to twelve children, within a year or so of each other in age, slept, ate, played and went to school in a single building, under the supervision of three adults (almost invariably women). Each kibbutz had ten or twelve large and well-appointed houses, catering for tightly knit little groups of children who changed house from year to year as they grew up, but retained their integrity as a group . . . In effect, each children's house was a miniature boarding school, which catered to a single grade, from the infant nursery through the primary school grades.[20]

This was supposed to reduce parental influence. Perhaps if the kibbutzniks had read Pierrepont Noyes they might have saved themselves some trouble. In a chapter about his mother he recalls a rare treat—the day she was allowed to arrange a birthday party for him. He was six.

There were only two at the party, Dick and I, but it was a real party and we had cake. I think my mother got even more pleasure than I did out of that party. The Community system was harder on mothers than on their children. Whenever I was permitted to visit my mother in her mansard room—once a week or twice (I have forgotten which)—she always seemed trying to make up for lost opportunity, lavishing affection on me until, much as I loved her, I half grudged the time taken from play with those toys which she had—I think somewhat surreptitiously—collected for my visits.[21]

Kibbutz mothers had an easier time than the mother of Pierrepont Noyes: they could see their children daily. But like her they kept trying to make up for too much time apart. At first they could only see their children briefly in the evenings; then, after 1964, mothers were also permitted contact during the "hour of love"—a thirty-minute period each morning when they took their children out of the children's houses to play and walk. As the kibbutzim became more prosperous the mothers tried increasingly to get separate houses of their own: they wanted their children with them overnight.

By 1955 a majority of kibbutz women supported family housing, though only 40 percent of the men agreed. Ten years later the gap between men and women had widened. In 1965, in the more liberal kibbutzim where the pressure for change was strongest, 75 percent of women supported nuclear family arrangements, while men's support rose to 53.6 percent.

The most doctrinaire collectivists were always men. They warned that a more individualistic system would burden the women, and they were right. When children stayed home overnight it was their mothers who had to take them each morning to school in the children's houses—their fathers were by then at work in the fields. Nuclear households also gave mothers more domestic work. But none of this weakened their determination to get houses for themselves. Their answer to every objection was the same: "We don't mind, we're ready to do anything to have our children with us during the night."[22]

Life at Cold Mountain Farm

Engels announced the necessary demise of the bourgeois family if any serious progress was to be made, and during the high tide of communalism in the 1960s and 1970s feminists said much the same thing. In 1971 Eva Figes wrote that "until marriage is either abolished completely or has become a hollow sham, I am afraid women are going to make far too little effort to improve their own positions." The following year anthropologist Eleanor Leacock declared: "it is crucial to the organization of women for their liberation to understand that it is the monogamous family as an economic unit, at the heart of class society, that is basic to their subjugation."[23]

Views of this kind were common among the communes of the time. Laurence Vesey's account of several communities from the glory days of the counterculture, *The Communal Experience*, reports on a 1960s project at Cold Mountain Farm in Vermont, where the woman in charge was Joyce Gardner. Like the rest of her team she looked forward to the abolition of marriage, monogamy, class society, and all other obstacles to self-realization. The location was right—Putney in Vermont had been the original home of Noyes's Perfectionists—and the site chosen was an inaccessible farmhouse without electricity "set in a secluded valley surrounded by an attractive rim of hills."[24]

Those hills were important. Twelve months later they were about the only attraction left, since the Cold Mountain farmers knew even less about what they were doing than Robert Owen. They bought a tractor which soon broke down. They waited for good weather to sow their seed, under the impression that planting only takes place when the sun is shining, and that farmers get a suntan while they work. Meanwhile the time for planting passed by. There were personnel problems because some of the residents regarded disruption as a right. People drifted in and drifted out. A few chose to work stark naked, a gesture the neighbors found picturesque but unnecessary.[25]

Though summer was passing nobody could be bothered cutting wood for their winter fires. Gardens went unweeded, a hepatitis epidemic struck them down, autumn chilled their spirits, and as falling snow deepened in the leafless woods the last surviving colonists vamoosed.

Vesey says the main difficulties of the community "came from within," meaning that their utopian ideals fell too far short of reality. This is putting it mildly. In an account she wrote around 1970 Gardner tells how she dreamed of "a family of incestuous brothers and sisters" sharing everything and everyone, a family "where energies would flow among and between everyone, and all relationships would be voluntary," a warm community of people "whose love of life and of each other would give us an almost superhuman strength for survival."[26]

Many communes call themselves "families," but what exactly is a family of incestuous brothers and sisters? Gardner plainly wanted the best of two worlds. On the one hand she wanted the intimacy and caring associated with the sort of family where there are children. On the other hand she wanted the more demanding intimacy of incestuous sex. But the two things are not compatible—and as usual in fantasized sexuality, no fathers and mothers are mentioned, and no children, and certainly no daily routine of child care. What we have instead is the immature guilt-free sexutopia of Jean-Jacques Rousseau.[27]

The naked savages roaming Cold Mountain Farm included only brothers and sisters horizontally related in time. They were not linked to any generation before, or to any generation after, because *generation* had nothing to do with it. As a form of association the community was both logically and biologically sterile—a peculiar family indeed. The people at Cold Mountain Farm were *being*, not *generating*, pursuing the narcissistic ideal of self-development, self-fulfillment, self-realization—and if self-realization didn't result, what reason would a resident have for staying on?[28]

Sexual bonds alone are not strong enough to hold a group together. But it is unclear what other rationale than sex the Cold Mountain farmers had. "We didn't become NEW people—we just became physically healthy people," Gardner concluded. "We weren't ready yet to put the blade to our own skins and expose the raw, tender, inner flesh inside; to plant the seeds of the people we wished to become; to grow new and beautiful skins from the inside out; to rediscover our tribal consciousness, our human brotherhood . . ."[29]

Atavism with Ezra at Rockridge

Tribal consciousness, and the xenophobia which is the other side of "human brotherhood," can be found in abundance at Rockridge in New Mexico. Its leader is Ezra, and in 1971 his view is thoroughly apocalyptic: the "outside" is plainly heading for catastrophe, and salvation lies only through strict adherence to the "inside" principles of Rockridge itself. Described as a tall and broadly built man of forty-two, Ezra's dark hair is short and parted, and he has the general aspect of a construction foreman or perhaps a farmer: "He is no hippie."

His southern drawl is "rich, deep, full of masculine energy, always the instrument of his purpose, even when he shouts in rage." There's a lot of shouting at Rockridge because it has a government of men rather than laws—or frankly, Ezra is the government himself.[30] And here we might look once again at that announcement for Dreamland we noticed earlier on the Web. The bitterest complaints of Dreamland's promoter today have to do with surveillance, power, and control. What he finds intolerable about contemporary America is the "invasion of privacy and personal life whether by drug or polygraph testing, or other means that result in a culture of suspicion and feelings of fear and inappropriate guilt . . . camera surveillance and access cards or timeclocks that your 'betters' use to monitor your every move and to subordinate or humiliate you." All this gives rise to "blame, accusation, yelling, insults and threats against your job and livelihood."

At Dreamland, he says, all this will be banished forever. In the year 2000 he has learned his lesson from Waco, Jonestown, and similar establishments: "I intend to retain some authority over the place, but I hope for the place to be very libertarian. I most emphatically do *not* intend to become the charismatic ruler, or anything like that." No doubt he sincerely means this, and perhaps Ezra himself began with similar noble intentions thirty years ago. Perhaps even the Reverend Jim Jones of Jonestown did too, though it didn't prevent around 800 people getting killed. The trouble is, that in the absence of separate roles for lawmaking, criminal inquiry, and the adjudication of independent courts, men yelling insults and physical violence is what communes always seem to get.

Ezra could have learned much from Montesquieu: "When the legislative and executive powers are united in the same person, or in the same body of magistrates, there can be no liberty . . . Again, there is no liberty if the judiciary power be not separated from the legislative and executive. Were it joined with the legislative, the life and liberty of the subject would be exposed to arbitrary control, for the judge would then be legislator. Were it joined to the executive, the judge might behave with violence and oppression."[31]

Each day at Rockridge showed the importance of these cautions. Absence of liberty, arbitrary punishment, hectoring and humiliation, were all routine. This was because legislative and judicial and executive power were joined in the one unmanageable personality of Ezra himself. The larger community of Oneida had witnessed similar public humiliations a century before, but despotism at Oneida was softened by discussions in which various men and women, high and low, young and old, expressed their thoughts; and although Noyes's opinion always counted most, gross injustice was generally avoided.

At Rockridge the situation was much worse. It was not just that happiness depended on Ezra's smile; one's very existence depended on it. As a result his followers would do almost anything to ensure his approval and goodwill—including false confession, if required.

One day near Rockridge a woman belonging to the commune lost a wheel off her convertible while driving into town. The man who had changed the wheel at the commune (let us call him Tom) had failed to tighten the wheel nuts properly. Vesey was present at the "court proceeding" to be recounted, and so far as he could tell there was no reason to believe the "crime" involved anything more than simple negligence. But in synthetic tribalism, as in real tribalism itself, misfortune cannot be explained by anything so simple. There is no such thing as an innocent injurious act. In primitive society there is always a world beyond the veil of appearances, and it is the task of supernatural explanation to search in that world for malignant motives. Ezra said hidden motives lay behind the loose nuts on the wheel—and Tom would have to confess to having them.

After placing the wheel on the dinner table as a centerpiece Ezra accused Tom of trying to kill the girl in the car. He said Tom secretly hated her, hated all women in fact. Ezra then attacked Tom's upper-class Protestant background, and said that it was because the girl was Catholic that he had not tightened the wheel; that it wasn't an accident, it was sabotage. Ezra said he believed that deep down Tom was driven by homicidal impulses and that if the truth were told it was a combination of religious and class motives, plus his dislike of women, which had led him to attempt murder.

"What followed next," writes Vesey, "was from an outsider's standpoint truly remarkable. Tom tearfully accepted the idea of his deliberate intent, without the slightest sign of resistance."

But that wasn't enough. Ezra said Tom was holding something back and demanded dramatic evidence of how Tom "really felt"—now was the time for Tom to bring out all his repressed inner resentments, in order to finally rid himself of his need to kill. At this point the accused seized a glass water jug from the table and smashed it against a wall. Later, all passion spent, a process of rehabilitation took place, the "criminal" was reunited with the community, and Ezra invited Tom to come and read them his favorite William Blake poems. Group solidarity, the *summum bonum* of cultural primitivism, was again restored.

Rousseau and the General Will

How is it that something more typical of the world of witches and sorcerers can spontaneously occur in a New Mexico commune in 1971? On one interpretation this represents a theatrical showdown between the claims of the group and the individual. Coerced public confession demonstrates that the right of the collective to assign guilt completely outweighs the right of the accused to defend himself. At the same time it dramatically denies the value of objective truth.

According to the political theory Rousseau developed in *The Social Contract*, the rights of the group and of the state flow from the General Will, which is infallible, and where the General Will conflicts with an individual will the latter must yield. In totalitarian politics this principle is important—it involves the authority of the state—and the striking parallels from Soviet history and the Moscow Show Trials of 1938 are plain to see. As they were fully intended to demonstrate at the time, nothing more spectacularly proves the majestic authority of a regime than the willingness, on the part of those it accuses, publicly to confess to things they did not do and to crimes they did not commit.

In a revealing book from around the same time as Vesey's, Rosabeth Kanter's *Community and Commitment*, the author argues that humiliation serves the purpose of group therapy. "In communities . . . the use of mortification is a sign that the group cares about the individual, about his thoughts and feelings, about the content of his inner world. The group cares enough to pay great attention to the person's behavior, and to promise him warmth, intimacy, and love . . . if he indicates that he can accept these gifts without abuse. Mortification thus facilitates a moral commitment on the part of the person to accept the control of the group, binding his inner feelings and evaluations to the group's norms and beliefs."[32]

This statement deserves to be framed and hung on the wall. Seldom can the process of collective intimidation, humiliation, and thought control, with all its indifference to legal process and its potential for unhinged sadism, have received such an upbeat academic defense—and from Harvard, too. But Kanter does indeed throw light on the tribal process which elevates solidarity above truth. If the group says black is white, then the willingness to agree that black is white vividly testifies to an individual's acceptance of "group norms."

Vesey also describes after-dinner exorcism procedures at Rockridge. As several women cried "out! out! while breathing with the rising involuntary rhythm that one associates with sexual climax, I began to think I was eavesdropping on pure and simple hysteria of a kind which might even suggest Salem in 1692."[33]

But this was not pure and simple hysteria. What Vesey witnessed, in 1971, in New Mexico, was the deliberate reinvention of belief in supernatural evil by a marginal psychopath working the romantic primitivist vein, using the whole thaumaturgical box of tricks including irrational guilt, devils, and the ritual casting out of spirits.

3

Enter the Noble Savage

Jean-Jacques Rousseau showed his genius in three ways. First, as a copywriter. Although the poet John Dryden might have been the first to be heard romantically speaking of "noble savages", nothing much happened until Rousseau picked up the idea and ran with it. Then the thinking of the literary intelligentsia was turned upside down. Before Rousseau savagery was obviously and unarguably ignoble, and tribal life was regarded in most places with horror. It was where you found despotic chiefs, absurd beliefs, revolting cruelty, appalling poverty, horrifying diseases, and homicidal religious fanaticism. After Rousseau, among progressive thinkers, all this had gone. No Big Ditch separated the civilized from the primitive. Savagery was noble, the tribal world was morally transfigured, and the savage himself had been redeemed.

Second, as a bohemian. Strikingly robed in his black Armenian cloak, an engaging parasite with tousled hair living amid flashes of self-advertisement, Rousseau was "a stranger in the world, a misfit, an outsider, a wholly unique being." He feared and envied the civilized urban world he exploited, and he despised the men and women he used. He was a gifted writer and publicist. He was vain, hypersensitive, and paranoid. Combined with a phenomenal ability to project Arcadian fantasies plucked out of thin air, all this made for an extraordinarily powerful, mischievous, and unstable mix. Not only did his strong imagination rescue the savage, it legitimized the lifestyle of the countercultural bohemian *litterateur*.

Third, as the founder of anthropology—or anyway the kind of anthropology we have today. This is moralistic rather than scientific, political rather than detached, hates modernity in a hundred different ways, and has taken a great interest in what it calls "writing" in recent years. This has always been the tendency of the romantic imagination—and when he launched the Noble Savage on his career, Rousseau himself did so out of a romantic, interior vision. In his philosophy that inner world was always more important than reality. Along with other spiritual exiles Rousseau regarded the archaic, the exotic, and the picturethnic as a *symbolic community*, an ideal association to belong to and admire in one's imagination, a speculative dream with none of the discomforts of the world outside.

He was disarmingly frank about the advantages this offered. As he confessed in a letter to his friend and protector, Malesherbes, after an initial painful encounter with reality "I withdrew more and more from human society and created for myself a society in my imagination, a society that charmed me all the more in that I could cultivate it without peril or effort and that it was always at my call and such as I required it. I peopled nature with beings according to my heart . . . I created for myself a golden age to suit my fancy."[1]

Rousseau and Bohemia

Bohemians originated with Diogenes and the Cynics, and if primitivism has always been the revolt of the civilized against civilization, then Diogenes was the walking proof. Whereas the more conventional citizens of Athens wore robes, Diogenes wore a beggar's rags. Where ordinary Athenians chose soft beds at home, he lay down in the street. And the point of it all for the Cynics was to exploit their individual liberty—the gift, be it remembered, of civil society—to provoke and antagonize more conventional folk. In this way Diogenes used privileges, which only the rules of civil society provided, to attack civilized life from within.

Politeness generally helps sales in the commercial world of the *bourgeois* (urban civility is a by-product of commerce: *Ou il y a du commerce, il y a des moeurs douces*, Montaigne). In contrast, bohemian flamboyance demands impoliteness come what may: the only commerce that takes place in this milieu is an exchange of egos. An admiring commentator tells us that the Cynics advocated incest, while "they reportedly were willing to 'be natural' about fornicating and defecating anywhere . . . Many of their self-conscious violations of commercial, bureaucratic and upperclass morals and manners suggest the Cynics as the first to intentionally *épater le bourgeois.*" If you pointed out that Diogenes was probably mad, they calmly retorted that "most men are so nearly mad that a finger's breadth would make the difference."[2]

That is a sobering thought. It's easy to overestimate the mental balance of one's fellows. And the issue of sanity in relation to the Cynics, to bohemian exhibitionism, and to the emotional wildness of romanticism more generally, cannot be lightly dismissed. Listing as the psychopathic equipment of "the ideal bohemian" such traits as melancholia, satyriasis, claustrophobia, hyperesthesia, apathy, and dyspepsia, not to mention numerous lesser disorders including alcoholism, another experienced observer of this milieu goes on to add:

> such are the leading characteristics of the traditional idols of bohemia: Goethe, Byron, Shelley, Coleridge, Wilde, Verlaine, Baudelaire, and the decadents on down to Van Vechten, Bodenheim, Hecht, and O'Neill. Much as the babbling of the village idiot is regarded by the illiterate as divinely inspired, so the incontestable work of genius or talent is traced directly, in bohemia, to such symptoms of psychological infirmity as we have listed. It is the final phase of Rousseau's romanticism—the theory of a "natural man": unhampered, original, spontaneous, as he was in the Garden of Eden.[3]

Rousseau's appearance at the foot of this list is ominous. But it's also inevitable: he was bohemia's exemplary original. Like his fellow Romantic, the German Johann Gottfried Herder, the tormented personality of the discoverer of the noble savage grew from twisted provincial (and semi-savage) roots. Both men found the civilization of Paris galling, and both suspected that France was not giving them the honor which was their due. In Herder's case this gave rise to an anxious concern for local cultures, while his resentment of Paris turned into a passionate defense of everyone disesteemed by France.

Rousseau's approach was more personal and egoistic. The touchy Swiss adventurer derived an entire egalitarian political theory from little more than his own injured pride—from that hypersensitive sense of *amour propre* which was a personal torment, and which his books and essays made of central political importance in the West.

Why were noble savages preferable to ignoble citizens in Germany or France? Why is natural man innocent and civilized man irredeemably "corrupt"? Why are the lives of illiterate neolithic farmers morally superior to the lives of you or me? Because in the Garden of Eden invidious comparison was unknown. No face was more beautiful than another, no body stronger, no knowledge truer, no way of life better (or anyway this follows from his ideas). And no one should feel bad as a result. In Rousseau's paradisal "state of Nature" everyone is broadly equal. This ensures that even the most exaggerated pride cannot be hurt.

If only he had the time, he wrote in his *Discourse on Inequality*,

> I would observe to what extent the universal desire for reputation, honours and promotion which devours us all, activates and compares talents and strengths, how it excites and multiplies passions, how in making all men competitors, rivals or rather enemies [note the paranoid shift from "rivals" to "enemies"] it causes every day failures, successes and catastrophes of every sort by making so many contenders run the same course; I would show that this burning desire to be talked about, this yearning for distinction, which almost always keeps us in a restless state . . . is responsible for a multitude of bad things and a very few good ones.[4]

He admits that high achievements in science and philosophy also result from the desire for honor. But they count for little. All in all, the bad things in civilization far exceed the good. The imaginary state of Nature he then proceeds to create—a state which he frankly admits "no longer exists, which perhaps never existed, and which will probably never exist"[5]—is merely a speculative philosophical fancy. But it was a fancy with wide appeal. In this way the neurosis of an interesting madman (as one of the women in his life described him) produced the most potent version of romantic primitivism ever.

Our Master and Our Brother

Claude Lévi-Strauss once expressed the view that Rousseau was anthropology's patron saint. In the penultimate chapter of *Tristes Tropiques* he asks:

Is it then the case that anthropology tends to condemn all forms of social order, whatever they may be, and to glorify a condition of Nature
which can only be corrupted by the establishment of social order? . . .
Turning over these problems in my mind [i.e., whether or not anthropology is properly viewed as a kind of atonement for the wickedness of
civilization, and a search for mythical alternatives to the present day] I
become convinced that Rousseau's is the only answer to them.
Rousseau is much decried these days; never has his work been so little
known; and he has to face, above all, the absurd accusation that he
glorified the "state of Nature" for its own sake. . . . What Rousseau
said was the exact contrary; and he remains the only man who shows
us how to get clear of the contradictions into which his adversaries
have led us. Rousseau, of all the *philosophes*, came nearest to being an
anthropologist. He never traveled in distant countries, certainly; but
his documentation was as complete as it could be at that time and, unlike Voltaire, he brought his knowledge alive by the keenness of his interest in peasant customs and popular thought. Rousseau is our master
and our brother, great as has been our ingratitude towards him; and
every page of this book could have been dedicated to him, had the object thus proffered not been unworthy of his great memory.[6]

Thus Lévi-Strauss. It was the view of the sage of the Musée de
l'Homme that we have all been misled about the Noble Savage. He
says Rousseau has been the victim of two hundred years of detrac-
tion, and that he never glorified the state of nature "for its own sake"
at all. We can happily agree with that: Rousseau certainly did not glorify the state of Nature for its own sake. He glorified the state of Nature in order to demean and denigrate Paris, playing noble savagery
off against civilization for polemical purposes. Romantic primitivists
continually employ this tactic, and the underlying psychology will be
considered in the final chapter of this book.

But the second allegation is more grave. According to Lévi-Strauss,
Rousseau has been lied about, travestied, caricatured. He says that
what Rousseau really idealized in his writing was not savagery at all,
but an entirely different social condition—what you might call Early
Advanced Man at an amiably almost-civilized stage.

This is a serious charge. Has the world misunderstood Rousseau?
Were the Polynesians admired by Bougainville and others in the eigh-
teenth century, or the Caribbean tribes said by Columbus to be like
Adam and Eve, or the heroic Iroquois idealized by writers on Amer-

ican Indian life, not what Rousseau meant by the Noble Savage after all? And how can we know? Fortunately the means lie close at hand. For in the already cited place in *Tristes Tropiques* Lévi-Strauss devotes several pages to this matter, and having explained exactly what it was that Rousseau meant he delivers the following judgment: what Rousseau meant when he wrote about "noble savages" were "neolithic farmers."

After this we can all relax. Because the Polynesians were neolithic farmers, and so were the Iroquois, and so originally were all the Amazonian tribes on which Lévi-Strauss founded his reputation for ethnography during his visit in 1941. So also were the Kayapo which Sting and his band visited on the Araguaia in Brazil, and which we see in television advertisements for South American rain forest Edens over and over again.

All of them originally used polished stone tools for gardening (which is what *neolithic* means); all grew crops to supplement hunting and fishing; all were preliterate and had no form of writing. And since those are the things most people have in mind whenever noble savagery is mentioned, the case is closed. If Lévi-Strauss is correct— and it was he who raised the matter—the world has not misunderstood Rousseau at all.

Whether or not Rousseau can be regarded as the patron saint of anthropology—except perhaps in its French version—may be arguable. But that he is the patron saint of romantic primitivism there can be no doubt. Defining it as a dream of the primaeval that never was, and of a community that will never be, Rousseau's already quoted passage from his *Discourse on Inequality* is in complete agreement with the argument presented here. He frankly admits that the imaginary state of Nature is one which "no longer exists, which perhaps never existed, and which will probably never exist."[7] And here is Rousseau on the evils of private possession:

> The first man who, having enclosed a piece of land, thought of saying 'this is mine' and found people simple enough to believe him, was the true founder of civil society. How many crimes, wars, murders; how much misery and horror the human race would have been spared if someone had pulled up the stakes and filled in the ditch and cried out to his fellow men: 'Beware of listening to this impostor. You are lost if

you forget that the fruits of the earth belong to everyone and that the earth itself belongs to no one![8]

Two Anthropological Traditions

Right from the start in 1750 two kinds of anthropology were being done; two contrasting ways of using the reports of sailors and explorers from around the world. While Rousseau was "peopling nature according to his heart," a different kind of enquiry was taking place across the English Channel. It was also interested in social and institutional origins; but it was less inclined to argue philosophical points.

One example was William Robertson's 1777 *History of America*. This advances the argument that because "similar causes always produce similar effects," like ways of life result from like conditions: "A tribe of savages on the banks of the Danube," wrote Robertson, "must nearly resemble one upon the plain washed by the Mississippi." Another work was Adam Ferguson's 1767 *An Essay on the History of Civil Society*. This relates the evolutionary stages of savagery, barbarism, and Civil Society to distinctive ways of life. Ferguson also introduces the idea that many of our social arrangements "are indeed the result of human action, but not the execution of any human design."[9] In sharp contrast to Rousseau he also emphasizes "that men in becoming civilized had gained much more than they had lost; and that civilization, the act of civilizing, for all of its destruction of primitive virtues, put something higher and greater in their place."[10]

Then there was the Scot, John Millar. His 1771 book *Observations Concerning the Distinction of Ranks in Society* describes why men and women sooner or later give up holding land in common (why, that is, they put in the boundary stakes and dig the dividing ditches which aroused such indignation in Rousseau). Supporting Aristotle's observations in our last chapter, Millar says

> they grow weary of acting in concert with each other, by which they are subject to continual disputes concerning the distribution and management of their common property; while everyone is desirous of employing his labor for his own advantage, and of having a separate possession, which he may enjoy according to his inclination. Thus, by a sort of tacit agreement, the different families of a village are led to cultivate their lands apart from each other.

Observers have seen this a thousand times—not least among the Serbian peasantry in the twentieth century. But my point is this: the vision of human society which these men presented was not just Anglo-Scottish but *bourgeois*. It assumed a social world in which the middle classes with their commerce and industry played a leading role, and in which middle-class virtues were the foundation of moral order.

Distilled into Ben Franklin's thirteen "useful virtues" these summarized the Protestant Ethic: temperance, silence, order, resolution, frugality, industry, sincerity, justice, moderation, cleanliness, tranquillity, chastity, and humility.[11] We can't of course be sure that Robertson, Ferguson, or Millar personally exemplified these values in their lives, or even bothered to wash behind their ears, but such values plainly stand as far as anything can stand from the sentimental, neurotic, declamatory milieu of the literary salons Rousseau frequented.

So two kinds of anthropology existed by the end of the eighteenth century. The Anglo-Scottish tradition of social enquiry grew out of the emerging conditions of economic and social modernity, and involved the thinking members of the professional middle classes, especially the law. In contrast, the romantic Franco-Germanic way of thinking about society launched by Rousseau in France, and by Herder in Germany, was the product of a nostalgic literary intelligentsia, whose tastes, for the most part, were neither liberal nor democratic, who resented their inferior status in the scheme of things, and whose *amour propre* was piqued by the traditional aristocracy which fed and housed them and everywhere held power. These romantic litterateurs feared science, despised industry, hated commerce, and, as men of letters of uncertain means, were resentfully dependent on a nobility they regarded with thinly veiled contempt.[12]

In England the number of men and women who listened to Millar and Ferguson was probably small. But the number in France—those who listened to the emotional sermonizing of the sensational preacher with the long locks and the black Armenian cloak—would soon be huge. In 1750 Rousseau had begun by showing in his *Paradoxical Oration on the Arts and Sciences* (or *First Discourse*) how science, art, and civilization were the cause of moral ruin. Spartan simplicity was the thing to aim for; science was ignoble; education and even printing were to be deplored. Only the ignorant were innocent in Eden, and only the innocent were truly virtuous. It was civilization which corrupted mankind.

In his *Discourse on Inequality* (or *Second Discourse*) Rousseau took the argument further, and in the words of a sympathetic commentator "revolutionized the study of anthropology and linguistics, and made a seminal contribution to political and social thought."[13] Perhaps. What is certain is that in the course of his dazzling paradoxes the literary bohemian from Geneva, whose vagabondage was comforted by sundry indulgent women, created a world which defined romantic primitivism from that day on.

Romantic Primitivism

With Rousseau two things may be noted. First, although we can't actually return to the state of nature, and are even willing to admit we can't (as he says it is a state which no longer exists, which perhaps never existed, and which will probably never exist), at the same time the exact opposite is steadily implied. Otherwise what would be the point of the critique?

Thus a hypocritical mode of reasoning arises in which people continue to talk *as if* it might be possible to revert to tribal life, since at a vaguely moral level it seems *as if* it might be a desirable option, and *as if* the rules of primitive society and civilization were reconcilable—although privately we know very well they are not. This creates a pervasive atmosphere of ambiguous make-believe and insincerity.

Secondly, Rousseau's autobiography reveals clear symptoms of psychopathology. When the great revelation regarding truth, liberty, and virtue suddenly came to him while walking in the forest of Vincennes, and he saw through streaming tears a vision of how humanity had failed, it is clear that a disturbing life crisis was taking place. Certainly, much more was involved than finding an idea among the leaves on the forest floor. Alienated, frustrated, embittered and desperate, it flashed upon him that all his unhappiness was to be blamed on Parisian society—it had nothing to do with himself. This rationale would prove hugely popular. In the future, a teary mix of self-justification, disgust with civilization, personal distress, and fantasizing about "Nature" would regularly figure in the historic confrontation of bohemian and bourgeois.

Of course not everyone found Rousseau convincing. After receiving his copy of the *Second Discourse*, Voltaire wrote to the author as follows:

> I have received, sir, your new book against the human species, and I thank you for it. . . . The horrors of that human society—from which in our feebleness and ignorance we expect so many consolations—have never been painted in more striking colors: no one has ever been so witty as you are in trying to turn us into brutes: to read your book makes one long to go on all fours. Since, however, it is now some sixty years since I gave up the practice, I feel that it is unfortunately impossible for me to resume it: I leave this natural habit to those more fit for it than you and I.[14]

Nevertheless, Rousseau's visions quickly inspired others. Morelly's *Code de la nature* of 1755 agrees with Rousseau that sociability would require the abolition of private property, and goes on to propose agricultural communes, austere controls on consumption, severe punishments for crime, rational work rules, and "strictly regulated conjugal relations."[15] In 1761 the amiable Benedictine Dom Deschamps (who had enjoyed several meetings with Rousseau described as full of good cheer) drew up a mad scheme for global unity with everyone leading totally communal lives.

In Deschamps's utopia there would be no envy or jealousy because it would be "enough to replace moral inequality and property with moral equality and community of goods to efface all the moral vices that reign over humanity." Intellectuals would be abolished, metal would be banned from a wooden world, and in communal groups "all men and women would live together in one hut, work together at simple tasks, eat vegetarian food together, and sleep together in one big bed of straw. No books, no writing, no art: all that would be burned."[16]

The date 1761 is worth remembering. It is a landmark of romantic primitivist fantasy. From this we know that on the eve of the scientific and industrial revolution which laid the foundations of the modern world, one hundred years from the opening of the Crystal Palace in London, a French Benedictine monk conjured up in his mind a human future in which the use of metal would be prohibited, books would be burned, writing abolished, community of goods would ensure the eradication of vice, and fraternity was to be guaranteed by putting everyone into a big straw bed together.

Bohemian Versus Bourgeois

Rousseau fired the first shot in the "culture wars," and it has been ringing in our ears ever since. With Herder he started a dispute dividing pre-industrial Continental Europe and its values from the values of democratic industrializing England—that country of shopkeepers and tinkerers with their unending inventions, rising incomes, cheaper commodities, thriving commercial life, and, as Dr. Johnson put it, the example they set in the late eighteenth century of "all the business of the world being done in a new way."

Trade and manufacturing were developing in France and elsewhere too. But England was first in the field, and it was in England and Scotland that social thought was able to keep its feet on the ground, to keep Benedictine monks and bohemians at bay, and to build the foundations of an anthropology worthy of the name. By the middle of the nineteenth century the Edinburgh lawyer John McLennan was theorizing about female infanticide. Was it related to the low status of women in hunting societies? Other questions were raised about close-kin incest taboos. The American Lewis H. Morgan had explained them as arising from a fear of the bad biological effects of inbreeding, but there were several other possibilities, and debate continues to this day. Beginning in 1851 with *Social Statics*, Herbert Spencer's works presented institutions in all their variety and range, and as an encyclopaedic compendium they remain important. While Edward Tylor's 1871 book, *Primitive Culture*, is widely regarded as the founding text of anthropology itself.

In contrast to the salon intellectuals across the Channel each of these men were professionals. They were broadly middle class in their values, and they brought to social enquiry habits of mind which were serious, civilized, judicious, and humane. Their political and social views were generally moderate. James Mill's *Essay on Government* argues that "'the middling rank' formed the sole appropriate guarantors of representative government because they were 'the chief source of all that is exalted and refined in human nature'—which was to say that they contributed most to civilization."[17] Whatever one may think of this interpretation, it is against Mill's perception of the role of the middle classes that the bohemian avant garde destructively hurled itself from Rousseau on.

In the 1830s "bohemia" made its first full-dress appearance with Henri Murger's *Vie de Bohème*. The writers and artists who called themselves by this odd name had taken it from the gypsies in part of the Habsburg domain—wanderers regarded as colorful outcasts from society. Parisian bohemia enthusiastically identified with these anti-bourgeois vagrants. Unlike the real ostracism endured by gypsies, the outcast state of the Parisian artistic fraternity would be voluntary—but they were determined to be as outcast as possible.

In his 1964 study, *Bohemian Versus Bourgeois*, César Graña shows how Paris bohemians claimed a more natural sympathy with other cultures than the bourgeoisie could possibly possess. They regarded the lives of the French commercial and professional classes as utterly degrading. Graña describes Stendhal's horror of the lowness and meanness of the middle class, and how "anyone who acquired a routine social obligation or worked at a profession received from Flaubert either casual scorn or mocking sorrow." This same contempt for the routine world of paid employment was pushed to an extreme by Baudelaire, whose attitude—"to be a useful person has always appeared to me to be something particularly horrible"—expressed pure aristocratic disdain.[18]

Flaubert's hatred for the bourgeois was at times extreme. After completing his second novel, *Salammbô*, in 1862, he wrote that "It will: 1) annoy the bourgeois; 2) unnerve and shock sensitive people; 3) anger the archaeologists; 4) be unintelligible to the ladies; 5) earn me a reputation as a pederast and a cannibal. Let us hope so."[19] While research into sexual behavior is a normal part of anthropological inquiry, it was mainly a personal interest in erotic experience—romantically justified as self-fulfillment—which drove literary bohemia on its escapades.

Graña tells how Flaubert and his friend Maxime Du Camp went to great lengths to pose as the "colorful aborigines" of the countries they visited. Participant observers, they tried to grasp the essence of foreign cultures from the inside. Flaubert claimed to carry within himself "the melancholy of the barbaric races (and) their migratory instincts, and the innate disgust with life which makes them forsake their country." Rather than a French intellectual, he said, he would rather have been an Andalusian muleteer, a Neapolitan rogue, or "at least the stagecoach driver between Nîmes and Marseille."[20] Soon neither Andalusia nor Naples would offer sufficient escape, and a search began for remoter lands where the life-destroying bourgeois had not yet strayed—the legendary sandy wastes of

> The East and its vast deserts . . . its palaces trodden by camels . . . mares bounding towards the sun-flushed horizon . . . blue waves, clear sky and silvery sand . . . the smell of the warm oceans of the South; and then, near me, in a tent shaded by a broad-leaved aloe, some brown-skinned woman with burning eyes who would hold me in her arms and whisper the language of the houris.[21]

While describing the enchanting absurdity of it all, and noting that Flaubert would have been just as unhappy in another cultural setting as he was in his own, Graña writes that the yearning for the exotic was highly significant nonetheless:

> For the alienated individual, the cultivation of cultural remoteness represented the entrance into a *symbolic community* to which he gave the fullness of intellectual loyalty without having to meet any demands for actual adjustment. There were three reasons for this. Remote societies were regarded as *undivided* and having a *natural wholeness*, thus intellectual membership in them was a comfortable thing which relieved the tension caused by actual social isolation. . . . Motivations in such societies were thought to come from *nonutilitarian* impulses, and entire cultures were thought to have the same *aesthetic integrity* which the literary man attributed to himself. In Brittany, Flaubert marveled at the primitive's instinct for emotional grandeur while watching a fisherman's wife weep over the body of her husband washed ashore by the sea. From Egypt, he wrote about the elegance of the natives' expressions and stances. In the case of nomads he assumed that they moved because, like himself, they were afflicted with *Weltschmerz*. Finally, being whole and 'inspired', these cultures were also *unique*, which meant that intellectuals could identify themselves with them without surrendering their personal originality.[22] [italics my emphasis]

The bohemian version of romantic primitivism is well anatomized here. Whereas designer tribalism results in the real nitty-gritty, with practical problems of organization and discipline, bohemian primitivism is more in the mind. The yearned-for community is symbolic, not actual. Its undivided natural wholeness is something imagined rather than observed. The unique aesthetic sensibilities remote communities embody are hypothesized—deduced from pretty textiles, attractive pots, and ceremonial costumes. And even if one takes the trouble to visit such places in the flesh, one is still only a tourist who briefly stays—like Lauren Hutton—before returning to the safety of a waiting metropolis with hot baths and digestible food.

But the cream of the jest is still to come for this is a tale of unrequited love. The French writer may admire the Andalusian muleteer, but the muleteer thinks he's mad. There may indeed be a brown-skinned woman with burning eyes waiting for Flaubert, whispering the language of the houris, but the words she whispers are "only for cash." True Arabs find Englishmen galloping about on camels in the heat of Arabia incomprehensible. True Masai know only that if they stand around long enough, posing with their spears, they will be paid. Ordinary Nepalese are scandalized by hippies. In the good old days, in New Zealand, if these dropouts from civilization had dropped in on the Maori, they would have been killed and cannibalized—probably before the sun went down.

The Big Ditch that yawns between the sentimentalism of the romantic primitivist and the pragmatism of the native is almost immeasurably wide. In fact the only thing that bridges it—despite the supposedly pristine precapitalist virtue of indigenes—is the cash nexus the Culture Cultists are fleeing from.

4

The Triumph of
the Litterateur

Bohemia has always known whom to hate (the dreaded bour-geoisie) but finding someone to love has been more difficult. If you loathe and despise the whole modern world of cities, and science, and commercial enterprise, you can end up in a psychological hole. But Rousseau long ago showed a way out—gaze wistfully at the horizon and bestow your affection on the picturesquely ethnic and remote, on Zuni and Samoa, on the Maori and Masai, on the denizens of deserts and the natives of snowcapped Nepal. This therapeutic love-at-a-distance is usually safe, and today it can be indulged in departments of anthropology. Here, on campus, the spiritual heirs of Rousseau mix freely with other alienated souls in an environment as far removed as possible from the everyday world of the bourgeois.

The conversion of many anthropology departments into refuges for the bohemian counterculture is unfortunate, though it needs to be emphasized that academic anthropology holds no campus monopoly in this. It is also a development which is very far from the ideals of the man—Franz Boas—who helped to bring it about. When he opened the doors of Columbia University's anthropology department to would-be writers like Ruth Benedict and Margaret Mead, he did so with the best of intentions, and before we look here at the way things turned out those worthy intentions should be recalled.

Today's Culture Cult can be seen, in part, as the unintended effect of a propaganda war which Boas knew had to be fought. Back in the

1920s race theories were in the air, and were increasingly popular in Germany, and Boas saw an urgent need for some opposing ideas to help stop Nazism in its tracks. Racial theory held that biology was destiny, and that if some cultures were inferior to others then inferior racial biology was the reason. An opposing theory would have to show that cultural factors, not biological, explained the diversity of human social arrangements; that was the advantage of culture theory at the time.

Biological determinism could be falsified by employing gifted writers to dramatize the variety of cultures made from the same human clay. And no one did this more effectively than Benedict and Mead. But the reason for showing this variety was widely misconstrued. Whereas Boas valued cultural diversity for its polemical value in the race debate, the literary folk loved diversity for its own sake even more. In their eyes all the colors and scents and petals in the great garden of human culture were beautiful in themselves—beauty, not biology, was all—while for Benedict aesthetics were almost as important as politics. What this reflected was largely the alienated romantic love of the other to be found in the world of Greenwich Village, and which, with the powerful contribution of men and women whose main interest was literature and writing, came gradually to prevail in much modern anthropology as well.

Columbia University, 1960

At Columbia University in the 1960s the divide was clear. The dominant anthropologists were male, wore tweedy jackets along with shirts and ties, and had loafers with a mature but unostentatious shine. They lectured on primitive law, or economic systems, or the pottery of northern Peru. They had a serious commitment to science, and most of them still knew what science meant.

Opposing them was a round bespectacled woman carrying a crook. She lectured on culture, and it seemed pretty much anything could be explained by culture—the culture of Bali, the culture of Samoa, the culture of the Arapesh, of the Chambri, of the Mundugumor. Each culture moreover was different and each unique. The tweed jacket crowd had little to do with undergraduates and no one knew where they lived. The woman with the crook was more accessible, and everyone knew where she lived—in Greenwich Village.

Her friends were artists, writers, photographers, filmmakers, off-beat psychologists, off-beat anything at all. It didn't seem to matter if the ideas which came her way lacked scientific credentials, as long as they were exciting and unusual to her. It should, however, be said in her favor that she showed no interest whatever in the notion, so popular today, that ethnographic description itself is impossible, or that it isn't even worth comparing different ethnographic accounts as true or false. Language had limits, but it was a serviceable tool all the same. Even Margaret Mead would have been surprised to see what anthropological navel-gazing would achieve by the year 2000.

Bohemia Enters the Academy

At the start, the divide between science and literature was deep. And for a long time the two fields remained distinct. You couldn't confuse George Eliot with Herbert Spencer, or Emile Zola with Emile Durkheim, though in America the writings of James Fenimore Cooper and the social enquiries of Lewis Henry Morgan, both treating Indian life, suggested that the two might eventually become one.

But this could only happen in the right setting. As anthropology became institutionalized after 1900 positions in museums and universities opened up. Literary folk with ethnographic interests now had good reason for moving away from the precarious life of the marginal writer and onto the campus. Struggling artists and poets in Greenwich Village usually lived on the edge, freezing to death in garrets still happened, and if that was your likely fate, then an academic appointment in anthropology was highly attractive.

For those with a consuming inner drive to romanticize the tribal world, the prospects were now encouraging. A post in anthropology brought together two things you liked—and one that you urgently needed. You could spend your time writing; you could work off your alienation and hostility to the commercial world around you by wistfully idealizing tribal cultures far away; and all of this could be done with regular pay. By 1920 all that was required for the marriage of anthropology and bohemia to take place was the right combination of available posts, alienated minds, frustrated literary talents, and a university man willing to bend the rules on accreditation.

And soon enough it did—the consummation coming in New York after World War I. Now the romantic heirs of Rousseau came into their own. A trickle of discontented literary intellectuals with their own private agendas—Edward Sapir, Elsie Clews Parsons, Ruth Benedict, and Margaret Mead—began to infiltrate anthropology, seeing in it both a career and a solution to their personal problems. Each of them benefited from the disorientation of the 1920s and from the tumult of ideas which were in the air—moral, political, and religious.

In a discussion of the overlap and blending between the American counterculture and anthropology, "The Ethnographic Sensibility of the 1920s," a historian of anthropology describes the thirty essays in *Civilization in the United States* as symptomatic. This 1922 book included contributions from anthropology, and announced that "there must be an entirely new deal of the cards in one sense; we must change our hearts. For only so, unless through the humbling of calamity or scourge, can true art and true religion and true personality, with their native warmth and caprice and gaiety, grow up in America."[1]

For two writer/anthropologists a new deal of the cards, allowing their native warmth and caprice and gaiety a good deal of scope, was coming soon. Professional rules of accreditation had hitherto discouraged the recruitment of dilettantes into anthropology, successfully keeping poets and writers out. But now a professor helped to get them in. Of continental background, he was about to change the face of American anthropology by welcoming the view that every culture is an organic whole; that each shows a distinctive pattern incomparable with other organic wholes; and that each is uniquely valuable too. With appropriate literary treatment this view would now be made available to the general reader, and eventually provide the foundations of the modern Culture Cult.

The professor's name was Franz Boas, and Margaret Mead and Ruth Benedict were the gifted women whose popularizations would soon be warmly received. In a familiar scenario, an ageing and be-whiskered academic, who enjoyed being treated as a god, bent the rules to bring two adoring female disciples under his wing. "Quickly sensing the vigorously imaginative mind veiled by her 'painfully shy' demeanor," writes Stocking, "Boas waived credit requirements to hurry Benedict through the Ph.D." For not dissimilar reasons Boas also exempted Mead from her final examination.[2]

Now two highly influential "would-be literati" moved close to the center of American anthropology. "Sapir implicitly believed that the poet might contribute to the poetic style of his/her culture," writes his biographer Regna Darnell, adding that "he was not alone in this fascination. . . . Benedict and Mead were also active in revising the Boasian model; all were engrossed in literary and aesthetic endeavors during the period their mature thought crystallized."[3]

Mead's life would eventually include everything from fieldwork in the South Pacific and New Guinea, to pop psychology, to an interest in cybernetics, to an international career as a media star, all the way down to a taste in her last days for the psychic healing offered by an Earth Mother named the Reverend Carmen diBarazza, and about the only common denominator in these activities was a willful determination to get her own way. But this willfulness explained a lot. And it would have dramatic consequences in Samoa. Between 1918 and 1928 the values of postwar Greenwich Village, filtered through Mead's enthusiastic rendering of the South Seas mystique, became incorporated into one of the most widely used educational texts of all time.

Drs. Benedict and Mead

At the age of seventeen Mead had a bad experience at De Pauw University. When she asked a university instructor about her prospects as a writer, he bluntly discouraged such a career. But this only made New York all the more magnetic. "I believed that the center of life was here in New York City where Mencken and George Jean Nathan were publishing *Smart Set,* where *The Freeman, The Nation, The New Republic* flourished, where F.P.A. and Heywood Broun were writing their diatribes, and where the theater was a living world of contending ideas."[4] In her first semester at Barnard she spent a lot of time at the other end of Broadway, going to numerous plays, and before long Ruth Benedict helped to confirm Mead's somewhat shaken belief in her own talent.

As the strongest influence on Mead other than Franz Boas, we are told that Benedict was someone who felt closest to "those who by age or sex or temperament or accidents of life history were out of the main currents of their culture." But this merely hints at the extent of her alienation and depression. Both these conditions affected her life and work. Mead's contemporary at Columbia, the anthropologist Ruth Bunzel, wrote that in the 1920s in America "some of us fled to the freer air of Paris. . . . Some of us joined radical movements and sold the *Daily Worker* on street corners, and some of us went into anthropology, hoping that there we might find some answers to the ambiguities and contradictions of our age. . . ."

She could also have added that another motive for going into anthropology was the hope of finding answers to one's own ambivalence and disarray as well. Anyway one thing was obvious. At the outset of their careers—as "their mature thought crystallized" in Regna Darnell's words—Benedict and Mead were worlds away from the nineteenth-century Victorian masters of anthropology in attitude, intent, and conduct, and almost as far from the new fieldwork being done by Bronislaw Malinowski and such disciples as Raymond Firth.

Aspiring to be known as writers, both women entered anthropology with literary designs. What they came up with in the 1920s and 1930s—a mélange of cultural patterns, personality types, and educational theory assuming that environmental conditioning was all important—would blend an attractive writing style with antimilitarist pacifism, with sexual liberation, and with Herderian cultural wholes, along with just enough science to reassure their academic colleagues. The effect on American anthropology would be to find a place within the discipline for a kind of heavily didactic semifiction. The effect on American manners and morals would be to legitimize the bohemian counterculture of Greenwich Village.

But what was that—what exactly *was* the culture of Greenwich Village around 1920? Malcolm Cowley said it embodied the following ideas.[5]

1. The idea of salvation by the child . . . Each of us at birth has special potentialities which are slowly crushed and destroyed by a standardized society and mechanical methods of teaching. If a new educational system can be introduced, one by which children are encouraged to develop their own personalities, to blossom freely like flowers, then the world will be saved by this new, free generation.

2. The idea of self-expression . . . Each man's, each woman's, purpose in life is to express himself, to realize his full individuality through creative work and beautiful living in beautiful surroundings.

3. The idea of living for the moment . . . It is stupid to pile up treasures that we can enjoy only in old age . . . Better to seize the moment as it comes, to dwell in it intensely, even at the cost of future suffering. Better to live extravagantly, gather June rosebuds, "burn my candle at both ends . . . It gives a lovely light."

4. The idea of paganism . . . The body is a temple in which there is nothing unclean, a shrine to be adorned for the ritual of life.

5. The idea of liberty . . . Every law, convention or rule of art that prevents self-expression or the full enjoyment of the moment should be shattered and abolished. Puritanism is the great enemy. The crusade against puritanism is the only crusade with which free individuals are justified in allying themselves.

6. The idea of female equality . . . Women should be the economic and moral equals of men. They should have the same pay, the same working conditions, the same opportunity for drinking, smoking, taking or dismissing lovers.

7. The idea of psychological adjustment . . . We are unhappy because we are maladjusted, and maladjusted because we are repressed.

8. The idea of changing place . . . "They do things better in Europe." England and Germany have the wisdom of old cultures; the Latin people have admirably preserved their pagan heritage. By expatriating himself, by living in Paris, Capri or the South of France, the artist can break the puritan shackles, drink, live freely and be wholly creative.

Regarding the first items in this list, salvation through educational reform accurately describes Mead's program. As she planned a trip to Melanesia in 1928, she wrote that two things were at the forefront of her mind: "the influence of the progressive education movement and 'a quick and partial interpretation of the first flush of success in Russian educational experiments.'"[6] Though as a general philosophy Benedict would not have agreed that "self-expression" was life's main purpose, poetry's self-expressive possibilities joined to anthropological romance did enable her to realize her own individuality.[7] Cowley's quote from Edna St. Vincent Millay's "Second Fig" in *A Few Figs from Thistles* consists of the very lines Mead chose as a motto while at Barnard College: "My candle burns at both ends; It will not last the night; But ah, my foes, and oh, my friends—It gives a lovely light."[8] Those lines were a clue to her life.

In the romantic anthropological variation on the pagan idea of the *body* as a pristine temple, pagan *cultures* are the temples in which nothing unclean is found, and which should be worshiped as shrines to the mystery of life: this is also a leading dogma of the Culture Cult. The crusade against American Puritanism inspired both women, in Mead's case blinding her to the obviously important fact of Samoan protestantism—not to mention its highly visible white-painted churches—in her search for evidence of adolescent promiscuity. If bohemia believed we are only unhappy and maladjusted because of repression, Mead's report on the absence of inner conflict in the Samoan girl because "all of her interest is expended on clandestine sex adventures" directly mirrors this view. Finally, instead of the bohemian conviction that "they do things better in Europe," the message of both Mead and Benedict—and the universal message of the Culture Cult today—was encapsulated in the idea that they do things better in Zuni and Samoa or wherever. Primitive culture everywhere possesses an inner wisdom civilization has lost.

To argue that the peculiar skewing of the pictures of Zuni painted by Benedict were just projections of her psychological needs would be absurd. Or would it? Sapir's biographer writes warningly of "the fit between Benedict's personality and the concerns of the discipline," and how "studying the exotic allowed her to avoid judgments of her own life."[9]

Added to this we find Mead reporting that "Benedict's characteristic conceptualization of culture as 'personality writ large' was worked out during the winter of 1927–28 in long conversations. . . ."[10] And further information provided by Stocking supports the claim that Benedict's portrait of Zuni was in truth the "anthropologist's personality writ large." He writes that "without implying that it had no basis in her own observations, or no confirmation in those of others, it seems evident that the picture Benedict painted of Zuni reflected the personal psychological set established at the moment the story of her life began, and the patterning and dynamics of her subsequent personal and cultural experience."[11] This is surely true of her account of the pueblo people in her 1934 *Patterns of Culture*, a book which sold a million copies in thirty years, and which is still selling to the public Benedict helped create. In writing about Zuni, "her personality had found a suitable niche," writes Stocking; and the fit between her needs and her description of Zuni was eerily close.[12]

She found Zuni to be a place of easy sexuality; where houses belong to the women; where marital jealousy is soft-pedaled; where divorce is just a matter of putting a husband's possessions on the doorsill; where there is no sense of sexual sin or guilt and where homosexuality is an honorable estate. Pacifism was another preoccupation, and we find that homicide hardly existed; that every day in Zuni there were fresh instances of mildness; that children were not disciplined; that there was no possibility of a child suffering from an Oedipus complex; that there were no cultural themes of terror or danger; and that the Pueblos "did not picture the universe, as we do, as a conflict of good and evil." But then how could they? In a culture so benign, so innocent, and so purely an embodiment of Rousseau's Natural Man, benevolence naturally prevailed. I am what I anthropologize. What I anthropologize I am. Zuni was indeed Ruth Benedict writ large.[13]

Over the years her mild and inoffensive Zuni, basking contentedly in the Southwest sun, passed into public consciousness as the classic image of Pueblo life. So much so that when the archaeologist Christy Turner II recently turned up grisly evidence of cannibalistic habits in the past, he was reviled for doing so and has been attacked by the Pueblo people themselves.[14] Is it any surprise that they much prefer the soft watercolors Benedict painted seventy years ago?

The moral transfiguration of Pueblo Indian life appears to have already been going on for a long time before Benedict appeared: she was surf-riding a much larger bohemian wave. Stocking reports that patrons of the arts "like Mabel Dodge, whose primitivist urges required a more 'genuine' culture than urban bohemia could provide," and whose salons in Italy and New York were frequented by John Reed, Lincoln Steffens, and Max Eastman, had already discovered the charms of the Southwest. When Mrs. Dodge heard the Zuni singing and drumming she felt herself "brought up against the tribe, where a different instinct ruled, and where virtue lay in wholeness instead of in dismemberment." For the British novelist D. H. Lawrence it was a place where "the slow dark weaving of the Indian life" went on still, "the old nodality of the pueblo still holding, like a dark ganglion spinning invisible threads of consciousness."[15]

Mead's Samoan Idyll

But whatever the Zuni gifts for spinning, no one spun invisible threads of consciousness more skillfully than Mead herself. The Samoan dream work began during a stopover at Honolulu. There she met Dr. Edward Handy, an expert on the culture of the Marquesan Islanders—the Polynesians Herman Melville had fixed in amber as the golden image of hedonistic South Pacific youth.

Handy told Mead that what she could expect to find in Samoa would probably resemble the premarital promiscuity reported in his Bishop Museum Bulletin *The Native Culture in the Marquesas.* There he vividly describes how "an old European resident of the Marquesas has told me that it seems an irresistible instinct with natives of both sexes to run wild for a few years after adolescence, in pursuit of amusement in general, but of the satisfaction of their abundant sexual appetite, in particular. A girl was looked down on in native society if she did not run wild in this way. . . ."[16] Girls like that were almost certainly to be found in Samoa, said Handy—for some reason ignoring the fact that there were well-known differences between the islands of eastern Polynesia (Tahiti and the Marquesas), and the western Polynesian islands of the Samoan group.

When she arrived in Pago Pago the romance intensified. Echoes of South Seas literary legend could be heard from every whispering grove. Robert Louis Stevenson was buried on one island, the hotel of Sadie Thompson stood right in the very place where Somerset Maugham had stayed while gathering materials for his story "Rain"—the same hotel where Mead stopped for a night or two. Always practical, she chose to stay at the U.S. Naval Dispensary on the island of Tutuila for most of her period in the field. In theory her research was to take nine months, and most accounts of her work report this figure. Yet no more than five months appear to have been actually spent on the island where the work was done. And Derek Freeman, who has made a day-by-day examination of how Mead used her time (from extensive collections of field notes, journals, and letters), concluded that "a total of not more than four or five weeks could have been spent in the actual 'investigation of the adolescent girl'" which she received a grant from the National Research Council to do.[17]

So how were the curious details in her book obtained? For the complete story the reader is referred to Freeman's *The Fateful Hoaxing of Margaret Mead*, especially chapter eleven, "The Ides of March." From the account he gives it's clear that a very bright and industrious young woman who had bitten off far more than she could chew, and had secretly undertaken more work than she could handle, triumphed despite running out of time. Burning her candle at both ends was now routine. In her personal life she was already doubly contracted to her husband and Ruth Benedict; she would be doubly committed to her first and second husbands before long; and in Samoa she had secretly agreed to do two research projects simultaneously.

Today when it is claimed that culture is something written by writers (rather than behavior which is described by social scientists), and that distinctions between truth and falsehood are illusory, it is revealing to look at the textual changes which occurred between Mead's field-notes and the appearance of her book. Worried whether her quantitative data would stand up, she had written to Franz Boas from the field asking whether "if I simply write conclusions and use my cases as illustrative material will it be acceptable?" Boas accepted her proposal without demur.[18]

Turning her field data into illustrative material was to be the first of a series of transfigurative steps. When her original manuscript was sent to the publisher George Morrow, he asked for something more likely to make a best-seller. She then made certain revisions, provided new material, and in her own words pushed speculation "to the limit of permissibility."[19] George Stocking writes that when *Coming of Age in Samoa* finally appeared in 1928, her worries about the way she had handled the data were relegated to an appendix, while "her new introduction confidently asserted the validity of the 'anthropological method' as the only option for those 'who wish to conduct a human experiment but who lack the power either to construct the experimental conditions or to find controlled examples of those conditions.'" However, she concluded, by using "simple, primitive peoples" she was able to answer the question "which sent me to Samoa."[20]

But the hard question—does her account of traditional Samoa truly describe the culture of "simple, primitive peoples," or is it how one thoroughly Christianized culture lived in 1926 after a century of mission activity and the forcible suppression of warfare, killing, and cannibalism?—was finally reduced to an appendix. On page 219, after eight and a half pages in very small print, in the second to last paragraph of appendix 3, and in notable contrast to the amiabilities found elsewhere, the following information about Samoan culture is vouchsafed to dogged readers:

> The new influences have drawn the teeth of the old culture. Cannibalism, war, blood revenge, the life and death power of the *matai*, the punishment of a man who broke a village edict by burning his house, cutting down his trees, killing his pigs, and banishing his family, the cruel defloration ceremony, the custom of laying waste plantations on the way to a funeral, the enormous loss of life in making long voyages in small canoes, the discomfort due to widespread disease—all these have vanished.

This glimpse of ugly historical realities reminds us of one of the more deeply repressed features of twentieth-century ethnography. This is that 99 percent of the studies made by anthropologists have been of defanged tribalism (after the teeth of the old culture have been "drawn," as Mead puts it), cultures pacified and neutralized by colonial authority—that same authority whose laws and police forces protected the anthropologists while they worked. Toothless tribalism did indeed give an impression of remarkably "pacific" ways of life. It could hardly be otherwise, since under the colonial authorities the penalty for unseemly mayhem and killing was severe.

Elsewhere the same thing was true. All West African anthropology in the twentieth century, for example, took place in such circumstances—circumstances very different from the 1860s, for example. Although Sir Richard Burton's mission to the Kingdom of Dahomey on behalf of Queen Victoria may not have succeeded in halting human sacrifice in 1864, by the end of the nineteenth century it had indeed been stopped. The French saw to that. As a result it was never witnessed by any professional anthropologist. Though some of the barbarities of initiation inflicted on young boys in the highlands of Papua New Guinea may well have continued until twenty years ago, in their more extreme forms they too have probably come to an end. Likewise in Samoa, Fiji, and New Zealand in the nineteenth century, the widespread practice of enslavement, the occasional practice of human sacrifice, and the invariable practice of eating prisoners, were all determinedly stamped out by governments in close alliance with Christian missionaries. No academic anthropologist ever saw them— or survived to give an eyewitness report.

As for Mead and *Coming of Age in Samoa*, those who in 1928 read it for the message of its subtitle (*A Psychological Study of Primitive Youth for Western Civilization*) found just what they were looking for, much of it in the opening pages: "As the dawn begins to fall among the soft brown roofs and the slender palm trees stand out against a colourless, gleaming sea, lovers slip home from trysts beneath the palm trees or in the shadow of beached canoes, that the light may find each sleeper in his appointed place. Cocks crow, negligently . . . "[21] The book was both an idyll and a tract for the times, and the public bought it in droves.

Bohemia Is Institutionalized

Growing Up in Samoa and *Patterns of Culture* represented a decisive breakthrough for romantic primitivism as an accepted form of ethnographic presentation in academic circles. Yet anthropology remained a productive branch of social science for many years after. It was only when the countercultural heirs and successors of Benedict and Mead took the stage in the late 1960s that a real decline set in. The history of those years is too well known to deserve more than a reference here. But if you pick up a book like Keith Melville's 1972 *Communes in the Counter Culture* it is still surprising to find how constantly the romantic primitivist refrain is sounded—escapism, tribalism, sweetlifeism on page after page.

Civilization being doomed, "it was my dream to belong to a tribe, where the energies flow among everyone, where people care for one another, where no one has to work, but everyone wants to do something . . ."[22] A millennarian note is sounded and the birth of the New Age announced: "We're retribalizing, and when we get it all together, the vibes are so high we know we're doing something right. And, like, so many people are getting turned on, it's the beginning of a whole new age."[23]

Retribalizing meant going back to Mother Nature and seeking the wisdom of America's aborigines. Those well-known pacifists, the Plains Indians, had much to teach about freedom, tolerance, and peace. One of its speakers saw Indian freedom of movement as a sort of negative Open Society—you were free to leave—especially if you were looking for a way out. In Indian encampments "if one is not happy where one is, one leaves, instead of telling someone else to leave. When the chief of the Plains Indians became too oppressive for his people, he woke up one morning to find that his teepee was the only one on the plain."[24]

Partly inspired by hippie vision quests, anthropological enrollments in the universities now took off. A department's prestige greatly depended on the popularity of its courses, and if students were keen on the sort of radicalism that looks to shamanism for inspiration why not give it to them? An interest in alternative medicine suggested that a solicitous administration should set up a subdepartment devoted to holistic healing, and invite practitioners to come and discuss their craft. A few women had formed covens in the city: witches and warlocks were said to walk at night. These, too, could be used as subjects for enquiry and research. Numbers swelled as a strange regiment of the immature and the confused, sometimes barefoot and occasionally dragging mangy dogs on strings, converged on the nearest anthropology department confident they would be warmly received.

Few could spell. Some could barely write. But they were reassured to discover that all could pass. And those who got a "good" AB might be encouraged to try for a higher degree. Endless academic hours were spent, and large quantities of public money were wasted, vainly deliberating as to whether or not the puerilities of Thesis A deserved a higher mark than the inanities of Thesis B. (Or should it be vice versa? Who could tell?)

One day a youth with a ghostly whitened face and ink-black clothing came to leave his essay. Rising from my chair to receive it I stretched out my hand . . . only to withdraw it, horrified, feeling something like a large spider brush my skin. I then saw that his fingernails tapered several inches to a feathery tip at the ends, and this is what had brushed against me. After he left the office I remembered the strong connection between bohemian dress habits and Veblen's theory of the leisure class. What those spooky nails unambiguously proclaimed was that their owner did not, could not, and would not do useful work.[25]

Majority opinion has long derided bohemia as a force for change. Marxists have been especially scathing about the ideal of "art for art's sake," treating bohemia's contempt for the bourgeoisie as a contradiction. Serious rebels were advised to read that well-known manifesto, join the Party, and give their lives to the cause. But in the year 2000 it is fair to ask who is laughing now, and who has been the more effective, the bohemians or the Marxists—especially after 1989?

A member of the counterculture once argued that "a gang that playfully corrupts the mayor's teenage son produces more important and enduring change than does the strictly disciplined, grim, and earnest assassination squad that gets his father."[26] Be that as it may, it is certainly true that bohemianism is more deeply hostile to the values of the bourgeoisie than Marxism ever was. To understand why this is so, remember Ben Franklin's useful virtues—temperance, silence, order, resolution, frugality, industry, sincerity, justice, moderation, cleanliness, tranquillity, chastity, and humility. Some of these values are compatible with social democracy. One or two of them found a place in the Communist world. But none are compatible with bohemia.

Anthropology's Decline and Fall

The little world of anthropology was to have its own crisis too—and its own literary transmogrification. As the old colonial world where fieldwork had been done fell apart in a chaos of guerrilla wars, the anthropologist retreated to the stacks. What interested him now was the usual sort of thing you find in libraries—books and writing. Sometimes it was his own writing on ethnographic matters, and sometimes other people's writing, and sometimes other people's writing about other people: almost anything at all would do.

With the waning of the primitive world the descriptive phase of ethnography was obviously self-terminating: you can't study old-time Aborigines or Inuit anymore. But anthropological *writing* always finds new ways to justify itself. Mortgage payments must be met. School fees must be paid. Husbands and wives and companions must be propitiated. In brief, income must be earned. The tradition of egocentric literary exoticism has no logical or practical conclusion. In academic sheltered workshops it can go on forever.

Cluttered with pretentious jargon, postmodern anthropology can be seen as a bizarre, scholasticized, and institutionalized variation of the romantic primitivism which originated with Rousseau. It signals the triumph of the litterateur. In the nineteenth century this expressed itself in the form of a narcissistic concern with self-realization and self-expression, fused with a romantic admiration for other times and places. Much the same takes place in the genre of academicized travel writing one finds today. As Ernest Gellner put it not long ago, "Sometimes . . . a social anthropological study degenerates from having been a study of a society into a study of the reaction of the anthropologist to his own reactions to his observations of the society, assuming that he had ever got as far as to have made any."

What you get often "tends to become a set of pessimistic and obscure musings on the Inaccessability of the Other and its Meanings. At other times the gimmick seems to be to exile the author from the text and to proceed to decode, or deconstruct, or desomething, the meanings which spoke through the author had he but known it." There are brave exceptions here and there. But in the year 2000 that is what much anthropology has become.[27]

PART II

ACADEMIC PRIMITIVISM

The Political Implications

5

What Karl Polanyi
Found in Dahomey

West Africa is not a happy place. Much of it has gone backward since 1960. In 1999 a well-known weekly described its most populous country—Nigeria—as lacking any of the structures which hold modern states together, being systematically undermined by "ethnic or religious loyalties, by networks of mafias or secret societies, and by bribery. Industries that should be making money have become instruments for the theft of billions of dollars." The economy is in tatters. Corruption is a way of life.[1]

Yet in 1960 Karl Polanyi believed that West Africa would lead the world. He was convinced that planned economies run by strong rulers were the coming thing, and he spent years searching all history for evidence supporting this view. He invented a scheme of economic analysis still influential in anthropology. He studied the economy of Mesopotamia in antiquity. And when his research led him to West Africa, he thought he had found, in the eighteenth-century kingdom of Dahomey, an example of central economic planning of amazing complexity. There was a method of record-keeping using pebbles and raffia bags—something he boldly compared with the achievements of IBM. Here, in a barbaric despotism featuring war, slavery, and human sacrifice, this romantic Hungarian found his political ideal.

Karl's brother Michael Polanyi was a very different man. He had a distinguished early career as a research chemist. As a philosopher he emphasized what he called "the tacit dimension" of knowledge—all the things we know without having to articulate them, or are even conscious of, and which underlie social life. But only his economic ideas concern us here, and these were original.

Michael Polanyi, whose thinking was close to Friedrich Hayek's, showed why Karl Polanyi's ideas about central planning wouldn't work. Hayek had said that the countless billions of calculations required in a modern economy couldn't be done by the state because they were noncomputable. Polanyi added that there were also physical constraints of time and energy, which made central planning impossible "in the same way that it's impossible for a cat to swim the Atlantic."

Along with the chapters on Isaiah Berlin, and on Karl Popper, we look here at the relation between romantic primitivism and academic thought. As so often, John Maynard Keynes's words are deeply relevant. Ideas, he said, "are more powerful than is commonly understood. Indeed, the world is ruled by little else. Madmen in authority, who hear voices in the air, are distilling their frenzy from some academic scribblers of a few years back . . ."[2] Used to glamorize West Africa and to make acceptable the unacceptable customs of the past, Karl Polanyi's academic writings on behalf of archaic Dahomey comprise one of the stranger examples of a twentieth-century university mind. But in this case the madman was the academic scribbler himself.

Presidential Dreams

President Clinton's visit to West Africa in early 1998 was an uplifting experience for all concerned—and as a photo-opportunity it was a huge success. Speaking to the thousands gathered in Accra's Independence Square he pointed out that he was not the first notable United States citizen to have visited Ghana. In 1957 Martin Luther King, Jr., had come to represent the United States at Ghana's independence celebrations, and the great civil rights leader was "deeply moved by the birth of your nation."[3]

The president also mentioned how the eminent black American W. E. B. DuBois, toward the end of his life, had become a citizen of Ghana, and had eventually died there as a friend of Ghana's leader Kwame Nkrumah. DuBois once wrote that "the habit of democracy must be to encircle the earth." The president invited the assembled crowd to "resolve to complete the circle of democracy; to dream the dream that all people on the entire Earth will be free and equal; to begin a new century with that commitment to freedom and justice for all . . . to find a future here in Africa, the cradle of humanity."[4]

No mention was made of Ghana's history under Kwame Nkrumah, or that he had ended up as an exile in Romania with Nicolai Ceausescu, dying in Bucharest in 1972. It was a time for looking ahead with hope and pride. The president and the first lady had come to learn from Africa, he said, concluding eloquently that his dream for Ghana was nothing less than a new African renaissance.

Nor did he dream in vain. A renaissance of sorts came to West Africa the very next year when Nigeria changed from military to civilian rule. Civilian rule is always expected to bring good things, and when in 1999 President Obasanjo lopped the top off the armed services, fired customs officials, and tried to restrain the looting of the treasury, these were taken as encouraging signs.

According to the world press it was all good news; and had Mr. Clinton wanted academic support for this upbeat view of Africa, all he needed to do was consult the numerous books published since the 1960s foreseeing a splendid future for the continent. Among these, a 1968 study of a country tucked between Ghana and Nigeria on the Bight of Benin would surely have been of interest.

The country was Dahomey (now known as Benin), and the book's author was Karl Polanyi. A man easily impressed by evidence in favor of his pet ideas, Polanyi was convinced that the eighteenth-century Kingdom of Dahomey was one of the administrative wonders of the world, and like Mr. and Mrs. Clinton he believed that Africa had much to teach us all. In his view Western ways were overrated. There were other models of governance, notably in Dahomey, and Polanyi hoped his book would make a contribution to meeting the problems of the modern age. Foreseeing an era of wise guidance by powerful African rulers (a renaissance, in fact, though he didn't use the word himself), he looked forward to a day when "high statecraft may reappear unexpectedly in the awakening countries of the continent"[5]— and in West Africa most of all.

Budapest

Karl Polanyi was born in Budapest in 1886 and had an unusual childhood. Much of it was spent in the isolation of a castle out in the country. There he and his four brothers and sisters received individual tuition in accordance with the precepts laid down by Rousseau in *Emile*. Inside the castle the children were to be shielded as much as possible from "the hypocrisy and corruption of society." It is possible that this permanently weakened Karl's grip on reality—he always seems to have found that ordinary people fell sadly short of his ideals.[6]

But all the Polanyi children had remarkable lives. The oldest boy, Otto, made a successful business career in Italy before serving as an adviser to Mussolini. After Otto came Adolph, a famous engineer and visionary promoter in Brazil. Next born was a girl called Mousie. No one ever called her by any other name, but in the years before World War I she played a leading part in the Hungarian folk movement associated with the music of Kodály, Bartók, and Dohnányi. If Peter Drucker is to be believed—and this author's sketch of the family is our only source of information—she not only pioneered Hungarian rural sociology, but also influenced the design of the early kibbutz. The youngest child was Michael Polanyi, born in 1891.

Drucker knew several members of the family personally and tells us that they all "enlisted in the same cause: to overcome the nineteenth century and to find a new society that would be free and yet not 'bourgeois' or 'liberal'; prosperous and yet not dominated by economics; communal and yet not a Marxist collectivism." This judgment is revealing—especially the view that both freedom and prosperity can be achieved by communal means—though it doesn't fit Michael quite as well as the others. In any case, what is most important are the political delusions which came to dominate Karl's mind.[7]

His gifts were recognized early—the Galileo Circle in Budapest made him its first president in 1908. This society of intellectuals hoped for the overthrow of the Habsburg monarchy, the advance of science, and the liberation of mankind. Its leaders were divided between those who looked to the English model of parliamentary democracy, and those more drawn to the communal traditions of Eastern Europe—but it was the Eastern prospect which fascinated Karl. Although he found refuge in England, and later in America, he never seems to have fully understood the West.

The Galileo Circle had been founded by a legal philosopher named Julius Pikler, who warned his followers that "scientific research and speculation must never give way to religious, social or political considerations." But his warning seemed to have gone unheard. In the words of one observer the Circle soon came to reflect "the spirit of revolutionary Russia, rationalism driven to its mystic extreme."[8]

Utopia Meets Ludwig von Mises

Extremes of one kind or another were typical of Karl Polanyi. But the unreality of his politics seems to have mainly come from a severely moralistic view of life. He believed that the whole of Hungarian society had fallen into such a state of dereliction that only idealism pitched at the highest level could save the nation. In a 1929 memoir he wrote of the Galileo Circle that, "For generations, moral standards were not imperative in Hungarian public life. The representatives of the working-class, whom the Hungarian moral quagmire finally entrapped, had also sunk into a profitable, or at least a comfortable opportunism. The Galileo Circle took upon itself that without which life becomes ignominious: self-sacrificing responsibility for the rights of others. . . . The Galileo Circle's assets were moral."[9]

Notice how the word "moral" occurs three times in four sentences. There is an air of extravagant high-mindedness about it all, and Polanyi seemed aware of this tendency when he berated himself for a lack of realism "which in the theoretical as in the practical field condemned me to futility. From 1909 to 1935 I achieved nothing. I strained my powers in the futile directions of stark idealism, its soarings lost in the void."[10]

With hindsight this might have been a good thing. If he had made a career in politics his highly unreal expectations and severe demands could easily have made for a terrible ruthlessness. There is a similarity between his attitude toward the shortcomings of the Hungarian people and Mao Tse-tung's attitude toward the shortcomings of the Chinese people. Mao once said of his countrymen that they had "accumulated many undesirable customs, their mentality is too antiquated and their morality is extremely bad . . . ," all things which "cannot be removed and purged without enormous force."[11]

But it is idle to speculate what Karl Polanyi might have done with political power. What is unarguable is that "stark idealism" (or maybe just a plain refusal to face the facts) accurately describes his reaction to the reports coming out of the new Soviet Union in 1920. Those were the days when the Bolsheviks tried to abolish money, to prohibit private trade, to introduce "socially necessary" forced labor (the beginning of the gulag), and to impose a comprehensive economic plan. Peasants who opposed the state had their entire crop seized and were publicly hanged by the hundreds to impress the rest. In the words of Richard Pipes:

> Commerce in cereals and other agricultural produce was outlawed. Such actions, unthinkable even under serfdom, embroiled Soviet Russia in the most ferocious civil war in the country's history, in which hundreds of thousands of Red Army soldiers fought pitched battles against hundreds of thousands of peasants. A communist economist described the economic collapse which followed these events as a calamity "unparalleled in the history of mankind."[12]

But there are calamities and calamities, and some have lessons to teach. Bolshevik policies focused the attention of Western economists on the economics of socialism as never before—one economist in particular. This was the Legal Advisor and Financial Expert of the Vienna Chamber of Commerce, Ludwig von Mises, whose essay "Economic Calculation in the Socialist Commonwealth" made a pioneering contribution to the subject. Appearing in April 1920, this "set the scene for the scientific discussion of the problem of socialization. . . . Just when the hopes of socialism seemed to be about to come true, Mises voiced the thoughts uppermost in the minds of so many who lacked the courage to speak out."[13]

In this essay Mises did two important things. On the one hand he argued that "socialism could not work or keep its promises . . . because under such a system economic calculations in terms of value were rendered impossible." On the other he asserted that the centralized organization of the economy inevitably "becomes transformed into a totalitarian regime."[14] These were prophetic words indeed—but they didn't go down well with Karl Polanyi. By then employed on a Viennese newspaper as a financial journalist, he decided to answer the "bourgeois economist" from the Chamber of Commerce in 1922.[15] The debate begun by Mises was of momentous consequence, and many in the German-speaking world were watching. Here was Polanyi's chance to respond to the most significant challenge yet made to socialist prophecy.

So what did he do? Dismissing Mises's criticism of socialist accountancy as irrelevant, he quickly moved discussion onto the idealistic plane where he felt at home, and where you don't have to worry about figures. In the words of an admirer, "Polanyi's socialism (argued in response to Mises) was more the conclusion of a humanist scholar than a matter of practical political action. . . . In that article he focused more on the moral superiority of socialism . . . than on the politics of creating socialism or the possibilities of economic calculation in a socialist economy."[16]

The tactic is familiar. Journalistic expertise meets genuine expertise, and rather than treat the issues it goes for the high moral ground.

The Sacred Hate

Polanyi was also showing more peculiar traits. After being seriously wounded in action during World War I, he had undergone major surgery in 1919, and it was in a Viennese hospital that he met the nineteen-year-old nurse's aide who became his wife. Ilona Duczynska was no dreamy intellectual waffling on about moral sacrifice. She was a tough revolutionary who had been a leader of the Communist Party underground in Hungary during the war, and after taking part in Bela Kun's short but bloody Hungarian Revolution of 1919 she had been forced into exile in Vienna. Where Polanyi was inclined to lofty impracticality, Ilona Duczynska was just the reverse. Her mentality was that of a Hungarian Red Guard, and her vocabulary had a coarse intransigence—for Ilona the emotion of hatred was a noble thing.[17]

Did she have anything to do with the strange manuscript her hospital patient Karl wrote during his convalescence? This huge and unpublishable work "traced the history of the capacity of the developing science of medicine to murder people, equalled only by the capacity of developing social science to do so."[18] There are plenty of reasons a wounded cavalryman might be depressed during convalescence, resentful of delayed recovery, discouraged by lingering deaths in neighboring beds, and suspicious of the reassurances offered by faceless surgeons he does not know or trust. But a large piece of writing about "the capacity of medicine to *murder* people" and the capacity of social science to *murder* people too? Strange, if nothing more.[19]

But stranger still is Peter Drucker's story of his Christmas Eve visit to Polanyi's house in Vienna. It was Christmas Eve, 1927, and the older man had invited his young associate on *The Austrian Economist* to join him and his family for Christmas dinner. "We took one streetcar line to its terminal way out in a slum district. Then we took another one that ran through an industrial zone of small factories and warehouses. And then, from the terminal of that line, we walked a good twenty minutes through tumbledown shacks, abandoned-car lots, and a few city dumps until we came to a solitary old and grimy five-story tenement, the lower floors of which were boarded up."

Lugging some valises he used as briefcases, Polanyi and his guest arrived on the top floor in total darkness, where a "door was opened and we were greeted by Polanyi's wife Ilona, her mother, an elderly widowed Hungarian baroness, and the Polanyi's only child, a daughter then about eight years old. We sat down to dinner immediately and were served what, without exaggeration, I can call the worst meal of my life: old, badly peeled, half-raw potatoes—there was not even margarine with them. This was Christmas dinner!"

Earlier that day Drucker had seen Polanyi's paycheck—"by Austrian 1927 standards it was enormous"—and because he had been shocked by his Christmas dinner he wondered aloud whether such austerity was strictly necessary. "All four stopped talking and were absolutely silent for what seemed an eternity. Then all four turned and stared at me. And all four said, almost in unison: 'What a remarkable idea; spend your paycheck on yourself! We never heard of such a thing!' 'But,' I stammered, 'most people do that.' 'We are *not* most people,' said Ilona, Karl's wife, sternly; 'we are *logical* people.'"[20]

Vienna had many refugees living in miserable circumstances at that time. Polanyi gave his entire paycheck from the *The Austrian Economist* for their support, and gave his family old half-cooked potatoes to eat. Such was the ethic by which logical people lived. It was a hint of things to come.

As things got worse on the Continent, Karl made his way to England in 1933. Arriving there as an unknown radical from Central Europe, he struggled for years to make a living, endured great poverty, and during visits to Wales saw grim workers' housing in the shadow of hills of slag. His mind turned back to the early days of the Industrial Revolution, and he began to gather documents for a book. In Ilona's account of this period she writes that it was in England that her husband acquired "the hatred of the classical species of class society in its classical homeland," adding that "it is given to the best among men somewhere to let down the roots of a sacred hate in the course of their lives."[21]

Ilona tells us this sacred hate was directed against market society and its effects, because they divested man of his human shape. No doubt hatred has occasional benefits for even the best among men, but Ilona's attempt to sanctify her husband's destructive obsession is not convincing. This so-called sacred hate of capitalism gravely distorted his work, fatally skewed his scholarly interpretation of the ancient world, and finally destroyed his moral sense.

Michael Polanyi Meets Bukharin

While Karl was in England reliving the Industrial Revolution, his younger brother Michael was in Russia asking questions about the Bolshevik revolution. Michael (1891–1976) had obtained a degree in medicine from the University of Budapest in 1913, and a Ph.D. in chemistry four years later. He spent some of World War I as an officer in the Austro-Hungarian army, and afterward did research in physical chemistry at the Kaiser Wilhelm Institute in Berlin, mixing there with Planck, Schrödinger, and Einstein. The rise of Hitler led to his departure for England in 1933, and by then he had more than a hundred papers to his credit and an international reputation for his work on chemical reaction rates.

The effects of inflation in Germany and the grim spectacle of the Great Depression made him curious about the "experiment" taking place in the east, and on a visit to Moscow in 1935 he decided to find out what Nicolai Bukharin thought about science in Soviet Russia. For Michael pure science was always best left to the spontaneous co-operation of researchers themselves:

> We recognize here that a large number of independent activities can form a system of close co-operation . . . This is the co-operation of independent minds devoted to the pursuit of an aim which, though it is beyond the perception of any, yet is jointly guiding their several thoughts. It is the co-operation which arises by the pursuit of truth and other parts of human culture.[22]

Bukharin saw matters differently. The commissar's view was "that pure science was a morbid symptom of a class society," and that under socialism scientists should work for the Five Year Plan. During his visit Polanyi was shown a report from a research institute telling the reader how "Each department draws up a plan for work from January 1 to December 31 of each year. The plan is given in detail for each quarter, and there must even be a suggestion of what will be done on each day. At the end of each month the research worker assesses what percentage he has accomplished of his plan. This is usually about 80 percent to 90 percent, and the assessments are notably honest."[23]

Michael later described this report as a "disgusting comedy." It was disgusting because it made a mockery of human nature itself, and it was a comedy because the whole work schedule was "only a pretence kept up for the satisfaction of official requirements; on my various visits to scientific institutions in the USSR I never heard it mentioned except in contemptuous jokes." Yet despite the laughable procedure, it had been solemnly reaffirmed as Soviet practice by the British communist and well-known scientist J. D. Bernal in his 1939 *The Social Functions of Science*.[24]

Michael Polanyi thought it was a great mistake of the Soviets to base their reforms on military organization. Like Hayek, he believed that loose guiding principles were needed in human affairs—not generals and guns and guards. An army was the classic example of large-scale organization directed by a single purpose, firmly controlling all its members. But coordinating the many parts of an army in the field was notoriously difficult. "No authority can co-ordinate the movements of its subordinates, unless they obey orders; discipline, therefore, is essential to planning." The assumption of military planning and military discipline meant that only a short distance separated the needs of the assembly line from the discipline of the firing squad. If central planning were adopted, this would

> imply the abolition of both the cultivation of guiding principles and the pursuit of commerce, with all the liberties inherent in these forms of life. Hence collectivist revolution must aim at the destruction of liberty, and in particular must suppress the privileges under which Universities, Law Courts, Churches, and the Press are upholding their ideals, and attack the rights of individual enterprise under which trade is conducted.

Critique Without Remedies

Karl Polanyi might have thrown back his head and laughed at this. Forms of life, guiding principles, the pursuit of commerce . . . these meant less than nothing to him. He hated commerce, and liberty was something he barely noticed. The politics he had learned in Budapest led him to regard parliamentary government with disdain. Indeed, military planning, of the kind Michael said was incompatible with life in a free society, was pretty much how Karl saw the road ahead.

Disturbing personality changes in Karl in the late 1930s began to be reported. At the *Austrian Economist* in the late 1920s he had been respected for his reluctance to speculate. But in England he began to invent news. He was absolutely sure that Hitler would not invade Austria. Though German troops were already massing on the Austrian border, something told him this was just a feint: Switzerland was the real target. With utmost confidence he told Drucker that a German invasion of Austria was "the one thing, Peter, you don't have to worry about just now." Hitler marched in ten days later. During the "phony war" two years later he said to Drucker, "It's crystal-clear that there is a secret agreement between Hitler, Russia, the English, the French, and Japan for an attack on China and an attempt to partition it. The European war is just a feint."[25] This turn of mind did not augur well. Matters would be equally "crystal clear" when he began reading about West Africa, treating questionable ethnographic sources as indubitable.

In 1940 Peter Drucker found a position for him at Bennington College in Vermont. There Karl Polanyi wrote a sweeping denunciation of the rise of industrial capitalism and all its works. *The Great Transformation* of 1944 parades the usual villains, from Adam Smith through Malthus and Ricardo down to his old enemy Ludwig von Mises, shows a sound grasp of nineteenth-century historical detail, and is written with color and passion.

Yet at the end the reader is left asking, "What next? What are you proposing? What should be done?" And to these questions Karl Polanyi had no answer. Despite his Soviet sympathies he was not an orthodox Marxist and there is therefore no call for revolution. Although its argument demands economic planning, the book lacks any concrete proposals. In England he had joined a number of churchmen and communists in writing *Christianity and the Social Revolution*, so was he urging a Christian Socialist Commonwealth perhaps? *The Great Transformation* contained a cursory treatment of pre-industrial arrangements. Did he think a return to the medieval era was possible?

Perhaps he did. There is a sense in which the entire indignant sermon of the book was a way of praising the virtues of the old medieval village community with its tied farmers and feudal lords; a way of nostalgically admiring the political administration of the ancient empires; a way of indulging the romantic primitivist dream of cultures that never were and pasts that have gone forever. Once upon a time all those exemplary cultures that romantics admire existed—ritualistic and rural, disciplined and predictable, and much more virtuous than anything the twentieth century can show. And if some of them had slaves, or practiced human sacrifice, and were conspicuously undemocratic, so what?

As it did for Rousseau two hundred years before, life in an imaginatively constructed past had several advantages for Karl Polanyi. After becoming a professor of economic history at Columbia University in 1947, an escape into the mists of classical history would neatly solve the problem of having no practical policies to back up his bitter critique. He wouldn't need them—romantics never do. He would play off the primitive against Western civilization, not in order to propose a genuine alternative, but to demean civilization itself. Like Rousseau he would argue analogically "as if" what he was describing were an alternative to modern life; "as if" a study of neotribal communalism in a despotic state could be of political service today; "as if" the way back into the past was the way ahead.

Back to the Future

Soon this became a pattern. His response to the crisis of the 1930s had been to bemoan the passing of the agrarian age, and to write scathingly about the rise of industrial capitalism, while offering the reader no obvious plan for reform. In much the same way, his response to the embarrassing capitalist prosperity of postwar America in the 1950s was to escape back into the ancient empires of the Middle East. And whatever he found would be interpreted in the light of his "sacred hate."

He forcefully argued that corruption of primordial, communal, organic harmony came first with trade and markets; and with a vigilant eye he began ransacking antiquity for documents supporting this. If the contempt of the scribe for the merchant is an invariable feature of human history, Karl Polanyi was its incarnation. In *Trade and Market in the Early Empires,* whenever he found that archaeology could not actually say for sure whether Babylon had market places he was delighted—here at last was a civilization without them. In Babylon, he announced, prices were not set by market mechanisms but by the administrative officials of the central government, and administrative price-fixing was exactly as it should be:

> As to market squares, I pointed to the archaeological proof of the almost complete absence of open spaces in the walled towns of ancient Palestine, as well as to the marketless layout of Babylon, attested by the finds in the library of Assur-banipal. In a separate study of the translations of the "Cappadocian" tablets available to me, I developed a conjectural sketch of the administrative functions of the *tamkar*, of non-market trade; of the riskless forms of administered foreign commerce and other requisites of treaty-trade, which appeared compatible with the postulate of non-market methods . . .[26]

The "postulate of non-market methods," and of prices being set from on high by public authorities whose job was to assure "risk-free" forms of commerce—this had become an *idée fixe*. The absence "of even so much as a word for 'market' in the Akkadian language," he crowed, "must raise many questions for Assyriology."[27]

Whatever could be defined as *good for the group*—whatever conformed with its customs however strange or oppressive, however heartless or cruel, however incompatible with the most rudimentary civil rights—this was by definition a good thing, since it helped to secure "solidarity" and "wholeness of life." Romantic primitivism consistently idealizes coercive tribalistic blood-based solidarity, and Polanyi was delighted to find this in the ancient world. Instead of independent work by free individuals, economic activity was governed by "blood-tie, legal compulsion, religious obligation, fealty, or magic"—each of them ensuring collective solidarity and therefore good things all.[28]

Michael Polanyi—
Why Central Planning Must Fail

While Karl plodded steadily on toward the ultimate revelations of West Africa and Dahomey, Michael refined his thinking on the Soviet Union. Taking a broad view of the matter, there seemed to be two universal principles of social order. "Deliberate order," for example, was what you found in the well-kept garden or the well-drilled regiment. It consisted of "limiting the freedom of things and men to stay or move about at their pleasure, by assigning to each a specific position in a prearranged plan." This was a good way of making gardens or regiments or rockets, but it was a hopeless way of making economic decisions about the goods ordinary people wanted or the products which factories should make.

In contrast was the more important principle of "spontaneous order." This could be seen in nature at a number of levels. You found it in chemistry when fluids, gases and liquids crystalized at low temperatures, and the molecules in a well-stirred mixture spontaneously sorted themselves out on their own. You could see it in biology where growth and form in plants were spontaneously regulated by internal processes. And in the world of men and women, "when order is achieved among human beings by allowing them to interact with each other on their own initiative—subject only to laws which uniformly apply to all—we have a system of spontaneous order in society."[29]

Friedrich Hayek was saying that spontaneous order was similar to the dynamic self-adjusting and self-regulating order of classical economic theory. Michael Polanyi agreed, and pointed to parallels in the scientific field. "My argument for freedom in science," he wrote, "bears a close resemblance to the classical doctrine of economic individualism." Scientific discovery will proceed best, and will be best coordinated, "if—and only if—each (researcher) is left to follow his own inclinations."

As for the questions raised by Mises in 1920, Michael said that the Bolshevik attempt from 1919 to 1921 to abolish money and eliminate the market "broke down in chaos as von Mises had rightly predicted."[30] But a question still remained. Why exactly was central economic planning, in principle, absurd? It was not just because the billions of transactions were beyond calculation. The comprehensive direction of a national economy for 100,000,000 people was downright impossible—"impossible in the same sense that it is impossible for a cat to swim the Atlantic" or a cow to jump over the moon.[31]

How so? Because of natural limits of energy and time. Buyers and sellers in a spontaneously ordered social system make millions of mutually agreed-on adjustments directly and simultaneously every second of the day. A social system with vertical lines of authority, by contrast, must make them indirectly, intermittently, and in sequence, involving many more stages and steps and far more time.[32]

Michael Polanyi had seen the Great Depression. He was not an uncritical advocate of markets. They have several shortcomings, he wrote in 1951, but "we must either put up with these deficiencies or forgo the operations of the system altogether . . . There exists no radical alternative to the capitalist system. Our modern high-standard economy was built up on this system and its elimination would reduce our economy to the level of subsistence farming."

Amazing Dahomey

But subsistence farming under a military bureaucracy was what Karl had just found in West Africa. Some of the statements in his 1966 book *Dahomey and the Slave Trade* are so strange, and their political assumptions are so hair-raising, that one needs to be sure this posthumously published work was entirely his own. In one obvious way it was not. The information about economic organization it contains is drawn wholesale from Melville Herskovits's 1938 *Dahomey: An Ancient West African Kingdom*. But there are other complications too. On the title page it says "in collaboration with Abraham Rotstein," and one wonders what this means in the case of a book appearing two years after the author's death. Nevertheless Ilona's clear statement that it was "given its final shape by Polanyi in the winter of 1962" would seem to absolve Rotstein from its wilder claims.[33]

An opening section titled "Perspective" is revealing for its complete unworldliness. The first paragraph announces that this account of an eighteenth-century, war-making, slave-owning African kingdom, which practices large-scale human sacrifice, has been "conceived as an economic historian's modest contribution to meeting the problems of his own age." Which particular problems did he have in mind? Overpopulation? The pros and cons of Bretton Woods? After this we are told that "The economic historian's critical interest in archaic society naturally lies in identifying the structures, institutions, and operations by means of which the economic process is implemented."[34]

The cast of mind this reveals is typical. Economic behavior does not happen because men and women need to feed and house themselves and their families. Instead it is "implemented" by state officials, the insinuation being that without state officials nothing would happen at all. It is a fact of common observation that interference by the state in the decision-making of small farmers about what to plant and when has time and again produced disasters. In Russia, China, Cambodia, and Ethiopia famines resulted. Yet Dahomey is said to have had hardly one famine throughout its history. How can this be?

According to Polanyi the reason is not at all what you might expect—that wise rulers had the good sense to leave their farmers alone. Instead it was because *the king and his ministers were telling them what to do.* "The King of Dahomey enforces cultivation over all his dominions," he quotes approvingly from a nineteenth-century source, while "the permanent administration of agricultural affairs was in the hands of the 'Minister of Agriculture,' the Tokpo." Under him were other administrative assistants, and "it was the duty of the agricultural officials to insure a balanced production of crops and adjust resources to requirements. . . . If there was overproduction or underproduction of any crop, the farmers were ordered to shift from one crop to another."[35]

No one knows how far Dahomey's bureaucracy actually succeeded in achieving any of these goals. But Polanyi clearly believes it did, seizes enthusiastically on any evidence of "an extensive apparatus of planning and administration," and jubilantly hails the taxes imposed to provide state revenue. He is particularly excited by a report that when the king was "about to set a new price for pigs" (did the royal personage have nothing better to do?) "a complicated system of controls was set in motion." The slaughter of sows, the movement of livestock, and both production and transportation, were monitored—so we are told—by state officials throughout the land.

Could a peasant who wanted a hoe just sit down and make one? No, he could not. "Twelve forges throughout the country were designated to make hoes; and production of hoes was limited to these forges, each of which was under the watchful eye of an official charged with supervising production."[36] Polanyi sees nothing wrong in the king having some 4,000 women attached to the court, 2,000 of them wives and the rest a regiment of female soldiers known in the literature as the "Amazons." That "people of rank engrossed the major part of the women" was not a worry, since other women were appointed by the king to provide sexual services to the public at large.[37] Plainly, no detail of public welfare was overlooked. As for security, this was attended to by an elaborate system of state spies.

But how were numerical records kept of all the taxes paid, the numbers of livestock, the men available for the annual war, of births and deaths and marriages? Here we come to Polanyi's remarkable claim that Dahomey possessed a system of enumeration representing, for its time, "an advance in communication comparable to IBM." It seems that when a citizen wanted to count he put pebbles one by one into raffia bags, the annual census-taking conducted before the slave-raiding wars being the main occasion for this, and the time when hundreds of bag-carriers bearing pebbles converged on the capital.

Because there was no way of indicating percentages of a total, each tally in the census—of women, of men, of male and female births during the year, of male and female children below the age of thirteen, of male and female deaths from natural causes during the year, of deaths in war, of the number of captives taken, and finally the number of slaves available for sale (a secondary matter compared to the number of captive "heads" or prisoners for sacrifice to the ancestral gods)—was conveyed independently in separate bags of pebbles.

As one tries to visualize the lines of porters toiling uphill under the blazing African sun, day after day and week after week to the capital city, with their burdensome raffia bags slung from their shoulders, and the innumerable pebbles they must contain . . . Well, it is impossible not to become suspicious. Perhaps Melville Herskovits himself did too. The arithmetic itself seems odd. And where are the earlier reports corroborating the account Herskovits obtained in the 1930s? There are none. To his credit Herskovits admits to finding "the system of bureaucratic control" he describes as "bordering on the fantastic." And when one considers all the complications it is not surprising to find it has been described by another authority on Dahomey as "almost incredible."[38]

The Logic of Slavery

As for Karl Polanyi, the kindest thing that can be said about his credulous acceptance of all he read is that only someone of the type set before us by Peter Drucker, with "a naive belief in the cunning, cleverness, and foresight of our rulers," filled with that sacred hate of the market system so admired by his wife, convinced of the impending downfall of modern capitalism, and simple-minded enough to see pebble-counting with raffia bags as analogous to the achievements of

IBM—only someone like this could have possibly fallen for it in the first place.

But let's be sympathetic. Consider the ageing scholar's situation in New York. Sitting in his "tiny faculty apartment on Morningside Heights, each of its grimy and ill-maintained rooms piled from floor to ceiling with books and pamphlets, articles and letters,"[39] never having done an actual day's fieldwork in Africa in his life, and with everyone talking up its prospects, it was perhaps understandable for him to wildly idealize this eighteenth-century state so long ago and far away—a despotic kingdom set before us as a model for the modern age. Seldom can the delusions of romantic primitivism have put a man so completely out of touch.

When Karl Polanyi moved west from Hungary, he carried some of the worst ideological baggage of Eastern Europe with him. He never learned to appreciate the principles of democratic government which defended his existence. He never understood the true nature of the economy which fed him and gave him the freedom to work. While Michael Polanyi deepened our understanding of civilization in *The Logic of Liberty*, Karl Polanyi was preparing a book which might have been called *The Logic of Slavery*.

In one place he casually mentions that after a military victory 4,000 captives were sacrificed to Dahomey's gods. How would Polanyi have felt if he had witnessed these killings? He was hardly a family man, but his relationship with his daughter seems to have been close. What would he have thought of the training procedure for future Dahomeyan executioners, where girls and boys were given knives to hack at the heads of their living victims?

In the eighteenth century thousands of slaves and prisoners were killed each year in Dahomey. At the only place in his book where he shows any concern about this, Polanyi writes that "admittedly, acts of repulsive cruelty, religious mass murder, and endemic techniques of treachery in the political field were the accompaniment of its high achievements. Nevertheless, Dahomey's was an unbreakable society, held together by bonds of solidarity over which only naked force eventually prevailed."[40]

That only naked force could break this culture is presented as its vindication. But as much might be said of Hitler's Germany. Such are the priorities of those who believe that the primitive moral claims of solidarity outweigh all others—simple humanity included.[41]

6

The Book of Isaiah

The Culture Cult holds three dogmas to be unquestionable: 1. each culture is a semisacred creation, 2. all cultures are equally valuable and must never be compared, and 3. the assimilation of cultures (especially the assimilation of primitive cultures by a secular civilization coldly indifferent to spiritual things) is supremely wicked. This chapter looks at a man who did more to popularize these notions at the highest level of discourse than any other thinker of our time—the Oxford celebrity Sir Isaiah Berlin.

It is rather odd that this is so. In the first place, he was certainly no anthropologist and showed no understanding of tribal societies. In the second place, his role as both a publicist and promoter of romantic primitivism appears to be completely unknown to his admirers—indeed, most people would say that coupling Berlin's name with anything "primitive" is absurd. Set him down among the Masai, and he would have fainted away at the sight of all that blood. To the best of my knowledge he never set foot in Africa, or anyplace else where he might have encountered the tribal world face to face.

Berlin showed a number of superficial resemblances to Rousseau—the romantic literary sensibility, the wordiness, the big reputation in salons, a man, in the words of his biographer, with "no children, no dependants, few official duties, who had consciously prolonged his adolescence." Yet he wasn't interested in Rousseau at all—instead he became infatuated with the eighteenth-century German Romantics and wrote a major essay on Johann Gottfried Herder, Rousseau's neurotic culture-cultist on the German side of the frontier. It is through Herder that romantic primitivism comes into play.

Herder believed that only within a culture could you find authenticity, truth, virtue, and the organic community which everyone should belong to—culture was king. Like other German Romantics he believed our traditions and outlook are indissolubly bound up with the culture "with whom we form an organic unity," and what he hated most—and this is central—was "the *assimilation* of one culture by another." But like Rousseau, Herder's love of ethnicity was largely an inversion of his hatred of civilization. And that is why for Herder civilization had to be denounced, demeaned, and diminished, while the cultures of the provincial, the backward, and the insignificant were raised up and praised up and generally elevated above their deserts.

Berlin wrote excitedly about romanticism, about its emotions, its enthusiasms, its dark restlessness, its illimitable will to doom. But did he have any idea what the romantic culture-genie would do when it escaped from its academic bottle? He seems to have only weakly understood the barbarous things that happen where culture is *really* king, not as airy theory but—look for example at Dahomey—as a brutal fact of life.

The Immigrant

There must be few more beguiling childhood pictures of famous men. Warmed by a Russian cap and a thick fur collar, a ten-year-old face of unusual beauty looks out from the dust jacket of Michael Ignatieff's 1998 biography, calm and assured, a portrait photographer's dream. Ignatieff tells us that Isaiah Berlin was the much-loved child of a prosperous Jewish merchant's family, and in that portrait on the dust jacket there is all the confidence in the world. You feel the presence of a "preternaturally bright and bubbling only child, sure that no one—certainly no younger sister or older brother—would interrupt his monologues."[1]

Berlin was born of Jewish parents in 1909. He was not just an only child but an uprooted child, born in Riga who spoke Russian, plus a little German, and who was transferred from this linguistic community to England at the age of eleven, where in the course of a lifetime "he took three conflicting identities, Russian, Jewish and English, and braided them together into a character at one with itself."[2] Not entirely at one with itself however. He remained ambivalent about his family and his identity to the end. To be Jewish was a continual burden; but not to belong to some kind of community would be far worse.

His biographer, Ignatieff, writes that "there was little nostalgia in him and, despite being an exile, no obvious sense of loss," and certainly Berlin tried to give that impression.[3] His father, Mendel Berlin, had written a memoir telling the story of his own upbringing in Tsarist Poland. Commenting on this in later years Isaiah was severely dismissive: "All very unreliable . . . Pure sentimental return to roots. He worked up all this Jewish feeling in old age."[4] On the matter of ancestry Ignatieff reports that Berlin always said that origins "are a fact, full stop, but nothing to be proud of. To take pride was to surrender to the dubious determinism of the blood." He could be derisive of modern Lubavich Hassidim: "with their three-quarter-length black frock-coats, wide-brimmed hats, beards and ringlets, he regarded them as alarming fanatics."[5]

Yet only a few pages away in Ignatieff's book other evidence suggests very different attitudes and feelings. In 1915 the family had been making its way eastward from Riga, trying to avoid the approaching German danger, when they stopped for a while at the logging town of Andreapol near Pskov. Here the boy went to Hebrew school and received his first religious instruction. Memories of the school and its rabbi, who taught Berlin the letters of the Hebrew alphabet, were still vivid eighty years later. Talking to his biographer at his home in Oxford, Berlin remembered the old rabbi saying, "Dear children, when you get older, you will realise how in every one of these letters there is Jewish blood and Jewish tears." For a moment Berlin was unable to go on. He stared out from the room in which they were sitting to the garden beyond. It took him a while to compose himself. Then, writes Ignatieff, "he looked back at me, equanimity restored, and said, 'That is the history of the Jews.'"[6]

Though all were of Jewish background there was a marked contrast between the childhood experiences of Berlin—suggested in this scene of Hebrew school in a Russian logging town—and those of Karl Popper and the brothers Karl and Michael Polanyi. The families of Popper and Polanyi had each converted, the first to Lutheranism, the second to Calvinism after Polanyi senior had spent time in Switzerland,

and in each case the children grew up as the secular citizens of a Western cosmopolis. Karl Popper felt so strongly about this that he went out of his way to dissociate himself from both Jewish ethnic identity and nationalist sentiments of any kind: "Racial pride is not only stupid but wrong, even if provoked by racial hatred. All nationalism or racialism is evil, and Jewish nationalism is no exception."[7]

Berlin's feelings were vastly different. And however much he wrestled with the ambiguous nature of nationalism in later years, and saw the deep connection it had with Johann Gottfried Herder, he was still trying to justify these feelings to the end. This perplexed his friend the pianist Alfred Brendel. "Brendel had grown up in fascist Croatia during the war and he found Berlin's willingness to speak positively about nationalism a mystifying bias, which he could only attribute to Berlin's Zionism. As an expatriate pianist making his living on the concert stages of the world, he had no similar longing to belong."[8] Referred to a little enviously as "the Paganini of the platform," Berlin was at one point almost as busy lecturing at academic venues as Brendel was performing in the musical world. But on this matter they were poles apart. Berlin's need to belong was unassuageable.

In 1921 the family moved from Riga to England. The upheavals of the preceding years included a spell in revolutionary St. Petersburg, so the move to the secure environment admired by his "Anglo-maniac" father was welcome. Here the eleven-year-old Isaiah began the British public-school education which was the foundation of his later success. He was taken into English life with a rush. "Isaiah always emphasized how rapidly the assimilation occurred: within six months he had a part in *Babes in the Wood*," and by the end of the first year, when another boy called him a "dirty German," he had his first experience of English fair play when his schoolfellows beat the culprit up.[9]

But his emotional response to the welcome at school was unusual. Instead of enjoying the ease of his acceptance it made him uncomfortable, as if it were in some way shameful. "He always worried that a Jew should not be so emollient and accommodating . . . Ingratiation, he maintained, was the characteristically Jewish sin . . . Paradoxically, of course, this extreme sensitivity to the dilemmas of assimilation made him uniquely successful at it. He became a master at fitting in, at the price of lingering self-dislike."[10]

Paradox and Equivocation

All this is not without interest. But the paradox here has broader consequences, and has less to do with his sensitivity than with his mind and thought. It links private dilemmas with public views, for the personal discomfort he felt about his right to the benefits of assimilation was then used to argue the case against assimilation in general. Berlin wrote in a letter to a friend that "all central beliefs on human matters spring from a personal predicament," and his own philosophical opposition to assimilation would seem to be a case in point.[11]

In response to his own perceived predicament he converted a private prejudice into a general principle—the principle that the assimilation by one culture, of men and woman from another culture, was always wrong. The odd thing being that this didn't come from one of life's excluded and ignored. It came from a boy who had been welcomed into the educational community of Arundel House School in southern England, had won early recognition for his talents, and then went on to a career at the highest levels of British life.

This contradiction became more striking with each passing year. Later on, as an enthusiastic sponsor of Herder's views, he authorized, at the highest level, general policies of "enlightened ethnicity" that provided intellectual aid and comfort to those opposing the assimilation of minorities. As an academic philosopher he rarely, if ever, addressed himself overtly to social policy, and had even less to do with formulating it. The lines of connection between public opinion and the ideas he promoted are obviously indirect, as the effects of teaching usually are. But as one who helped popularize the value of cultural identity, along with the dogma that no culture should be compared with any other, he did much to promote the Culture Cult in our time.

"Herder's fame," writes Berlin at the start of his essay on this eighteenth-century figure, "rests on the fact that he is the father of the related notions of nationalism, historicism, and the *Volksgeist* . . . ," and his three cardinal ideas, ideas "which go against the mainstream thought of his time, I have called Populism, Expressionism, and Pluralism." The pluralism Berlin attributes here to Herder is significant: he later adopted it as his own. Herder was famous as "the most formidable of the adversaries of the French philosophes," a man who had a "vast general influence" upon the world.[12]

The distinctiveness of clans and hamlets and villages, of tribes and nations, was for Herder the most important value of all. He agreed that humanity shared certain universal features, but universals bored him as much as they bore anthropologists today. Much more interesting were the divisions in mankind, particularities of language and belief, of clothes and custom, and different ways of wresting a living from geographical niches around the world. Herder also thought that each human culture drew its inspiration from the spirit of the *Volk* (the folk or local community), a community with deep roots in the soil. Each culture was an expression of the unique and unassimilable traditions of the *Volk*; thus it followed that each *Völkisch* political unit had a quasi-divine right to grow and develop and fulfill itself, without interference from anyone else, for these peculiarities all derived from an overarching religious design.

The vague vitalistic philosophy contained in these ideas plainly had biological roots. But it would be for later thinkers to tease out the racial implications of Herder's views. In the eighteenth century these features of his thought seemed entirely benign. He was like a well-meaning schoolteacher who piously believes everything the United Nations says about itself, pins up on the classroom wall its latest exhortations, and would be deeply shocked by the suggestion that the glorious self-fulfillment of culture X might lead it to brutally annihilate cultures Y and Z. Cultural autonomy and cultural assertiveness were straightforwardly good things.

Berlin always denied that his sympathy for Herder's ideas had any personal significance. He described himself as just an interested interpreter who found a certain piquancy (the thrill of a masquerade perhaps?) in discussing views the opposite of his own. He even claimed, in 1992, that his true affinity was for the Old Guard eighteenth-century Progressives. "Fundamentally I am a liberal rationalist. The values of the Enlightenment, what people like Voltaire, Helvétius, Holbach, Condorcet, preached are deeply sympathetic to me . . . I do not share, or even greatly admire, the views [of Herder et al.], but I have learnt a good deal from them."[13]

Michael Ignatieff says much the same thing, telling us that Berlin "defended his own commitments by writing about those who were its sworn enemies." It is possible that this was what was going on, although it seems an unusual form of defense. Anyway, the supposedly "deeply sympathetic" Voltaire, Helvétius, Holbach, and Condorcet were regularly damned for their failings, while Berlin warmly praised the opposing Herderian view which prizes each culture as an exquisitely unfolding flower in God's creation.

The inconsistency is obvious. One of his students said that Berlin liked "to venture out into the Romantic irrational by day, but always returned to the Enlightenment at nightfall." This at least shows a sense of self-preservation, but a harsher view is that he was a socially opportunistic man. "Throughout his steady ascent through the upper reaches of English life he had run with the hares and hunted with the hounds . . . had wanted to be thought a man of the left, but actually felt most comfortable among the right."[14] What is fairly clear from the numerous friendships he formed with artists and writers is that on balance Berlin's temper was romantic and emotional, rather than philosophical, and that he often allowed an aesthetic sensibility to weaken or confuse his political judgment.

This can be seen in the pages of *The Roots of Romanticism*, a book that was published in 1999 and consists of the belatedly edited transcript of his 1965 Mellon Lectures at the National Gallery of Art in Washington. It is equivocal in many places, and his last words are characteristic:

> What romanticism did was to undermine the notion that in matters of value, politics, morals, aesthetics there are such things as objective criteria which operate between human beings, such that anyone who does not use these criteria is simply either a liar or a madman, which is true of mathematics or physics. This division between where objective truth obtains—in mathematics, in physics, in certain regions of common sense—and where objective truth has been compromised—in ethics, in aesthetics and the rest—is new, and has created a new attitude to life—whether good or bad, I shall not volunteer to say.[15]

Altruism or Spite?

The main ideas Berlin thought he had found in Herder concerned the multiplicity of human values, and the plurality of incompatible ends. As he presents it, cultural pluralism is a doctrine inspired by the highest motives. That is what most people intuitively feel, and that is what Herder's commentators tell us when they portray him as compassionate and humane. But it is far from the whole story, and evidence that this seemingly benign philosophy is compounded of elements altogether more twisted, dark, and strange, can be readily discovered in the account of Herder provided by Berlin himself.

He reports that Herder was agitated and unbalanced, "by all accounts a deeply divided, touchy, resentful, bitter, unhappy man, in constant need of support and praise, neurotic, pedantic, difficult, suspicious, and often insupportable. . . . Goethe said that he had in him something compulsively vicious—like a vicious horse—a desire to bite and hurt."[16] That might seem enough for our purposes. The historic father of multiculturalism was plainly not at ease with himself. But why? What galled his self-esteem? What made the man so insupportable? It then transpires that France and the French and Parisian civilization as a whole were to blame. When this gauche and touchy provincial visited Paris he failed to make an impression on the *philosophes*, and consequently "suffered that mixture of envy, humiliation, admiration, resentment and defiant pride which backward peoples feel towards advanced ones, [and] members of one social class towards those who belong to a higher rung in the hierarchy."[17]

All of this could be perfectly true, but what conceivable link can there be with multiculturalism, the most spiritually uplifting doctrine of our time? In fact the link is direct and strong. For the modern attack on the high achievements of Western civilization by Herder's romantic heirs, on academic standards, on parliamentary government with its tiresome uncertainties and delays, on judicial impartiality, and along with this the leveling primitivism of the claim that despite very different levels of achievement all cultures are "incommensurable" and must never be compared—all this flows naturally from a neurotic need to pull down whatever impairs one's self-esteem. It grows precisely from resentment and defiant pride, and as a social philosophy it most strongly appeals to those driven by such emotions. Resentment is the natural by-product of the strain of trying to meet high standards (one of the strains of civilized life pointed to by Popper, Hayek, and Freud), while as any reader of *Mein Kampf* will quickly find, wounded pride compounded with populist rage is what *ressentiment* politics are all about.

Berlin's comments on this matter were ambivalent, and varied from time to time and place to place. In "European Unity and its Vicissitudes," a lecture given to the European Cultural Foundation in 1959, he looked into the abyss of the Nazi era and wondered if any such thing as universal human nature had survived.[18] Some years later, by the time of his essay "The Bent Twig,"[19] he was more than willing to make *ressentiment* the key to nationalism itself: "The infliction of a wound on the collective feeling of a society" is a necessary condition for its birth.[20] "The first true nationalists—the Germans—are an example of the combination of wounded cultural pride and a philosophico-historical vision to stanch the wound. . . ."[21] "Nationalism . . . is in the first place a response to a patronising or disparaging attitude towards the traditional values of a society, the result of wounded pride and a sense of humiliation, . . . " a sense so extreme, dangerous, and unmanageable, that he does not shrink from describing it as a "pathological inflammation of wounded national consciousness."[22]

But if this is true of *nationalism*, what about the chauvinistic excesses of *culturism*, the philosophy so popular today? Don't both of them draw on the same emotions and ideals? Isn't culture-assertion and culture-aggression nationalism's neurotic younger brother, an unstable sibling just as likely to become pathologically inflamed? The connection is not new. The core idea of nationalism itself is a "shared culture," wrote Ernest Gellner in his own last thoughts on the subject,[23] and comparisons of the assertive *Völkisch* themes in Herder, and those to be found in the literary/political soil of Nazism, show striking similarities.

But Berlin won't hear a word of this. According to him Herder's commitment is to something quite different—what might be called *pluralistic populism*. This is "deeply anti-political," profoundly democratic, and downright shocked by war. "Populism may often have taken reactionary forms and fed the stream of aggressive nationalism; but the form in which Herder held it was democratic and peaceful."[24]

Herder delighted in bringing out the individual shape of each culture and "the fullness of human experience they embodied; the odder, the more extraordinary a culture or an individual, the better pleased he was." Generously open-minded, he cannot "condemn anything that displays colour or uniqueness; Indians, Americans, Persians, Greece and Palestine, Arminius and Machiavelli . . ." All of these are equally fascinating. And what does Herder hate? Only what any sensible man would hate—"the forces that make for uniformity," not to mention that worst of all possible outcomes, *"the assimilation of one culture or way of life to another."*[25]

While Karl Popper was working on *The Open Society*, and Hayek was preparing the critique of totalitarianism that became *The Road to Serfdom*, Isaiah Berlin was on a boat bound for Russia in the company of the famous Cambridge spy Guy Burgess. This however is not nearly as significant as it seems—he had no idea what Burgess was up to. They had met at Cambridge in 1934, Berlin taking an immediate liking to this "amusing, energetic, vulgar but irrepressible Trinity Graduate," and kept in touch through the 1930s.[26] Then, in June 1940, he arrived in Oxford at a time when Berlin's career in philosophy appeared to have reached a dead end. Burgess said he was off to Russia, working for MI5, and wanted the fluent Russian-speaker Berlin to join him as a press officer at the British Embassy in Moscow.[27] Permission was obtained, and in July they set off by ship on a route taking them first to America, after which they intended to cross the Pacific to Vladivostok.

But it all fell through in New York. Burgess was recalled to Britain and dismissed from intelligence (he wound up in the BBC), while Berlin eventually stayed on in America where he was to spend the rest of the war. Ignatieff concedes in some discomfort that "It does seem extraordinary that he should have thrown up his teaching job, crossed the North Atlantic in the middle of a war and set off for Moscow, without visas or official letters of accreditation, in the company of a man known to be both unorthodox and unstable. It never occurred to Berlin that Burgess might not be all he claimed to be, putting down the haste with which the trip had been set up and the suddenness of its collapse to the chaos of war-time."[28]

Perhaps it never occurred to Berlin because in Moscow, at last, he would be able to escape the ordeal of philosophy seminars in the daunting company of top-level philosophers. The shadow of the Kremlin was less intimidating than the quirky brilliance of Wittgenstein. And, once in Moscow, he hoped to meet the writers he knew about and regain his old undergraduate pleasures with Burgess, the "dishevelled, homosexual adventurer" with whom he used to break out the whiskey and "talk into the small hours . . . about books, cinema and music."[29]

He was aware of the failings of the Soviet regime. He had spent five years on a biography of Marx, published in 1939, which "gave him a lifelong target, for he genuinely loathed Marxian ideas of historical determinism and was to argue that they served as the chief ideological excuse for Stalin's crimes."[30] He could in no possible way be regarded as an apologist for the Soviet system. But the Burgess episode did show an extreme degree of unworldliness which might become a handicap when he later turned to the history of ideas. A taste for airy abstraction would make him the least likely person to bring lofty thinking down to earth, or grasp what goes on in tribal politics at ground level.

The Abstract and the Concrete

In New York, and later in Washington, Berlin worked very successfully for the British Ministry of Information as "a propagandist, working with trade unions, black organisations, and Jewish groups."[31] Living at first in midtown hotels on Manhattan, he worked in an office on the forty-fourth floor of Rockefeller Center, lobbying editors, meeting influential businessmen, rabbis and politicians, shepherding delegations of British trade unionists into meetings with American union bosses. But his greatest challenge by far was keeping American Jewry sympathetic to the British cause. The 1939 British White Paper which banned further Jewish Immigration to Palestine was a source of deep resentment to American Zionists, and, as Berlin collaborated with his friend Chaim Weizmann, he was drawn into a situation where his loyalties to his adopted country on the one hand, and to Zionist efforts to create a Jewish state on the other, were put to the test.[32]

Berlin's identification with the cause of a Jewish homeland is fundamental to understanding his sympathy for nationalism, for eighteenth-century romanticism, and for Herder. Whenever he was expounding Herder's ideas on the cultural and political destiny of "peoples," the cultural and political destiny of the Jews was never far from his mind. Yet if ever there was a case that exposes the romantic illusions at the heart of Herder's thinking, it would have to be the history of Israel. Taking what might be described as a horticultural view of things, Herder saw the world as a kind of enormous garden in which each nation or culture should be free to fulfill its natural destiny to grow and blossom: "The practical understanding of man was intended to blossom and bear fruit in all its varieties: and hence such a diversified Earth was ordained for so diversified a species."[33]

But what if the growth of one culture took place at the expense of the next? What if one culture overran its neighbor in search of *lebens-*

raum? To these questions Herder had no answer. Lacking any practical sense of territory—surely important in political thought—his discussion of "pluralism" took place in a spatial void. And when Berlin
interprets Herder he too has nothing useful to say about this. "Variety does not entail conflict,"[34] he informs us on Herder's authority,
presumably because it has something to do with a belief that "genuine cultures" are at peace with themselves and the world. Holding
fast to this optimistic dogma we're supposed to concern ourselves
with the conditions in which a rich diversity of cultures thrive. It was
Herder's view that a culture is a living organism, a unified thing, a
natural and spontaneous social growth containing no contradictions,
with each part vital to its overall well-being, so that thought and language, cognition and belief, fact, value, law, and livelihood, are all in
healthy and harmonious balance.

But the dogma of organic cultural harmony is absurd. This is obvious
when you take a wider view than Berlin and Herder were willing to
do. It is not enough to say with Herder that "each culture is a harmonious lyre—one must merely have the ear to hear its melodies,"
for what anthropology teaches is that many cultures are lyres with
broken strings, and the noise they make is far from musical.[35]

"All societies are sick, but some are sicker than others" begins
Robert B. Edgerton's book about "the myth of primitive harmony"
and the realities it conceals.[36] Take the peoples of highland New
Guinea for example. As Edgerton says, before Australian contact
most "societies throughout highland Papua New Guinea required
that boys go through initiation ceremonies in which they were forced
to drink only partly slaked lime that blistered their mouths and
throats, were beaten with stinging nettles, were denied water, had
barbed grass pushed up their urethras to cause bleeding, were com-
pelled to swallow bent lengths of cane until vomiting was induced,
and were required to fellate older men, who also had anal intercourse
with them."[37]

Reliable witnesses report that the psychological climate was not
just one of fear but of terror. How might the tender susceptibilities of
Berlin have felt about this? "Cultures are comparable but not commensurable; each is what it is, of literally inestimable value in its own
society, and consequently to humanity as a whole," writes Berlin,
smoothly imparting Herder's view.[38] "Herder believed that every cul-

ture has its own irreplaceable contribution to make to the progress of the human race . . . that their function is to enrich the universal harmony between nations and institutions, for which men have been created by God or nature." Indeed. But what would happen if the boys could choose to leave this culture of literally inestimable value which is making its irreplaceable contribution to the progress of the human race at their expense? What then?

Bringing Berlin's thoughts to bear on real-life material can be illuminating: it's a great pity he never did it himself. In a 1992 interview he quotes the comments of Alexandre Kojève on Stalin. Noting in response to his interviewer that Stalinism was not at all what Hobbes had in mind ("Hobbes wanted rigorous laws, but only the minimum necessary for preserving public order"), Berlin pointed out that Stalinist terror consisted of complete and arbitrary lawlessness—of smashing society to a pulp, a jelly, where people accused of breaking laws they didn't even know existed become incapable of complaint, much less resistance. "Hobbes conceived the law as something which if you obeyed, you could survive. Stalin made laws which you would be punished for obeying or for not obeying, at random . . . Nothing could save you."[39]

Now the terrifying rites performed on the socially malleable social substance of initiates function in tribal cultures in much the same way. Mere obedience to "custom" or to "tribal law" is not the point. Total acceptance of every demand of the elders, no matter how arbitrary or lawless, as proof that you have surrendered your previous identity and are now ready to accept whatever adulthood requires— that's the point. That's what tribal "hazing" is about. If the elders say black is black, then black is black. If they then say black is white, then black is white. By compliance with manifest contradiction the initiate signals his docility and acquiescence. In such cultures the condition of a slave, unresisting submission, is the price a child pays to join the adult world.

In Herder's exalted vision pluralism is inseparable from peaceful co-existence. Each people driven by its own *élan vital* is eagerly fulfilling its destiny as part of the great kaleidoscope of cultures, but it never collides with its neighbors, is never in conflict, and never argues about elbowroom. This abstract romantic notion looks ridiculous enough in the Middle East. But how does it stand up alongside the historical evidence more generally?

The Aztecs provide us with the most revealing commentary on
Herderian pacifism. Nowhere else was there a culture with such a
built-in drive to perdition. Estimates of the number of sacrificial victims killed and eaten vary, though it was probably over 20,000 per
year, while many of their continual wars had no other reason than the
capture of prisoners for sacrifice. When, in 1519, the Tlaxcalans saw
a chance to be revenged on this tyranny, their warriors eagerly joined
the conquistadors to pull the Aztecs down.

Given the least encouragement, Herder's disciples in anthropology
will rhapsodize for hours about the glories of Tenochtitlàn, its buildings, its poetry, its art. But as for that vision of pluralistic peace, about
all Mexico proves is how one culture's sociopathic flourishing can be
remorselessly at the expense of the next. By what supracultural values
should we decide the claims of each? Here Berlin is silent. He warns
that Herder did not think all cultures were equally valuable. He cautions that Herder too believed in progress of a kind.[40] But how
should we deal with the fact that in the garden of humanity some cultures strangle other cultures in their beds? Neither Berlin nor Herder
has anything useful to say.

Positive and Negative Freedom

Let us give credit where credit is due. Isaiah Berlin's forays provided
delight and instruction for more than sixty years and introduced
many readers to books they might never have heard of. His best essays have zest, and his early book on Marx is still rewarding. Authorities agree that no one interested in the history of the nineteenth-
century Russian intelligentsia should overlook what he wrote on the
subject. His discussion of two concepts of liberty was timely: it served
to concentrate people's minds on the ruling illusion of the era—the
Marxist belief that human liberty could only be achieved by first making all men slaves. However hard it may be to assess the net effect,
the blows he struck for political sanity, and against the bandmasters
of "the March of History," must have helped to make the world a
better place.

Yet as the years went by he remained unaware of the mounting
contradictions in his thought. If the central question of politics was
"the question of obedience and coercion," then how did this question look alongside the cultural nationalism he also admired? He had

argued that freedom from constraint required a minimum of personal liberty, lest the individual "find himself in an area too narrow for even that minimum development of his natural faculties which alone makes it possible to pursue, and even to conceive, the various ends which men hold good or right or sacred." This sounds wise. But now that he was embracing anthropology via Herder, how much sense did this make on the banks of the Orinoco, or in the home of the Noble Savage more generally?

It was all very well for Herder to announce in the eighteenth century that "cultures are comparable but not commensurable; each is what it is, of literally inestimable value in its own society, and consequently to humanity as a whole." But for Berlin to be repeating this in the 1960s required taking account of what we have learned since. Not to mention the fact that his discussion of liberty implied that freedom was not a relative value, but something universal, and one which some cultures and political systems had and other cultures and political systems did not. How much "freedom from constraint" was there for example among the Yanomamo of South America, where "everyone gets placed into some sort of kinship matrix which, to a large degree, specifies 'in principle' how one is expected to behave . . ."

As in most tribal societies, individual Yanomamo do not freely decide how to behave and what to do and where to live: expected social behavior is determined by one's location on a kinship map. This has serious consequences. "To be outside the kinship system is, in a very real sense, to be inhuman or nonhuman; real humans are some sort of kin. It is in this sense that anthropologists say that primitive society is, to a large degree, organized and regulated by kinship."[41] Among the Yanomamo it makes no sense at all to speak of freedom as "individual freedom from constraint," for there are no individuals, and not even a value of privacy, in the Western sense. And this is equally true of all those bewitching rain forest Edens that anthropology students hear about in their lectures and catch enchanting glimpses of in film after film.

Nor did Berlin notice the connection between the idea of "positive freedom" and the idea of "culture." Where "negative freedom" had been largely the freedom admired by J. S. Mill—"the desire not to be impinged upon, to be left to oneself"—Berlin pointed out that "positive freedom" was compatible with extreme coercion. From what he and others have said on the subject, positive freedom is perhaps best understood as the view that human potential is too important to be left to itself. It must be directed toward its own fulfillment, and, if men decline to take direction, then they must be driven with whips, and, if necessary, enslaved. In the phrase associated with its Marxist incarnation, they must be "forced to be free."

This was no merely theoretical matter: in 1918 a Bolshevik poster told Russian recalcitrants how "with an iron hand we shall drive you to happiness." Positive freedom emphasizes two things: an ideal form of society which is known in advance, and an ideal of human development and ultimate happiness which sees conformity with this ideal as the only path to true self-realization.[42]

But this is what pre-modern cultures think too. That is why endless initiation ceremonies are performed on the socially malleable substance of individuals to force them into categories and classes; that is why a thousand minute taboos or prohibitions govern every aspect of life; that is at least one reason why in India the social form of the caste system is still—in the year 2000—a coercive structure within which nearly a billion people live out their lives. When it is said that unless one has been assigned a position within the kinship system of the Yanomamo one is not even considered "human," this illustrates exactly what Berlin was talking about. In brief: *Positive freedom is the acceptance of cultural necessity.* The plain fact is that the Herderian culture-worship Berlin espoused in one period of his life had suffocating political implications for the libertarian political theory he advanced in another. But he seems to have been quite unaware of this. His ideas about liberty, and the ideas he took from Herder, were kept in separate boxes and never examined side by side.

Incommensurability

After *Four Essays on Liberty*, Berlin's analytic abilities and his literary style both declined. The care, attention, and scrupulosity he once gave even to routine philosophical work slipped away. In its place was something that at best looked like overeager promotion; at worst, hyperbole and gush. Adjectives proliferated—no noun could stand alone. Synonymous phrases piled on top of each other. Inventory sentences ran as many as ten impressive names together, and then rushed on.

Contradictions and inconsistencies appeared which went unnoticed by editors—and which his admirers simply ignored. Something as apparently trivial as a footnote could be revealing. His Herder essay contains a curious aside regarding Mao Tse-tung. In the midst of a comment on Herder's relativism, Berlin touches on the challenge of managing political order amid cultural diversity, each cultural unit having to be simultaneously advanced "towards a final universal harmony, each moving by its own path toward the self-same purpose. . . . This is Lessing's conception, embodied in the famous parable of the three rings in *Nathan the Wise.*" He then adds at the foot of the page, apparently without irony, that this self-same conception "found an unexpected re-incarnation not long ago in Mao Tse-tung's celebrated image of the many flowers."[43] Celebrated it was indeed, but not for being a sincere embrace of pluralism.

Passing remarks sometimes reveal either misunderstandings or surprising ignorance, and not in minor matters. Discussing Herder's "populism" (which is admired for being pluralistic), he claims "it is based on a belief in loose textures, voluntary associations, natural ties, and is bitterly opposed to armies, bureaucracies, 'closed' societies of any sort."[44]

The "closed society" allusion can only be to Popper. But when had he last read *The Open Society?* There is nothing in that book to suggest that Popper's "closed society" had anything to do with armies or bureaucracies. These are mere organizational parts of the polity as a whole, and it is the polity and not its parts that Popper was writing about. No doubt armies are unattractive in many ways, but to drag them into a discussion of pluralism is very odd—though perhaps it is something worse. For it suggests that an idea central to Popper's thinking on this issue has gone completely unnoticed by Berlin. This is the view that tribal cultures are "closed," that civilization is "open" in ways they can never know, and that history shows a general evolutionary trend from tribal to civilized social forms. If he hadn't noticed it this would make perfect sense. Social evolution from lower to higher, and ethical progress from bad to better, are things which both Herder and romantic primitivism stoutly deny.

But perhaps the most striking feature of Berlin's enthusiastic essays on the Romantics is his reiterated claim that all cultures are "incommensurable." In the Herder essay it occurs several times only pages apart,[45] despite the fact that it was a term not much heard in the eighteenth century, and it would seem to come instead from the disciples of T. S. Kuhn and Clifford Geertz. Whatever the provenance, its importance in Berlin's discussion cannot be overestimated: it is fundamental to his arguments for pluralism, along with the asserted wickedness of the "assimilation of one culture by another."

It is nonsensical nonetheless, flying in the face of everyday observation and contradicting all we know about human history and social evolution. Far from being unmeasurable, the difference between London today and the world inhabited by the Ice Man 5,000 years ago in Europe can be studied on a hundred different scales, and the difference between Paris and the Palaeolithic likewise. *Et vive la différence!* People do not travel from Heidelberg to Rangoon to pursue higher degrees because the difference in results can be measured, and it doesn't take an Einstein to do the sums. They do not fly from New York to Ayacucho for heart surgery because the facilities in Ayacucho don't measure up. Nor will Professor K. Anthony Appiah be abandoning his comfortable post at Harvard to take a chair in Sierra Leone. Despite the rhetoric which comes so easily to his lips, he has checked out the salary and knows in his heart it would be foolish.

Critics will argue, however, that this is all painfully naive. Running a tape measure over a grass hut alongside a skyscraper will tell us nothing about the measurability of cultures—Berlin's ideas are vastly more subtle than that. His claim is ethical, not empirical. When he says that cultures are "incommensurable," his argument rests on a belief that values and ideals cannot be usefully compared, and that some are downright incompatible. An example he used for more than forty years to make this point is that of Freedom and Equality, two goods which cannot be maximized at the same time. This is presented in his 1956 essay "Equality" and was often referred to later. We can all agree that it is a good example of the imponderabilia of moral choice, politically considered, and that its either/or lies at the heart of much decision-making by modern governments.

But what about the situation among *premodern* governments in the *premodern* world? What is their main concern? What about the traditional cultures of Africa, or Asia, or the Islamic nations of the Middle East? You don't have to know much about these to realize that it isn't the conflicting claims of Freedom and Equality that keep their leaders awake at night. It is the demands of Fraternity and the exorbitant expectations of kin.

This case is central to Berlin's argument regarding incommensurability, but he never recognized it right to the end. Again and again he sets before us the Freedom vs. Equality paradigm of incompatibility, continuing to use it long after his discussion has moved into anthropological terrain. But it is the ideal of fraternity, not equality, and all the unending demands of fraternal communalism, which is where traditional cultures prove irreconcilable with the ordered impartiality of modern life—their incompatible kinship obligations, the natural ties mentioned as inherent in Herder's populism, the demands of brotherhood, and the myriad duties to an extending network of relations all of which expect material and other favors to come their way.

Berlin's high-flying philosophical altitude obscured these realities from him. Freedom and Equality are abstract desirabilities floating around in the blue. But Fraternity is woven into the fabric of tribal life, and you have to be down at ground level to see it. It is a matter of so many yams or camels or oxen due; so many men needed for work or worship; so many warriors needed for successful war. Fraternity is part of the deep moral structure of premodernity.

Perhaps Berlin was constrained by some inner fear that admitting the third great revolutionary principle could prove risky, might point to matters embarrassing to the Herderian culture-admiring point of view—tribal nepotism, corruption, the preference given to connection rather than ability, to blood rather than merit; in other words, all the things that clash with civilization and make the assimilation of traditional cultures into the modern state so difficult. At Oxford, no doubt, these problems seemed rather remote. But that is not how things look when the neolithic is your neighbor, and the Stone Age was only yesterday.

Berlin several times described the ideas of Herder and Co. as important, original, and profound. But his evidence is unpersuasive. Instead, in the guise of rescuing "higher thought" from oblivion, he appears to have devoted his considerable gifts to raising lower thought far above its deserts. Indeed, Herder's concept of the comity of nations as a garden of wildflowers may be the most childish notion ever to have imposed itself on the credulity of an influential mind. Whatever he may have imagined, the garden of human cultures contains just as many stink-lilies as violets, strangling vines as primroses, sick societies as those with rosy cheeks—and too many problems in the modern world come from sentimentally denying this fact.

In anthropology, Hamann's exaggerated view that language is coterminous with cultural consciousness and that "we can only conceive what our culture permits" led eventually to the extravagant linguistic theories of Benjamin Lee Whorf. The emphasis this placed on uniqueness and particularity was pushed to such an extreme that universal human understandings were said to be untranslatable from one culture to another.

At least the upward evolution of primitive forms of social organization received a leading place in Vico's scheme—those who have seen artist's impressions of the four-million-year-old *Australopithecus anamensis* will enjoy the Italian's entertaining picture of "the first men, stupid, insensate, horrible great beasts, the impious progeny of Noah, wandering the vast forests of the earth"—but as so often the original thinker's contribution gets buried under Berlin's adjectival hype, being variously trumpeted as bold, audacious, revolutionary, and profound. Vico's view that civilizations rise and fall in cycles of achievement and decay is noted but set aside as "the least interesting, plausible, and original of his views." Instead Berlin goes to extraordinary lengths to find support for his personal hostility to cultural assimilation. After an account of the uniqueness of past civilizations, he derives from Vico's philological writings the view that "equally authentic, yet autonomous, cultures. . . cannot be assimilated to one another."[46]

According to the dogmas of the Culture Cult, the enemy of the *particular* is the *universal,* and the universal is always Bad News. In various essays on the failings of the Enlightenment we read Berlin saying that "universalism, by reducing everything to the lowest common denominator which applies to all men at all times, drained both their lives and ideals of that specific content which alone gave them point." Yet, so far as I know, he never stood back from this heavy charge and stopped to think whether it made sense.

In what way is the Amerindian student who moves from the particularities of his native culture in Patagonia in order to join the universal project of modern medicine, and to Buenos Aires to undertake a medical degree, reduced, lowered, and drained of all that gives life meaning? How was V. S. Naipaul reduced or degraded by winning a scholarship which led the author from Trinidad to England and on to universal fame? In what way was Ernest Rutherford culturally deprived, his life and ideals impoverished, by traveling from parochial

New Zealand to the wider world of Cambridge in order to participate in the scientific project of modern physics? Even more to the point, how was the culturally isolated eleven-year-old Isaiah Berlin reduced, his prospects stunted, by leaving Riga and St. Petersburg behind him in order to make a career as an authority on European civilization at Oxford?

The real puzzle is how Berlin could ever take a cranky German provincial like Herder seriously in the first place. Why did someone who as a boy arrived in England from Latvia via Russia, whose gifts were soon recognized and rewarded, who received at Oxford all the honors which scholarship, intellectual eminence, and a charismatic speaking presence can achieve—a man as completely assimilated to the highest levels of civilized university life as anyone could hope to be—devote so much time to such a dismal collection of second-rate minds as the Romantics, most of whom were neurotically defensive about their own little patches of turf?

We know that Herder himself had a dark side, resentful and hurt. We know that Berlin's account of nationalism points repeatedly to the psychology of humiliation, injured dignity, and wounded pride, and as recently as his book-length interview with Ramin Jahanbegloo in 1992 he does so again on page after page. It isn't hard to imagine what a young boy torn from his linguistic roots and transferred to England may have endured in the immediate aftermath to World War One. There must have been both injuries and wounds—and the intensely personal way he describes the importance of belonging to a group one can call one's own cannot be disregarded (in the following quotation Herder's voice, and the the voice of Berlin, are surely the same):

> To be lonely is to be among men who do not know what you mean. Exile, solitude, is to find yourself among people whose words, gestures, handwriting are alien to your own, whose behaviour, reactions, feelings, instinctive responses, and thoughts and pleasures and pains, are too remote from yours, whose education and outlook, the tone and quality of whose lives and being, are not yours.[47]

It is a towering irony that this widely admired and not unattractive man should have struggled all his life against the belief that assimilation, adopting the superior civilization of one's host, might not only be best but could be honorable, too.

7

Karl Popper in New Zealand

How nice and peaceful New Zealand is—said Czech president Vaclav Havel when he visited a few years ago. Meanwhile, back in the Balkans murderous tribes were killing each other again, and bodies were being exhumed from mass graves every day. But there was nothing like this in New Zealand, as far as he could tell, and he wondered what the secret of this country's success might be.

Havel reminded his audience that Karl Popper had written *The Open Society and Its Enemies* in New Zealand during World War II, when the latter took refuge there from the "tribal fury" of Nazism. Popper's book made an important distinction between the open society of modern civilization and the closed societies of the primitive world, and as Havel recalled these matters he cast his mind back to Czechoslovakia's neighbors to the south and east. For the last two thousand years, he said, wave after wave of aggressive tribalism had persistently threatened Western civilization.

Although there is nothing you could call the "political theory" of romantic primitivism, certain themes are fairly obvious. Isaiah Berlin, for example, combined the highest liberal ideals with a decided weakness for tribalistic chauvinism and nationalistic sentiments. Polanyi's sympathy with the ideal of solidarity, come what may, led him to enthuse about the barbarous regime of Dahomey. Politically speaking, by "tribes" we mean large groups of people bound by some kind of notional kinship, usually by a common language, under a generally hierarchic arrangement of power rising to an apex of elders or chiefs. By "states" we mean large groups howsoever composed, enjoying laws and government equal for all within a common territory.

Humanity made a big step forward when it moved on from polities of blood to polities of geography: "as a result of this evolution, the informal practices of kindred groups, based on private law, gave way to formal public law." A world of *societas* (where men were tied by personal bonds) was superseded by the world of *civitas* (where territorial bonds were paramount). This occurred in Babylon in 1750 B.C., in England about A.D. 900, but not in faraway New Zealand until 1840.[1]

In the political sphere, too, a Big Ditch separates tribal society from civil society. On one side you have a social order which is "closed"—closed intellectually, socially, and politically, and ruled by kinship and "blood." On the other side you have a generally progressive social order which is "open"—open to new ideas, to new people taken on their merits as individuals, and to forms of political membership based on adherence to codified law. This important distinction was first formulated in a general way by Popper, in New Zealand, fifty years ago.

The Captain Cook Age
in New Zealand

New Zealand is a small country about the size of England in the southwest Pacific. It is famous for its scenery, has about three million people, and on the whole it's a prosperous and pleasant place. However, signs indicate that it could fall apart, bitterly divided between the 15 percent who are Maori Polynesians and the 85 percent who are white (known in the Maori language as *pakeha*). If open conflict breaks out this will be largely a result of the divisive, backward-looking, antiassimilationist doctrines spawned by the heirs of Herder. In fact, it is hard to think of any other reason. Given the least encouragement—as Kiri Te Kanawa shows—the Maori enjoy modern life and hugely contribute to it. But under the dispensation of the ruling Culture Cult in New Zealand it's a different story. Culture is king. And since it has the best claim to historic priority Maori culture is the anointed King of Kings. Under the widespread proposals for Maori education today, neither the glorious voice nor the spectacular career of a Kiri Te Kanawa could ever happen.

The Maori arrived in these remote islands by canoe some eight hundred years ago, about the time the Gothic cathedrals were being built in Europe, and the environmental impact they had on the region was devastating. There may only have been a handful of Maori at first—around a hundred or so—but within a short time nearly 30 percent of New Zealand's bird life became extinct. Originally there had been large geese, along with snipe, ducks, quail, pelicans, falcons, and an enormous eagle (*Harpagornis moorei*) with a wingspan of three meters.

Unfortunately the most unusual birds were also highly edible—the twelve species of moa. Large and flightless, looking like massive ostriches, moa ranged from about the size of commercial turkeys up to the 3.5-meter-high Giant Moa (*Dinornis giganteus*). Heavily boned and muscled, these weighed up to 250 kg. But all of them carried lots of good meat. Moa had never faced any land predators before, and they were very easily killed. Butchering sites all over the country record where Maori ate them—or did until they became extinct more than 600 years ago. The extermination of all twelve New Zealand moa species, in less than a century after the first Polynesians set foot on the island, is believed to be the fastest megafaunal extinction the world has ever seen.[2]

At the same time huge areas of forest were burnt: "Lowland podocarp forests were particularly affected, with the distinctive dry forest and shrub of the Canterbury Plains and adjacent interior regions being virtually wiped out." The burning of these forests was done in the course of moa-hunting, and since the forests were also the best areas of moa habitat it also hastened their decline.[3] By the time of Captain Cook's arrival in 1770, 50 percent of the forests which had been growing in New Zealand when Polynesians first arrived had disappeared.

As for Maori themselves, their neolithic culture was like many others. They lived by hunting, fishing, and gardening; they dwelled in small, windowless, dirt-floored huts; and they were politically organized into several tribes with numerous subdivisions. But far and away the most notable feature of Maori culture was the incessant warfare. Exactly when this began is hard to say (without any written history of their own, the Maori past must be pieced together from the evidence of archaeology), but by around A.D. 1500 heavily fortified villages, or "*pa*," indicate that it was already a well-established part of native life. These tribal strongholds contained earthworks, ditches, palisades, and dykes. The greater part of Maori economic resources were spent on war, on building giant canoes for sending war parties around the islands, and on fort construction.

Few people in the ethnographic record were more aggressive. The "welcome" dance they presented to visitors was a display of ferocious hostility, while their wood carving snarled and grimaced. All gargoyles without any redeeming piètas, it was the art of a violent and demon-haunted world. By the time the first Europeans arrived, in the words of the New Zealand Maori anthropologist Bruce Biggs, "intertribal warfare was endemic and male children were dedicated at birth to 'bearing the spear and the club, fighting and raging, killing war-parties and destroying forts.' Warfare was said to be *he taonga tuku iho* (a treasured heirloom)."[4] Prisoners were routinely baked and eaten. Authorities report that when Abel Janzoon Tasman visited in 1642, "cannibalism was already occurring. Certainly, by the late eighteenth century, the bodies of those killed in war were a prized source of food."[5]

To someone with a sense of history there's nothing surprising about any of this—similar things were probably going on in Europe and many other places between five and ten thousand years ago. It was, after all, only two thousand years ago that the Romans were stamping out human sacrifice among the German tribes. What *is* surprising, however, is the complete suppression in New Zealand today of all public reference to the way of life described above.

A long century of moral transfiguration has finally reached its apogee. With the cosmetic improvements of sundry members of the Culture Cult, only the most decorous and edifying version of the Polynesian past is allowed on public view—a genteel world of wise ecologists, mystical sages, gifted artists, heroic navigators, and pacifists who wouldn't hurt a fly.

A Visitor from Austria Arrives

When the Viennese philosopher Karl Popper arrived in New Zealand in March 1937, it was partly as a result of a misunderstanding. He had been in Copenhagen in 1936 visiting Niels Bohr in the course of a congress for scientific philosophy. While in Copenhagen a man named Warren Weaver introduced himself to Popper as the European representative of the Rockefeller Foundation—a charming gentleman, wrote Popper, who took great interest in him. But the Rockefeller Foundation itself was a mystery. It "meant nothing to me; I had never heard about the foundations and their work. (Apparently I was very naive.) It was only years later that I realized that if I had understood the meaning of this encounter it might have led to my going to America instead of to New Zealand."[6]

Instead of going to America he went off to the other end of the earth. There Popper became a lecturer in the Department of Psychology and Philosophy at Canterbury College, Christchurch, a provincial town in the South Island of New Zealand. In Christchurch the Nazis and the Communists were far away, and the furies about to descend on Europe were inaudible. Those like myself who grew up in Christchurch at the time remember students in blazers poling flat-bottomed boats on a stream called the Avon, passing beds of daffodils as it wound toward the sea.

But all of this was deceptive. Taken as a whole New Zealand was much closer to old-time tribalism than Vienna. It had been fifteen hundred years since Goths and Vandals had rampaged around Austria. But it had been less than a hundred years since a treaty was signed with the Maori chiefs—the Treaty of Waitangi—the beginning of law and order in a land torn by intertribal wars. The Treaty would soften the effect of conquest and subjection, and would be both misunderstood and neglected, and would in no way deal with the conflict between settlers and Maoris over land. Nevertheless it was a vital step in bringing the Maori people from the neolithic into the modern age.

Maori culture had a number of interesting customs. The institutions of *muru* and *tapu*, for example, embodied tribal conceptions of property and law, and they show how wide the ditch was dividing Maori practices from the way we live today. In the words of an observer of the 1830s *muru* consisted of "the regular legalised and established system of plundering as penalty for offences, which in a rough way resembled our law by which a man is obliged to pay 'damages.' Great abuses had, however, crept into this system, so great, indeed, as to render the retention of any sort of moveable property almost an impossibility, and to in great measure discourage the inclination to labour for its acquisition."[7]

In Western eyes one of the stranger aspects of *muru* was that it was often inflicted for accidents—events in which malice aforethought was wholly absent. If a child fell into the fire and was badly burned, and the mother's family came to hear of it, "the father was immediately plundered to an extent that almost left him without the means of subsistence: fishing nets, canoes, pigs, provisions—all went."[8] Once more we see the general rule in tribal society that there is no such thing as an innocent injurious act. Everything is moralized. Accidents don't just happen. But if they do, someone is held responsible and must pay a price.

Counterbalancing *muru* was *tapu* (this being the Maori form of the generic Polynesian "taboo"), which tended to secure property against predation. In fact *muru* was usually the penalty for some violation of *tapu* itself. Although "earth, air, fire, water, goods and chattels, growing crops, men, women, and children—everything absolutely was subject to its influence, the original object of the ordinary *tapu* seems to have been the preservation of property. This personal form of the *tapu* was permanent, and consisted in a certain sacred character which attached to the person of a chief and never left him." The sacred aura of *tapu* forced everyone to keep their distance, never to touch, and perhaps not even to look—sometimes on pain of death.

A chief's fighting men and associates were also "more or less possessed of this mysterious quality. It extended or was communicated to all their movable property, especially to their clothes, weapons, ornaments, and tools, and to everything in fact which they touched."[9] This had practical value. But *tapu* was combined with a range of prohibitions making innovation in thought or deed difficult, if not impossible. It closed off whole areas of the mind to new ideas.

As he worked away on the manuscript of *The Open Society*, Karl Popper was aware of this feature of Polynesian life. There are a number of places in his book where taboos (forbidden actions and unthinkable thoughts, in contrast to Socrates' ideal of the examined life) were singled out as a characteristic feature of tribal psychology. Since the clash between Maori *tapu* and secular European society has often figured in New Zealand ethnic conflict (and still does today), that might have been a good example to use in *The Open Society*.

But it was not to be. His classical training and his determination to expose Plato's role in what had gone wrong with the world (the subtitle of Volume One of *The Open Society and Its Enemies* is *The Spell of Plato*) meant that Sparta and Athens were where Popper's thoughts about taboo naturally belonged. Above all, Greece was where the first spontaneous transition from tribalism to civilization took place, and the parallels he saw between Sparta and the neotribal ideals of both fascism and communism in 1940 were striking. Fascism and communism were reactionary forms of "arrested tribalism." In a similar way "the ultimate aim that dominated Sparta's policy was an attempt to arrest all change and to return to tribalism." Any attempt of this sort was doomed to failure, for "innocence once lost cannot be regained,"[10] but you could learn a lot from Sparta just the same.

To begin with, the Spartan goal of an "autarchic" (self-sufficient) foreign policy was a caricature of foreign policy Nazi-style. Its first command was to "shut out all foreign influences which might endanger the rigidity of tribal taboos." Equally dangerous was the threat of egalitarianism: where democratic ideas were in conflict with tribalism these had to be firmly suppressed. Protectionism was another area where similarities could be seen, and the cumulative effect of Spartan policy overall was to produce an obsession with power and the maintenance of power—in order to be strong enough to enforce its rules a tribe always needed to strive for mastery, enslaving its neighbors when possible, dominating them when not.[11] It all sounds not unlike West African Dahomey.

Popper agreed that tribalism was not the same all the way across the map. There were variations, and the New Zealand Maori represented one of these. But the power of taboo meant that tribal cultures everywhere tended to be cognitively static and incapable of intellectual advance. "When I speak of the rigidity of tribalism I do not mean that no changes can occur in the tribal ways of life. I mean rather that the comparatively infrequent changes have the character of religious conversions or revulsions, or of the introduction of new magical taboos . . ."[12]

The social effect was clear. Within a tribal setting mental life is so dominated by taboos that there is no real equivalent to the moral problems of modern consciousness, let alone the freedom to speculate about good and evil. For Popper the tribal world is a world without doubts, and the average tribesman "will rarely find himself in the position of doubting how he ought to act. The right way is always determined, though difficulties must be overcome in following it. It is determined by taboos, by magical tribal institutions which can never become objects of critical consideration."[13] These thoughts then crystalize in a statement which sets out the theme of his book:

> the magical or tribal or collectivist society will also be called the *closed society*, and the society in which individuals are confronted with personal decisions, the *open society*.[14]

Tribalism and nationalism both embodied the culturally particular—the sort of thing admired by German Romanticism and Isaiah Berlin. Popper, on the other hand, hoped to see nationalism wither away in the years ahead. He had been a Social Democrat in Vienna for two decades, and he remained loyal to some of its ideals. The parochialism of Herder was something he would have found repellent. But the philosophy of Herder's contemporary Immanuel Kant was sympathetic. In fact few words describe Popper's general outlook better than those of Ernest Gellner describing Kant:

> It is the universal in man which he revered, not the specific, and certainly not the culturally specific. In such a philosophy, there is no place for the mystique of the idiosyncratic culture. There is in fact hardly any room for culture in the anthropological sense at all.

The Maori Situation

But "culture in the anthropological sense" was very important to the man who was Popper's departmental head in New Zealand, the anthropologist Ivan Sutherland, and Sutherland was soon at loggerheads with his newly arrived lecturer from overseas. A man of missionary impulses, Sutherland was typical of those who spend their earlier years searching for a faith to believe in and a vocation to follow. He first wanted to be a Methodist minister. Then in London he studied under the sociologist and political scientist Graham Wallas. After this he turned to psychology, and by the time of Popper's arrival in New Zealand in 1937 he had become a specialist in Maori affairs. He disapproved of capitalism, deplored the stress and strain of modernity, saw much to be admired in the old communal world, and like Karl Polanyi he looked forward to a socialist future.

Sutherland's books and writings on the Maori were significant. They combined down-to-earth reports on modern conditions with the *sotto voce* promotion of traditional ways. His sympathy with the Maori cause was genuine and not unreasonable. Maori sufferings had indeed been real enough. Land wars in the 1860s had led to large-scale confiscations, and for decades afterward many Maori were demoralized and depressed.

But white settlement in New Zealand had been rather more complicated than today's energetic myth-making suggests. While the settlers had wanted land, thousands of Maoris had also wanted European goods, and both parties behaved much as you'd expect. In the early days Maori chiefs actively encouraged white colonization since they gained both economic benefits and prestige (*mana*) from having whites on their lands. The New Zealand historian James Belich writes:

> The settlements employed Maori labour and bought Maori food—initially they had very little agriculture of their own. They provided Maori with a regular source of European goods, as against the sporadic one of ship visits, or even the intermittent and limited supplies provided by trading stations. This was especially important for consumables such as gunpowder, tobacco and sugar. Planting Pakeha instead of potatoes on part of your land made economic sense, as well as boosting *mana* as the latest currency of rivalry.[15]

One chief wrote to Governor George Grey in the nineteenth century "offering to sell land and asking him for European settlers direct from England for a larger town." Another chief planned a town big enough to contain 104 European families. A third chief declared: "Should the Pakeha (the white man) wish to purchase land here, encourage him; no matter how small the amount he may offer, take it without hesitation. It is the Pakeha we want here. The Pakeha himself will be ample payment for our land, because we commonly expect to become prosperous through him."[16]

Much has been made of large acreages paid for with a few guns or trinkets plus a blanket or two. Belich comments: "The guns, cash, blankets and trinkets laid out or promised at the sale ceremonies were merely a bonus, though sometimes a valued one. Beneath this overt price was a tacit one: an ongoing relationship with the cluster of settler neighbours created, and intended to be created, by the sale."[17]

But settler pressure for land never let up. Misunderstandings multiplied. Reckless and rapacious transactions took place—20 million acres of the empty South Island changed hands for £2,000. Gradually, as they came to realize that what was happening was irreversible, Maori resistance grew to both land sales and settlement. War broke out in the 1860s, and in their eventual defeat the Maori were subject to the full confiscatory power of the state. Many had their lands taken from them—the powerful Waikato tribes (who had themselves murderously enslaved and expropriated their neighbors for many years) now found themselves expropriated (but not enslaved) in turn.

Maori who still owned land still wanted the new life. But the economic rules of the game had changed. Trapped in old ways and old habits they were unaware of this. Their communal arrangements made it hard to convert the capital which accrued from the sale of land into permanent productive assets. They never understood how the modern economy worked. High spending on prestige items continued, and chiefly profligacy went uncontrolled. As the nineteenth century drew to an end, after one hundred years of culture contact and the establishment of schools and a modern economy, ostentatious tombstones were being ordered by wealthy Maori, costly bridal dresses made by expensive dressmakers, and buggies bought for chiefly transport: "A buggy became the status symbol of a *rangatira* (chief) . . . Such things cost money, of which land selling was increasingly the easiest source."[18]

From Belich's account several things are clear. Underlying the Maori situation was the profound contrast between Maori communal and white individual ownership and rights, between casual and sustained activity directed to the goal of a better life, between the impulsive adoption of some innovation (a plow, a new livestock breed) and continuous technological modernization, all of it aimed at self-improvement by private households and small families within a framework of modern property law. With their erratic incomes communally dispersed, and their land communally owned, Maori could not progress. The emerging pattern of Maori disadvantage rested on irreconcilably opposed forms of landownership, enterprise, and economic understanding. The Big Ditch once again.

This was still the physical situation of Maori in 1940. But what might be called the metaphysical situation of the Maori—in other words, the interpretation of their condition by intellectuals who had taken it upon themselves to explain the Maori situation in moral terms—was rather different. As active men and women playing their part for better or worse on the historical stage, and making decisions for better or worse on their own behalf, Maori would from now on be increasingly replaced by abstract ciphers, symbolic figures out of Rousseau, brown victims cast in a morality play to illustrate white guilt.

Maori traditions would be idealized beyond recognition. With not a battle or a broken head in sight, let alone cannibal feasts, their culture would be portrayed as something that had been tragically "taken from them" like the land itself. This dual expropriation would then be used to explain every imaginable failing. Colonial history would be rewritten as a purely moral drama of villains and victimhood, while the script for this drama incorporated a common sentimental illusion much favored in progressive circles—the moral superiority of the oppressed.[19]

The Strain of Civilization

Throughout his stay in New Zealand, Popper's conflict with Sutherland grew steadily worse. And, as it did so, Sutherland's personality became more disturbed. Upholding the old-time communal Maori past, he recommended preserving it on broadly psychiatric grounds. If Maori were widely regarded as feckless, or lacking in will or direction, he attributed this to the disrupted "equilibrium" of their traditional life. In 1940 in *The Maori People Today* he claimed that they had originally lived in a state of primitive harmony:

> When a people is living in a state of established equilibrium with its natural and social environment, and when each generation is inheriting a stable tradition, mind and character are patterned in terms of this tradition and mental and moral stability are thus achieved. This was the state of the Maori people before the advent of Europeans. Mind and character reflect the outward forms of social and cultural life. When these latter are progressively destroyed, as they were in this country, minds progressively disintegrate . . . [20]

However sympathetic this may seem, it is little more than the old organic harmony myth once again. In the case of Maori culture it is amply clear that "the state of established equilibrium with its natural and social environment" never existed—certainly not in pre-European times. That was when wildlife was destroyed on a Herculean scale, and when Maori depredations reduced vital food resources so seriously that there must have been grave economic consequences when the last moa bit the dust and the last seal swam away from the coast.

As indeed there were. After using up all the large birds and mammals, the Polynesians now began to eat each other. "By the fifteenth century the Maori living in the north had begun to build great *pa*, or forts. One function of the *pa* was to protect stores of sweet potato. . . . Another, more fundamental function was to protect people themselves from predation by other hungry humans."[21] Following these developments came levels of warfare which meant that in any given week a man might or might not be killed, captured, enslaved, or eaten—and a woman raped as well. The landscape of New Zealand resembled medieval Europe. There may not have been mailed knights on horseback, but there were Polynesian castles throughout the land.

No doubt some kind of "mental and moral stability can be achieved" in such circumstances. But one is tempted to retort to Sutherland: shouldn't mental equilibrium be rather more easily achieved under the conditions prevailing in the New Zealand of 1940, with all the provisions of a pioneer welfare state including free medicine, family benefits, education, and universal peace?[22]

But this misses the psychological point. Increasingly disturbed, Sutherland was by then a potential suicide who in the years ahead would take his own life. His sympathy for the mental health of the Maori appears inextricably confused with his own deteriorating mental state. When he proposed that they strengthen their traditional communal roots as a solution for their problems, it is possible that a deeper and unacknowledged reason for doing so was a feeling that in the security and protection of Maori community life he too could find relief. It was not the Maori but Sutherland himself who faced disintegration. That is where breakdown loomed.

In *Civilization and Its Discontents*, Sigmund Freud notes with a certain ironic surprise the suggestion that our own social arrangements are the source of our discontent. "When we start to consider this possibility," he writes, "we come across a point of view which is so amazing that we will pause over it. According to it, our so-called civilization itself is to blame for a great part of our misery, and we should be much happier if we were to give it up and go back to primitive conditions."[23] How has this come about? he asks. What explains "this attitude of hostility to civilization"?

He gives two reasons. First there was the effect of voyages of discovery, such as Captain Cook's, when "men came into contact with primitive peoples and races. To the Europeans, who failed to observe them carefully and misunderstood what they saw, these people seemed to lead simple, happy lives—wanting for nothing—such as the travellers who visited them, with all their superior culture, were unable to achieve." This view was baseless ("later experience has corrected this opinion on many points") but it was widely believed, being "erroneously attributed to the absence of the complicated conditions of civilization."[24]

The second cause of communal yearnings and hostility to the modern world is more recent, writes Freud, and derives from speculation about the origin of neurotic disorders. "It was found that men become neurotic because they cannot tolerate the degree of privation that society imposes on them in virtue of its cultural ideals, and it was supposed that a return to greater possibilities of happiness would ensue if these standards were abolished or greatly relaxed."[25]

Later than Freud, Popper too suggested that the idealization of tribal life is an unconscious reaction to the "strain of civilization." Acknowledging Freud's contribution, he wrote on the very first page of Volume One of *The Open Society and Its Enemies* that his book "attempts to show that this civilization has not yet fully recovered from the shock of its birth—the transition from the tribal or 'closed society'. . . to the 'open society.'" In Volume Two he wrote again that a fact with "grave political and institutional problems, is that to live in the haven of a tribe, or of a 'community' approaching a tribe, is for many men an emotional necessity," the "strain of civilization" being "partly a result of this unsatisfied emotional need."[26] As his last days would soon show, the haven of a tribe was something Sutherland seems to have been seeking too.

Friedrich Hayek had similar things to say about romantic communal yearnings, and although there were wide differences between them, Freud and Hayek and Popper all shared a common theme.

This suggested that the profound emotional longing for the security of a communal environment was a permanent feature of our psychic life—every bit as hard to renounce as the Freudian renunciation of sexuality. Romantic primitivism was no mere midsummer madness. For better or worse Rousseau will be always with us because fantasies about tribal life will never die.

Anthropology and Its Discontents

A combination of cultural anthropology (which tends to normalize the primitive while treating civilization as aberrant) and psychology (which may seek to normalize Freud's "primordial, deeply buried mental states") seems to be a very unstable mix. Some can handle it and some cannot, and the evidence from Margaret Mead on has not been encouraging. Stanley Diamond's claim that anthropology is the most alienated of the professions is also worth noting. This suggests what ordinary observation confirms—that a schadenfreudian delight in the failings of civilization, and deep discontent with its rewards, is for some anthropologists a stronger motive for joining the discipline than a positive interest in tribal life. Fieldwork brings added complications, putting the researcher in a close personal relationship with communities where detachment is hard to maintain. In this situation the anthropologist often softens his portrait of the people he has come to study, idealizes their customs, abandons all objectivity, and jettisons questions of truth and value in the process. The treatment by Benedict of Zuni, and by Mead of Samoa, are only two of innumerable examples.

In Sutherland's day anthropological truth had not yet been relativized as "truth," and facts had not yet been ironized as "facts." But the school of cultural anthropology he belonged to generally denied that civilization was superior to anything else. It therefore denied that there was any reason whatever to celebrate the change from a "closed" to an "open" society. For Sutherland such a distinction would have been either meaningless or false. This being so, need one look any further to explain the intense dislike he came to feel for Popper, and which Popper believed had something to do with Sutherland's suicide?

Opinion differs—some are disinclined to see any connection—but it was an unusual situation. On the one hand the disputatious Popper was engaged on a magnum opus, *The Open Society*, in which the failings of tribalism were comprehensively laid bare. On the other hand Sutherland was writing papers that were largely a defense of the tribal world and that called for its support. Cause enough, perhaps, for departmental war? Soon Sutherland instigated a campaign of harassment against Popper, eventually alleging to the police that the visiting European was probably an agent of influence for the Axis powers—if not an actual spy. The Viennese philosopher had a thick accent, and to the average New Zealand constable during wartime this was very suspicious.

When the police came to his door Popper was able to dissuade them from making an arrest. But he was shocked at their ignorance, and he was seen the following day carrying armfuls of books down to the police station to bring the officers up-to-date on the real nature of Hitler and the Nazis. For this episode Sutherland was forced to apologize to Popper by the college Rector. And his vendetta intensified from that day on.[27]

Popper regarded New Zealand as an outpost of the Open Society he admired, years later declaring it to be "the freest country" he knew. Yet it is unlikely that he grasped the complexities of the racial situation. Few Maori lived in Christchurch. Most of them lived elsewhere, and it is quite possible that in 1940 Popper was not well informed about the historical background to their situation. Yet the message he brought remains pertinent today.

If Popper is right, then a discontented nostalgia for the communal is a widespread reaction to the difficulties of modern life, and there is a singular irony in his being tied to a man in New Zealand who embodied that discontent. By 1945, however, relief was in sight. *The Open Society* had been published and he would soon leave for England. In the teeth of Stalin's postwar triumphalism, as if to spite the "revolutionary" governments being imposed by the Red Army in the east, he argued that far and away the most significant historic change had been "the transition from the closed to the open society," and that this itself was "one of the deepest revolutions through which mankind had passed."[28]

In 1951 Sutherland took his own life. Toward the end he was more and more preoccupied with maintaining Maori traditions, and we are told that he was increasingly drawn into the flesh-and-blood lives of Maori communities, with all their reciprocal bonds and human responsibilities, "deepening his studies of present day Maori life, on the East Coast with his oldest Ngati Porou friends, in the Waikato and the Urewera, in North Auckland, in Taranaki."[29] But whatever support he found there does not finally seem to have been enough.

If it is true that anthropology is the most alienated of the professions, it is equally true that the vocational choice of anthropology is sometimes a signal of personal distress. In addition to this, the conflict between the obligations and duties of the tribal world he studies and the wider civilized world he belongs to sometimes produces a strain in the anthropologist's sense of identity—his sense of who he is and where he belongs and what his duties are—and it would be surprising if this did not play a part in Sutherland's breakdown. When an obituarist wrote that "the strain told," one feels that the split, the crackup, the decision to end it all, came also from conflicting allegiances that had become unmanageable.[30] The cause of his fierce personal struggle with Popper and its final crisis might be seen as yet another symptom of the strain of civilization itself.

The Maori People Today

And the Maori People? What has happened to them? Most have got on with their lives and joined the modern world. Everyone knows of the opera singer Kiri Te Kanawa. But thousands like her in much humbler situations have made their own contribution to New Zealand today. However, this is not what you will hear if you visit the country. A local observer writes that "the fact that many Maori run hundreds of highly successful enterprises in the professions, tourism, entertainment, retail, farming and contracting" goes completely unnoticed. Those successfully assimilated to Western commercial life are the very last to attract attention. Indeed they are almost invisible. Instead, educational curricula and numerous governmental publications ceaselessly glorify the Polynesian ways of the past.

It's all very strange. Any visitor to New Zealand can see that modern Maori have the same needs for housing, education, and jobs as everyone else. And given a chance they are just as capable. But as we have already seen in Australia, indigenous attempts to succeed are handicapped by a pervasive hostility to market society across broad stretches of the white middle class. A miscellaneous army of teachers, academics, government servants, clergy, radical lawyers, progressive judges, journalists, and numerous other *bien pensants* promote the revival of traditional Maori culture even more fanatically than the Maori do themselves. Not of course the blood-stained pre-European Polynesian world. Instead, an unending routine of communal basket-weaving, accompanied by traditional dance and song, seems to be more what they have in mind.

A typical collection of essays provides a glimpse of these attitudes. An Anglican priest rails against "the monocultural grip on all our institutions" that British colonization secured; deplores the "institutional racism" that sees the schools, the broadcasting system, and parliament itself all propagating Western values; commends the way Maori "communal values encourage the sharing of resources"; asserts that "for Maori and many other cultures, spirituality encompasses all things," a fact which means that "instead of destroying millions of acres of natural bush . . . Maori spirituality treats the land and bush as sacred in the first place"; and threatens that unless Maori rights are recognized and appropriate restitution made, Maori will be entitled to "take the law into their own hands."[31]

A teacher says that New Zealand should "hand over the education of Maori children to Maori authorities—probably to tribally based authorities to run tribally based schools . . . The agenda of such schools must be Maori, the methods Maori and Maori *mana* (that is, power and prestige) must be paramount." Ignoring the modern world of the Internet, the need for literacy and numeracy, the ever-increasing pressure for specialized training and technological expertise, he claims that, "It's my bet that with these ingredients" (i.e., a fully tribalized Maori-language education, presumably in a setting of native rain forest, to the singing of native birds) "future Pakeha/whites will have to look to their laurels when it comes to jobs, politics, and every facet of New Zealand life which will truly fulfill the hopes of partnership implicit in the Treaty of Waitangi."[32]

Similar goals are embraced by the official policy of "bi-culturalism." This supposedly combines the modern legal and economic arrangements of New Zealand society in general with Maori collectivism, with a revival of tribal social organization, and with the reassertion of communal taboos as forms of pseudo-legal control. It is said that where all else has failed, bi-culturalism will at last achieve

"social justice" and "equity" and the alleviation of "economic dispar-
ities" between white and black. And if it doesn't . . . ?

Well, then something more muscular may be tried. A recent document from New Zealand's Maori Development Ministry warns that if
demands for "rapid improvement" are not met, there may well be violence in the streets. Not of course that either the Maori minister or
his ministry advocates violence—not at all. But he and his friends in-
sist that all future New Zealand social policy must ensure that Maori
traditions are "fully functioning and respected." The view expressed
seems to be that as long as your culture is "respected," then success
is inevitable and your bank account will grow.

It is almost as if Sutherland has finally triumphed fifty years after his
death. For the analysis he made of Maori problems bears an uncanny
resemblance to the psychological insistence on "respecting" Maori
culture found today. It is of course absurd to suggest that "respect"
for Indian or Chinese culture has anything whatever to do with Indian and Chinese success on the one hand, or Maori failure on the
other. (Bitter resentment of Asian immigrant success is expressed in
the same government document.)

The reason Chinese and Indians succeed in New Zealand and elsewhere is that they bring with them more successful entrepreneurial
cultures, and aim at more successful financial outcomes, which are repeatedly shown to be more successful than communal traditions at
achieving the desired results. And as we shall see in the next chapter,
the general causes and conditions of cultural success and failure are
steadily becoming better known.

PART III

CIVILIZATION

AND ITS

MALCONTENTS

*The Economic and
Cultural Implications*

8

Why Cultures
Succeed or Fail

How did the rest of us cross the Big Ditch? Why was it that the West successfully achieved both peaceful and open societies while the East got something very different, often worse, and whole continents became arrested at the tribal level? If you take the eleventh century as a starting point—as David Landes does—then the amount of violence in Europe at that time differed little from the level in New Zealand in Cook's day or in West Africa about 1750.

In Jan Huizinga's *The Waning of the Middle Ages*, it is clear that at the beginning traditional tribal values still ruled Europe. His opening chapter, "The Violent Tenor of Life," says that until the fifteenth century the central dominating motive for most men "was the thirst for revenge." Every traditional Maori would agree. "There can be no doubt that no other political motive could be better understood by the people," writes Huizinga, "than the primitive motives of hatred and of vengeance."

Commerce was under a cloud too. An influential wing of the Church was hostile, and remained hostile for centuries. The "rigorists" stood for virtuous communalism, and even opposed the purchase of loaves from bakers by those rich enough to pay bakers to make their bread. Cardinal Robert of Curzon wrote in 1213 that all men should be instructed "under pain of excommunication . . . to eat only their own bread, that is, the bread won by their own labour, as the apostle commanded, and that there be no idle or pushing fellows among us." The intention was egalitarian social justice. The result was to discourage the specialization of trades and to slow the growth of towns.

But this process couldn't be stopped. Unlike pre-Columbian America, or the Polynesian world, or India, or China, the essential foundations of European success had been laid in classical times. The contrast between Greece and Rome and oriental despotism was the contrast "between private property and Ruler Takes All." And in most of the rest of the world, the rulers and their families took all. Only in the West did a free and independent bourgeoisie grow up. Only in the West were the warrior classes effectively tamed and controlled.

For this reason, wrote David Landes, "the very notion of economic development was a western invention. Aristocratic (despotic) operations were typically squeeze operations: when the elites wanted more, they did not think in terms of gains in productivity." They just squeezed harder. But in Europe, by the fourteenth century, cultures allowing multiple initiatives, with fewer taboos and freely inventive minds, having enhanced security and low costs of doing business, and with continually increasing specialization, and division of labor, and rising productivity—were making it across the Big Ditch toward civil society.

Origins of the Present

What is the most remarkable achievement of modern science and technology? Is it the unscrambling of the genetic code? The communications revolution? Or that robot nosing up to rocks on Mars? My own choice from engineering would be the townships built on oil platforms in the middle of the North Sea. To hear the men at work constructing these rigs, Norwegian and English and Scottish voices shouting through the gale as piles are driven and barges floated into place above the waves, is to be reminded of the various strands which came together to make Western civilization the creative marvel it is— just as the 5,000-year-old Ice Man found in the Alps of northern Italy, untouched and undiscovered since some early excursion went awry, reminds us of that civilization's long history.

The Ice Man wore leather shoes stuffed with dry grass against the cold, a leather tunic and leggings, a cap of chamois fur, and a cape loosely braided from grass to protect himself against the cold, rain and snow. He carried a short flint knife, a small copper axe, a bow, and some arrows in a quiver. It seems he was caught in an early winter storm while crossing a mountain pass.

A primitive shepherd perfectly suited for romantic fantasizing, he was as innocent of civilization as you could wish—a man who had been wandering in some Mediterranean Eden only the day before. Here was just the sort of creature idealized by Rousseau, a late-neolithic tribesman from a time when agriculture was starting in the valleys below. His people grew einkorn and wheat—particles of wheat and barley were found on his clothes.

But he was not nearly as primitive as someone like Rousseau would have us believe. Back home in the Ice Man's village, trade was thriving: only Adam Smith's "propensity to barter and exchange" could explain the axe he carried. Far from the prehistoric simplicities of Eden, cast in copper by *çire perdu*, his axe suggests all those long centuries of trial and error, of fires and molten ore, of ingenious metallurgical experiment leading eventually to the furnaces of the Industrial Revolution—the decisive development which put the West ahead of the rest. The method of trial and error used for centuries to establish the ductility of alloys is only now yielding to modern computer techniques.[1]

What this progress suggests—from neolithic hunting to the oil rigs in the North Sea—is that cultures differ profoundly, and these differences have profound effects. Cultures differ in the kind of questions people ask about the natural world, they differ in the way it is explored, and they differ in their ability to produce useful adaptive results. Not all cultures value truth and empirical inquiry, facts rather than fantasy, the practical rather than the theatrical in social life. Cultures also differ in their capacity to adapt and learn and change almost as much as in their attitudes to work—and work was changing for the Ice Man himself, as hunting gave way to agricultural routines.

Social behavior varies too. There are cultures that allow high levels of overt aggressiveness: others regard this as intolerable. How powerful is the man at the top? Must it always be a case of ruler takes all? This has been a Russian problem for centuries. Other cultures seem to have never discovered the secret of peacefully settling disputes. Conflict that should be manageable tends continually to expand into violence or war, and insecurity and shaky communications make regular production and trade impossible. Economic historians tell us that what might seem a recent problem in Africa has deep historic roots.

Such cultural differences are crucial—they may decide a people's fate. Like it or not, some cultures succeed and others fail because some are better able to provide law, security, order, prosperity, freedom, and the institutional pluralism that people in the year 2000 expect. To deny this is to deny the facts of life.

Innovation Versus Tradition

The most widely imitated successful culture of all time is the civilization of Western Europe. Classical Greece and Rome two thousand years ago were the foundation. The Dark Ages brought a period of disorder, insecurity, and decline. Then around the eleventh century the "European Miracle" got under way, power became less centralized, and commercial towns escaped from the authority of the king. A balance developed among relatively free social groups and institutions, each forming alliances with the other when threatened. In John Powelson's words:

> Over time, the weaker groups—peasants, craftspeople, financiers and traders—demanded a greater share of both power and resources. They acquired it by organizing themselves into corporate groups contesting each other. In this they were helped by an increase in material output which they controlled.[2]

The political environment was favorable. But technical innovation plus science was just as important. In his *The Wealth and Poverty of Nations*, David Landes writes that if any one thing gave Europe an early edge it was the eleventh-century "invention of invention." Adam Smith said that specialization in a widening market encouraged innovation, and this is "exactly what happened in the Europe of the Middle Ages—one of the most inventive societies that history had known."[3] In 1066 one might have expected Britain to be mechanically backward, but the Domesday Book, compiled by the Normans after their conquest, listed 5,600 waterwheels and mills. With a bit more research and development and a bit more savvy, the full potential of water power and mills was discovered. Soon they were used to manufacture woollens, to hammer metal, to mash hops for beer, and mangle rags for paper.[4]

Now compare this dynamism with China. The Chinese had known how to make paper by hand for a thousand years, and they continued to make it that way. Coarse art paper is still handmade in places. But as soon as paper-making arrived in Europe in the thirteenth-century, manufacture was mechanized.[5] Mechanization saved time, and time-saving itself was done by new mechanical clocks. No one knows who first made them or where, though it is said of the escapement mechanism that "whoever invented it must have been a mechanical genius."[6] China had built a few astronomical water clocks, "complicated and artful pieces that may have kept excellent time in the short run, before they started clogging."[7] But the European escapement mechanism was far superior, and it changed time-keeping forever.

Freedom is needed for innovation, but in China, knowledge was a monopoly of the emperor. Because knowledge was power, only the emperor was supposed to have it, and he wouldn't share it with others. In John Powelson's study of successful economic development the diffusion of power is of critical importance. But "the main purpose of Chinese law was to preserve the power of the state, not the rights of the individual,"[8] and the imperial power monopoly was secured by a series of tightly run dynastic regimes.

In 1306 a man in Pisa wrote, "it is not twenty years since there was discovered the art of making spectacles that help one to see well, an art that is one of the best and most necessary in the world."[9] European priority in the making of corrective lenses lasted between three and four hundred years, led to microscopy, and from there to important discoveries about the microcosm. It was the same with printing. Invented in China in the ninth century, it didn't really catch on there, and according to one authority it was only in the twentieth century that printing with moveable type replaced the older method—five hundred years after the West.[10]

In China the free circulation of printed material was blocked by the emperor. Again the contrast with Europe is striking. When Gutenberg produced his bible in 1452–55, the first Western book made by movable type, the pent-up demand for books was already huge: "Within the next century, printing spread from the Rhineland throughout Western Europe. The estimated output of incunabula (books published before 1501) came to millions—two million in Italy alone."[11]

The merchant classes in Europe developed in the towns. But in China traders were attached to the central bureaucracy, were a part of the state, and never had fully independent individual ownership. Merchants in China were always an arm of officialdom itself, and the attitude of a Chinese official was quite different from that of a Western entrepreneur. "The tradition in China had been not to build a better mousetrap but to get the official mouse monopoly."[12] John K. Fairbank adds that the bureaucracy lived by "systematized corruption, which sometimes became extortion"; that all money transactions involved "squeeze" in the form of gifts; that nepotism was universal since "even classic texts extolled duty to family, and particularly filial piety, as superior to any duty to the state"; and that those holding high office were expected to use it to enrich themselves. Moreover, it was difficult for anyone to keep track of what was happening since "budgetary and accounting procedures were rudimentary."[13]

Not so in Europe. If traders were to make a profit, they had to keep proper accounts—and the technique for this began early. Double-entry bookkeeping first showed up in a work published by the London branch of an Italian firm in 1305, and in 1494 it was given a full presentation in what is described as the "masterwork" of Luca Paccioli in Milan, a treatise with the title *Summa de arithmetica, geometria, proportioni et proportionalita*. But whatever its source, writes Peter Bernstein in *Against the Gods*, "this revolutionary innovation in accounting methods had significant economic consequences, comparable to the discovery of the steam engine three hundred years later."[14]

Even medieval monks were excited by machinery. A member of the Abbey of Clairvaux in the twelfth century thanks God for devices which "can mitigate the oppressive labor of men and spare the backs of their horses." But what exactly lay behind this European delight in discovery and innovation? One suggestion is the Judeo-Christian respect for manual labor. Another is the subordination of nature to man in Western thought, this marking "a sharp departure from widespread animistic beliefs and practices" involving naiads and dryads in every field and stream. A third explanation points to the European linear sense of time in contrast to the cyclical conceptions found elsewhere.

But in the end David Landes comes back to Adam Smith. "In the last analysis, however, I would stress the market. Enterprise was free in Europe. Innovation worked and paid, and rulers and vested interests were limited in their ability to prevent or discourage innovation."[15] That is why Western Europe became rich while many other places stayed poor. That is also the answer to the problem which provides an epigraph for Landes's book: the need to determine "the causes of the wealth and poverty of nations—the grand object of all enquiries in Political Economy."[16]

Communal Order Versus
Market Prosperity

Several studies show that the contrast between the wealth-producing cultures of Western Europe and the poverty-producing traditional cultures admired by romantic primitivism goes back for centuries.[17] And they also show that the break with communal arrangements was the essential first step forward. Ernest Gellner writes that in most communally organized social systems a man "can sometimes escape the tyranny of kings, but only at the cost of falling under the tyranny of cousins, and of ritual." Everyone knows the delight anthropologists take in pointing to examples of the "kin-defined, ritually orchestrated, severely demanding and life-pervading systems," that they have admiringly documented among primitive societies over the years.[18]

But in England anticommunal rules kept kin and cousins in their place; separated ritual from economic life; guaranteed private property in land against the demands of relatives; gave rights to transfer family property to nonfamily members; and enabled men and women to think their own thoughts, however suffocating the *idées fixes* of the tribe—and all of this went back hundreds of years.[19]

After studying sixteenth-century England, Alan Macfarlane went off to Nepal to do fieldwork in a Himalayan village, and what he found surprised him.

Two things especially struck me when comparing it to England in the past. The first was the very great difference in *per capita* wealth in the two societies. Historians kept talking about England in the pre-industrial period as a "subsistence" economy, with people on the verge of starvation, technologically backward, economically unsophisticated. But when I compared the technology, the inventories of possessions, and the budgets of a contemporary Asian society with those for English sixteenth-century villagers, I found that there was already an enormous gap. The English were, on the whole, an immeasurably wealthier people, with a far higher investment in tools and other productive forces. To think of India or China in the early twentieth century as directly comparable to England just before the industrial revolution [in the years when Adam Smith was gathering material for his book] appeared to be a serious mistake.[20]

This mistake was spectacularly made by Karl Polanyi. *The Great Transformation* claimed that a vast change had taken place in England after the sixteenth century, which had seen a nonmarket economy destroyed. What is absolutely clear, wrote Alan Macfarlane, contradicting Polanyi,

> [I]s that one of the major theories of economic anthropology is incorrect, namely the idea that we witness in England between the sixteenth and nineteenth centuries the "Great Transformation" from a non-market, peasant society where economics is "embedded" in social relations, to a modern market, capitalist, system where economy and society have been split apart.[21]

In Macfarlane's view the split was ancient. England's evolution in the direction of a market economy had gone on for centuries, and what Smith was laughed at for inventing—*Homo economicus*—appeared to be little more than a truthful depiction of the world around him:

> According to Polanyi, such a man had only just emerged, stripped of his ritual, political and social needs. The implication of the present argument, however, is that it was Adam Smith who was right and Karl Polanyi who was wrong, at least in relation to England. "Homo economicus" and the market society had been present in England for centuries before Smith wrote.[22]

The main argument of Smith's *The Wealth of Nations* (1776) was straightforward. Specialization and division of labor were essential to economic success. So was a growing population which obtained millions of new jobs, and so was capital accumulation and the private investment of capital in productive ways. If economic success is the goal, that's the way to go. In a modern economy we all benefit from the work of millions of anonymous people we never meet, and, instead of being a handicap, this uncommunal impersonality is a very good thing. Each contribution, coordinated by market signals alone, adds to the wealth of the whole. As Smith says at the end of his first chapter:

[I]f we examine, I say, all these things, and consider what a variety of labour is employed about each of them, we shall be sensible that without the assistance and cooperation of many thousands, the very meanest person in a civilized country could not be provided, even according to what we very falsely imagine the easy and simple manner in which he is commonly accommodated. Compared, indeed, with the more extravagant luxury of the great, his accommodation must no doubt appear extremely simple and easy; and yet it may be true, perhaps, that the accommodation of an European prince does not always so much exceed that of an industrious and frugal peasant, as the accommodation of the latter exceeds that of many an African king, the absolute master of the lives and liberties of ten thousand naked savages.[23]

England Versus Russia

What about Russia? Can its unending misery and backwardness be due merely to bad luck and bad weather—or do unmistakable historical factors explain the situation there too? Three dates make an interesting comparison with England. First, the year 1215; second, the year 1649; third, the year 1728, when Daniel Defoe's paean to England's middle classes and their culture of commercial success was written.

In England, the year 1215 was the year of Magna Carta, and of the limits this charter placed on royal power. The word "consent" now entered the relations between the English king and his subjects, and it is usually seen as part of the nation's political history. But Richard Pipes says that Magna Carta's economic consequences were just as important—if not more. Fiscal matters were central: the year 1215 decisively marked the end of ruler takes all in the British Isles. When King John agreed not to levy taxes without "the consent of the realm," this meant that the king was prevented from robbing his subjects of their private wealth and assets whenever some ill-advised military campaign went astray.[24]

In 1297 this agreement was incorporated into the Confirmation of Charters, which "restated the principle that the king had no authority to impose nonfeudal levies without a parliamentary grant." The effect was to provide "fundamental guarantees of the security of private property in England." Kings could no longer freely wage war and pay for it later by seizing the wealth of their subjects. Unless the people consented to a special levy, the king would have to pay for his military adventures himself. Pipes says that England, guided by Magna Carta, represented a classic illustration of how private wealth restrained public authority.[25]

Now for Russia in 1215. Genghis Khan and his Mongols were overrunning the land. They had no interest in occupation. Instead the Mongols forced Russia's princes to pay tribute to them, turning them into servile tax-collectors for three hundred years. Just as the princes were wholly at the mercy of their Mongol overlords, the peasants were at the mercy of their Russian "owners." Peasants were merely chattels, and consent had nothing whatever to do with their acceptance of aristocratic authority.

But it is the upshot of this system that matters, for its effects lasted right up until 1989—Russian Rulers Take All. The Prince or King or Czar was always regarded as the sovereign in his domain: private property was never secure and was always held conditionally. Civil society couldn't develop, and institutional pluralism was something the country never knew. An early historian noted that "the sovereign was the possessor of all Russia and private property derived from the sovereign." The private sphere was entirely dependent on royal favor. Where such favor was lacking—and that was throughout most of Russian history, and conspicuously under Ivan the Terrible and Peter the Great—a private sphere did not exist.[26] This blocked the rise of Civil Society, and it became impossible for Russia to cross the Ditch.

The next date is 1649. In this year serfdom was confirmed by law in Russia. Throughout Russian history no peasants had either property or legal rights—nor for that matter did their masters. All of them together, nobles and gentry, peasants and slave-like serfs, were legally "servants of the state."[27] Because confiscation was a punitive possibility, they had no incentive to try new farming methods, build better housing or improve farm buildings, or do anything else that might have given superior comfort levels of amenity a permanent base. Cultural failure again.

Compare this to the situation in England. The year 1649 saw merchants, free farmers, and the commercial and professional middle classes in general, dramatically asserting their rights against central power and royal privilege. After his exactions became intolerable, a free and independent property-owning citizenry arose in anger to cut off King Charles's head. Pipes compares the rural situation in Western Europe and in Russia as follows: "[I]n respect to the farming population, as in respect to landed property, the evolution of Russia proceeded in a direction opposite to that of the West. In the West at the close of the Middle Ages, serfs became freemen; in Russia freemen turned into serfs."[28]

Which brings us to 1728, only a short time after the death of Peter the Great. Peter cut off the Boyars' prodigious beards, and by forcibly educating the aristocracy and making them adopt Western dress he superficially civilized the Russian elite. But economic life was never more insecure. Under Peter, Russian land, assets, factories, and all products, were continually threatened with state seizure. In 1729 a Chancery of Confiscations was established in Russia, "an office that may well be unique in the annals of government institutions."[29] The czar's property-grabbing had been so insatiable that a special division of government was set up to handle the accumulating estates—the Chancery of Confiscations was that division.

In England in 1728 the contrasting economic spectacle was vividly depicted by Defoe. A freely enterprising citizenry was building and buying and making and selling—and then buying and selling again. Living without fear of confiscations, an independent middle class was flourishing, while more and more people lived in towns, free of both the lords in the countryside and the intrusive authority of king and court. The institutions of government and commerce were pluralistic, not unitary. Here was a culture of success, not failure. The Big Ditch had been well and truly crossed. "It is upon these two classes of People," wrote Defoe,

> the Manufacturers [not the employers, but rather those who labor in industry] and the Shopkeepers, that I build the hypothesis which I have taken upon me to offer to the Public, 'tis upon the Gain they make either by their Labour, or their Industry in Trade, and upon their inconceivable Numbers, that the Home Consumption of our own Produce, and of the Produce of foreign nations imported here is so exceedingly great, that our Trade is raised up to such a Prodigy of Magnitude, as I shall shew it is . . .[30]

Black Markets and White

For hundreds of years the private sector has been a barely tolerated semilegal presence cowering in the shadow of the Russian state, and in the absence of established and enforceable property law, and a legal structure securely protecting trade and commerce, that is pretty much the way it remains.

But ordinary Russians stubbornly pursued a better life regardless. Although Peter the Great imposed the death penalty in 1703 for cutting down a single oak tree without permission, people still cut down oaks. In 1932 Stalin imposed the death penalty for private trading in grain, but people still bought and sold grain.[31] In 1961 the death penalty for "economic crimes" was re-introduced under the Soviet regime as an attempt to control the "black market." But nothing could stop the "black market"—which is, of course, merely what the police call the market in goods and services, which spontaneously arises as a result of absurd policies, when the state makes goods and services legally impossible to obtain.

Nothing like Russia's communist economy was ever seen before, and nothing like it is ever likely to be seen again. Under the Soviet system an entire "counter-economy" came into existence with several names—though *na levo*, translated as "on the side" or "under the table," was the most common. Before 1989 virtually all retail items had a "black" component. There was the price a customer paid to the shop, and then there was the under-the-counter extra price paid to the shop employee—the total often being up to twice the advertised price. State employees spent half their time privately dealing in public property. As numerous Russians told Hedrick Smith in the 1970s, "Everyone in the retail trade is a thief and you can't put them all in jail."[32] By banning every sensible human transaction, the state made all its citizens criminals, and the effect this had on public morals leaves it an open question whether Russian life will ever be the same again. The universal distrust produced by the Soviet system was a recipe for cultural and economic failure on a titanic scale.[33]

Countless security police were employed and countless informers worked for the police day and night, but nothing could stop what was going on because most of it was accepted by ordinary Russians. What the formal economy was unable to provide, the counter-economy provided on the side. Despite continual threats, fulminations, prosecutions, and denials by the Communist Party that things were as bad as they seemed, glimpses of the underlying reality did occasionally appear in the official controlled party press: "One venturesome newspaper commentary in *Komsomolskaya Pravda* in October 1974, dared to imply that the system is at fault for *not meeting the basic needs of consumers.*"[34]

Although nothing as perverse as the Soviet system has been found anywhere else, we do find almost exactly the same words being used more recently to describe the Peruvian economy. The writer is novelist Mario Vargas Llosa. "In countries like Peru," he wrote in 1989 in the preface to a book by Hernando de Soto, "the problem is not the black market but the state itself. The informal economy is the people's spontaneous and creative response to the state's *incapacity to satisfy the basic needs of the impoverished masses.*"[35] A few pages later de Soto himself tells us that when migrants coming from country districts poured into Peru's cities, they found the barriers of a corrupt legal system raised high against them: "Thus it was, that in order to survive, the migrants became informals"—"informals" being the term used by the author to distinguish the "illegals" working in the so-called black market from those in the "formal" economy.

> If they were to live, trade, manufacture, transport, or even consume, the cities' new inhabitants had to do so illegally. Such illegality was not antisocial in intent, like trafficking in drugs, theft, or abduction, but was designed to achieve such essentially legal objectives as building a house, providing a service, or developing a business. . . . We can say that informal activities burgeon when the legal system imposes rules which exceed the socially accepted framework—does not honor the expectations, choices, and preferences of those whom it does not admit within its framework.[36]

In contrast to Russia, Peru's laws and formal economy bore a superficial resemblance to those of Western Europe, the United States, and other developed countries. But this was misleading. The names of its institutions "were mere facades; Latinate separation of powers, political parties, Treasury Departments and Reserve Banks that mimicked their North American counterparts. Mechanisms such as news media scrutiny, public rule making, encouraging accountability in the United States, barely existed at all. A vast corruption enabled a privileged few to dismember and privatize foreign investment."[37]

De Soto's research took him into Lima's shanty towns, and there he found something strange but revealing. A district on the two sides of a river, both occupied by Peruvian Indian migrants who had arrived in the city equally penniless, was really two utterly different communities. As Tom Bethell tells the story, each community covered about three acres and had about 500 people. "On one side were crude huts of mud-brick or cardboard; on the other, brick homes with shops, neat gardens, sidewalks, and merchants living above their businesses. Both were founded by Indians who had come from the same part of Peru."[38] So how was the difference between cardboard and brick, for example, to be explained?

From a retired employee in the Housing Ministry, de Soto learned the history. The difference between the two sides of the river was the same as the difference that separated the English farmer and the Russian serf—security of title to property, a desire to improve whatever property one has, and freedom to act. Both Indian communities had settled on vacant land as squatters. Both wanted secure title. But in Lima there was no easy way to do this. "Titling and registration was the preserve of the ruling class. . . . Over the decades the ruling class had made access to these registers so expensive that most people did without." The two settlements developed differently, "because the leader of the more prosperous one had persevered with Lima's officials for six full years until his residents finally received legal titles; across the river, such protection had not been extended. Owners on one side felt secure that the fruits of their labor would be protected; squatters on the other had no such reassurance."[39]

De Soto next simulated the setting up of a small garment factory, revealing the burden of bureaucratic costs weighing on every legitimate small business. It took ten months to acquire government permission, there were ten demands for bribes, and the cost of the whole procedure was $1,231, which was thirty-two times the minimum monthly wage in Peru. In a parallel test conducted in Tampa, Florida, "complete legal certification of the same business took less than four hours."[40] A study of the costs of access to housing showed eighty-three months were needed to secure permission for a community

housing development to proceed, and each member of the association wishing to build would have to pay $2,156. "In other words,"
writes de Soto, "someone who at the time was earning the monthly
minimum living wage would have to pay out his or her entire income
for four years and eight months."[41] As Peruvian law operated, it was
a built-in institutional recipe for failure.

African Agonies

"Why has East Asia emerged as the model for economic success,"
writes Keith Richburg, "while Africa has seen mostly poverty, hunger,
and economies propped up by foreign aid? Why are East Asians now
expanding their telecommunications capabilities when in most of
Africa it's still hard to make a phone call? Why are East Asian airlines
upgrading their long-haul fleets, while bankrupt African carriers let
planes rust on weed-strewn runways because they can't afford fuel
and repair costs? Why are the leaders of South-east Asia negotiating
ways to ease trade barriers and create a free-trade zone, while Africans
still levy some of the most prohibitive tariffs on earth, even for inter-
regional trade?"[42] Richburg claims there was nothing inevitable
about Asian success and African failure. In 1956 Nkrumah's Ghana
had a higher GNP than South Korea, and Korea was recovering from
a four-year war.

> Today South Korea is recognized as one of Asia's "dragons," an eco-
> nomic powerhouse expanding into new markets throughout the region
> and the world. Ghana, meanwhile, has slid backward. Its gross national
> product today is lower than it was at independence.[43]

Is there some flaw in African culture? asks Richburg. The answer
being yes indeed—and not just one but many. At a reportorial level,
they can be viewed in the pages of his book *Out of America: A Black
Man Confronts Africa*. Based in Kenya, Richburg was the chief cor-
respondent on the continent for the *Washington Post* from 1991 to
1994 when events in Rwanda, Somalia, and Liberia were at their
worst. At a more theoretical level they can be studied in the three
chapters about Africa in Powelson's economic history. According to
Powelson it is the all-powerful state with its all-powerful Big Man
which is Africa's main problem. For as long as anyone knows "the

state was governor, producer, trader, executive officer, and judge, with no separation of powers."[44] African politics desperately needed a variety of nongovernmental institutions. After listing a score of examples Powelson concludes that they all "support the generalization that African states have dominated production and trade from early centuries, often to the exclusion of other groups or private enterprise."[45] Another case of ruler takes all.

The list of African liabilities is long. Tribal rules meant that there was no way to transfer land from less efficient to more efficient uses. No independent labor market developed. "Slavery and marriage were employed to move labor from areas of its abundance to those where it would be more productive. Neither is an efficient means of allocating labor." There was no easy way of telling if consumer preferences changed. Traders did not write contracts, and trade was conducted in an atmosphere of general mistrust. Not enough independent groups were able to challenge the authorities or compete with them. This left them inexperienced at compromise. And if you don't compromise what do you do? You go to war, and war becomes the regular outcome of disputes.[46]

"Fundamentally it was endemic war, waged for millennia in all parts of the African continent, that set the norm of the territorial state. War and preparation for war summed up the purpose of the masculine life."[47] Violence governed both external and internal relations: "Violent force was the weapon of choice to gain labor (by enslavement) and capital (cattle). While peaceful transactions may have taken hold in some places after independence in the 1960s, in others the tradition of legitimate violence returned."[48]

If Powelson is correct then war and violence as routine procedures for settling differences are the deep foundation of the chaos we see today. But to understand the African leaders who emerged after independence back in the 1960s, we need to glance at their education, too. Schooling had made huge strides in British West Africa by the time independence came in 1960. Literacy had advanced from the near-zero levels of the 1880s to a point where hundreds of men and women were sent to universities overseas. But what did this "higher education" consist of?

Thomas Sowell warns that "human capital must not be confused with formal education, which is just one facet of it, and still less with the growth of an intelligentsia."[49] The very opposite may be true. Intellectuals trained in politics and nothing else can be a serious handicap. Much depends on their attitude to the productive classes in society—which in Ghana meant their attitude toward the tens of thousands of peasant farmers on whom rural production rests. Would orators like Kwame Nkrumah who held peasants and small traders in contempt be the right men to run the new African states?

The militant new leaders were recruited almost entirely from humanistic intellectuals, and intellectuals from a small range of fields. "Few nationalist militants were engineers, or economists or professional administrators." Nkrumah made a name for himself as an activist with a line in incendiary prose, Jomo Kenyatta of Kenya had anthropological training, Léopold Senghor of Senegal was a poet. A leading characteristic of such people is that they take economic productivity for granted. Confident that the wealth of nations is entirely unproblematic, they assume that governance is just a matter of sharing the cash that comes pouring in. Once their colonial masters had been expelled there was sure to be lots of spending money. Not a recipe for success—just evidence of complete incomprehension.

Another problem with post-colonial intelligentsias, writes Sowell, is that they have often been "prominent among those fostering hostility toward more advanced groups, while promoting ethnic 'identity' movements, whether such movements have been mobilized against other ethnic groups, the existing authorities, or other targets."[50] Moreover, "newly educated and semi-educated classes have often sought positions in government bureaucracies, rather than in industry and commerce, for which their education has usually given them few skills likely to be useful in the marketplace." Such well-paid positions provide a useful base for agitation. In one country after another surplus political intelligentsia "have played a central role in promoting intergroup and international animosities and atrocities—and in trying to artificially preserve, revive, or fabricate past glories."[51]

It will be recalled that in his last years Karl Polanyi developed an enthusiasm for the African state of Dahomey. He looked forward to it becoming a model for administrations elsewhere, one in which the glories of "high statecraft" would re-emerge to lend dignity and honor to a new era of prideful self-sufficiency and self-esteem.

But what really happened? In the first twelve years of independence there were eleven changes of government, five military coups, and two changes of constitution. In 1973 a Major Kérékou seized power, changed Dahomey's name to The People's Republic of Benin, nationalized most enterprises, and established a one-party state. The gazetteer in which these facts were found tells us that the legal system of Benin is based on the French civil code and customary law, and that the death penalty applies to murder. Assume, however, that it was not applied when the president of Benin murdered his foreign minister.[52] Nor are we told much that is useful about Benin's economic or financial state, the gazetteer blandly reporting in its 1998 edition that "the 1994 budget of 204 billion CFA francs was in balance."[53]

David Landes however is more forthcoming. "This country's biggest products from 1960 to 1989 were Marxist-Leninist propaganda and political coups. The official statistics showed product and trade as almost nonexistent." This was misleading—in fact the planting and harvesting of palm oil and peanuts went on as usual. But the farmers of Benin had learned that the only way to survive was to keep their crops out of the hands of the ruling "kleptocracy" of Kérékou and his friends. So they didn't sell their produce "to the authorities or to official markets. Just about everything moved in parallel channels. These yielded the farmer more than he would ever get from an official marketing board, and the farmer bought off the swollen bureaucracy. On the record, then, Benin is an empty husk with big negative trade balance and negative growth; but it's really a smuggling machine."[54]

"Corruption is the cancer eating at the heart of the African state," writes Richburg. "It is what sustains Africa's strongmen in power, and the money they pilfer, when spread generously throughout the system, is what allows them to continue to command allegiance long after their last shreds of legitimacy are gone."[55] This is true. But it's important not to lose sight of an even more important point. Regardless of the problem of corruption, everywhere in sub-Saharan Africa the state is controlled by a powerful, parasitic, and extremely violent politico-military élite largely indifferent to whatever productive classes the devastated continent still retains. Production takes place with neither the help of the state nor in the presence of an indifferent state: it occurs in spite of the state. Scarcely the rudiments of Civil Society exist.

Civil Society Versus the Warrior State

Restless military men have long been a problem. We all know that generals are grand when in their element. Looking north from the

Capitol at the noble spectacle of Julius Caesar beating up Gauls and Germans, or trying to knock sense into the Celts, the citizens of Rome saw a capable man doing what he did best. The defense of Roman territory was in good hands. But what if Caesar turned and marched on Rome? This is something that happens time and again in Africa today—and it is also the question that kept Adam Ferguson awake at night.

Ferguson was a colleague of Adam Smith in the eighteenth century who published *An Essay on the History of Civil Society* (1773). He too believed that specialization was the coming thing, and that in a commercial civilization the arts of peace were more important than the arts of war. He agreed with Montesquieu that it was commerce which had sweetened the manners of the barbarous warrior élites of northern Europe. But he still worried when he saw large numbers of army men with nothing to do. Perhaps, if they had a mind to do so, a cabal of colonels would usurp the place of parliament and make its own uncivil values prevail—as it does throughout Africa today. Democracies, he noted sadly, seemed blind and heedless things.[56]

But what if there's no democracy to start with? Africa today is filled with cultures lacking any firm tradition of electoral government as a counterweight to military ambition. Suppose, also, that there exists no deeply rooted respect for law rather than power, no respect for political procedure to outweigh charismatic appeal. Traditional African culture was entirely without checks and balances since legislative, judicial, and executive powers were usually combined. No lengthy experience of negotiation and compromise inhibited resort to force. Force came naturally. After the colonial powers had departed "confrontation and war became the principal means of 're-solving' disputes"—indeed disputes were not meant to be "settled" in a western sense at all. They "might only be contained, indefinitely," until a Savimbi or a Kabila felt there was more to be gained by striking than by sitting still.[57] It all sounds very much the way things were in eighteenth-century Dahomey—a recipe for disaster.

Successful cultures are not in thrall to violent, powerful, irremoveable military elites. They have found a better way. Even during World War Two, when "a curious coalition of warriors and industrialists" tried to take over the world, they were eliminated. In both Japan and Germany, the transition from the *samurai* ethos of their respective military castes to modernity had not been complete. All the fascist convulsion of the 1930s proved, according to Ernest Gellner, is that

"Military rule characterizes *unsuccessful* rather than *successful* nations. . . ."[58] Civil Society is something else again:

> to define our notion of Civil Society effectively, we must first of all distinguish it from something which may in itself be attractive or repulsive, or perhaps both, but which is radically distinct from it: the segmentary (i.e., tribal) community which avoids central tyranny by firmly turning the individual into an integral part of the social sub-unit. Romantics feel nostalgia for it and modern individualists may loathe it; but what concerns us here is that, whatever our feelings for it may be, it is very, very different from our notion of Civil Society . . .[59]

In Gellner's view three choices exist. First is the tribal world, "cousin ridden and ritual ridden," and although free of centralized political tyranny "not really free in a sense that would satisfy us." Second is the world created by the arrested pseudo-tribalism of the Nazis and Communists. This involves a "centralization which grinds into the dust all subsidiary social institutions or sub-communities, whether ritually stifling or not."

Third, and finally, there is a world which is far removed from both, and which grew up in Western Europe and America before spreading around the globe. This "excludes both stifling communalism and centralized authoritarianism."[60] It rejects both militarism and labor camps. It is broadly democratic, and, in contrast to numerous national cultures which have failed, it is highly successful. It is, in fact, the civilization we have today.

9

Civilization and
Its Malcontents

Cultures are one thing—but "civilization" is something else again. A leading aim of the Culture Cult is to ennoble the first, to denigrate the second, and to make the very notion of civilization superfluous. This is understandable enough in the case of chip-on-the-shoulder communards and bohemians, who tend to blame all unhappiness on the world around them. But songs in praise of cultural parochialism are a good deal harder to understand from men like T. S. Eliot and Ludwig Wittgenstein.

To read Eliot's poetry is to encounter a range of reference which only the very literate could hope to grasp. To read Wittgenstein is to meet something equally rarefied in philosophy. Yet both of them were drawn to the all-inclusive anthropological concept of culture, something which is the antithesis of High Culture, and which would undermine its status and fatally weaken its defense. One wonders whether the strain of civilization was too much for their refined but fragile minds. And what motive drove them to pushing the anthropological concept so enthusiastically?

Over the years the terms "civilization" and "culture" have both been the victims of a deliberate, strategic, dumbing down. It was the prestige of "civilization" which galled Rousseau and Herder two centuries ago, and the Culture Cult's assault on civilization in our own day took up where they left off. More significantly, for university life, it was the high reputation and esteem accorded the ideal of High Culture in the humanities—culture as literature and music and art—which drew the resentful attention of Raymond Williams. In each case the terminological attack and the semantic leveling attempted have been driven by a neurotic and destructive *ressentiment*—and Williams's efforts were damaging in the extreme.

The process of semantic leveling has three stages. First a word like "culture" is resented for being too exclusive, pretentious, élitist, or injurious to public pride, and for wounding the self-esteem of whoever feels left out. Next, sensitive citizens offer new definitions which expand the meaning to include things hurtfully excluded. Last *reductio ad absurdum* operates until nothing is left out—everything is art, everything is music, everything is literature, science, or whatever. Mozart, meteorology, and meatpacking all mean much the same.

Unable any longer to endure the humiliating discomforts of High Culture, Williams anthropologically expanded the meaning of the term to give the British Labour Party a creative status equal to the plays of Shakespeare and the poetry of Keats. The result was predictable. Once everything was included, the original term "culture" was nullified as a measure of quality; it was no longer able to confer distinction of any kind; and the world was ready at last for cultural studies.

Civilizations Don't Rise

In August 1999 *National Geographic* magazine tackled the subject of "culture"—or maybe the real subject was "cultures," it's hard to say. The editors appeared spread-eagled between two meanings that are miles apart and in several ways are flatly opposed. On the one hand there was the familiar plural use which gives us a multicultural and many-costumed world. This is what *National Geographic* has successfully traded in for many years. A reader of its August 1999 issue who understood this meaning would expect to turn the pages of a pictorial atlas showing a spread of peoples from Amish to Zulu, dropping in on the Maori along the way. And that is partly what the August 1999 issue was about.

But this plural use of "cultures" was muddled in with a very different meaning. This second sense of the word is found when we speak of "human culture" to distinguish humanity from the rest of nature.

It is universal, not particular. It also has a built-in evolutionary perspective and looks back over thousands of years. When we speak of the history of human culture, or the evolution of human culture, we mean a universal adaptive process of social change and institutional improvement. The meaning is general, and cosmopolitan, and applies to all humanity all around the globe.

Sometimes *National Geographic* seemed to mean this. Its first chapter about "Global Culture" (singular) suggested that a universal global process was involved. The pictures dealt with some of the cosmopolitan trends around us, from Thai Buddhist monks breakfasting at a Denny's restaurant in California, to a girl in a black plastic catsuit sitting next to her mother wearing a red sari in Bombay, to Big Bird flapping around a kindergarten in Shanghai. On the contents page the reader was referred to a supplementary foldout with the title "culture" (singular), again implicitly universal. But as soon as you found the foldout accompanying this issue and opened it, confusion followed. Now we were being told about "cultures" (plural), all of which are admirable, and some of which were said to be on the wane. So what did the editors actually want to say? And how was a reader to know?

There was indeed an obvious way out of this muddle—a well-known term for general, world-wide, universal human development exists. But it isn't "culture," it's "civilization." It has been widely used for the past two hundred years, and it has no satisfactory substitute. But nowadays it is no longer used. The Culture Cult has made sure that civilization can only be used negatively as the mortal enemy of all those waning particularities in their colorful folk costumes—if indeed it can be used at all—and although it lurked invisibly in the background throughout this issue of *National Geographic*, and could be glimpsed between the lines on page after page, the editors were careful never to include the actual word in the main text.

There was also a "time line" in the supplement, and here the evasion and confusion was even more striking. As time lines do, this showed a grand sweep of evolutionary development starting with the splendid cave paintings from France 34,000 years ago, touching down in Mesopotamia for cuneiform, in Alexandria for the Great Library, and at Mainz to see Gutenberg, before ending with the invention of the CD. What it showed was "the rise of civilization," and up until about twenty years ago that is how the editors would have described it. Now, civilization having become unmentionable, the time line carried *no title at all*. And we all should know why. To speak of the "rise" of anything is impermissible. It might be taken to mean that some cultures didn't rise but stayed put. It might imply that in those cultures where you don't find writing and libraries and the wheel, because they never had them, there had been no advance, no improvement at all. And someone's feelings would be hurt.

The August 1999 issue of *National Geographic* also included many true and useful things, among them a chapter on the invention of writing. But the taboo on the word "civilization" made it impossible to give a coherent account, in historical and evolutionary terms, of the world we live in today. Or even an account that made sense.

Culture Versus Civilization

Cultures are good: civilization is bad. Those six words tell all you need to know about the moral judgment we have inherited from Herder and Rousseau. Each of these terms have had their ups and downs over the past 250 years, but "civilization" has generally stood for a world marked by accepted freedoms and respected courtesies, both private and public, not found in ruder forms of life. "The terms *civilité, politesse*, and *police* (meaning law-abiding) go back to the sixteenth century," wrote Adam Kuper in a recent review of Lucien Fèbvre's discussion of the matter. "Throughout the seventeenth century, the terms 'savage' and, for more advanced peoples, 'barbarian' were current in French for people who lacked the qualities 'of civility, courtesy, and, finally, administrative wisdom.'"

Then by the eighteenth century, "Fèbvre suggested, there was a need for a new substantive term to describe a new notion. Born at its hour, in the 1770s the neologism *civilisation* 'won its papers of naturalization,' and in 1798 it forced the doors of the Dictionary of the French Academy." By 1800, and for a long time thereafter in France, "normally civilization was valued, and identified with progress. In general usage, the term took on a sacred aura."[1]

In France perhaps—but not among those who felt ignored by Paris. For many both inside and outside France the sacredness and aura were little more than a challenge and affront, and the long assault by a resentful provincial clerisy on behalf of "culture" against "civilization" began. In eighteenth-century Germany the opposition was felt intensely at a regional level, and was first formulated in the terms we know today. It again became important a century later with the collapse of the Habsburgs, an irruption of angry nationalities, and in Nazi Germany in the 1930s and '40s something much worse than that.

Now, in the year 2000, the conflict is felt globally, and is expressed in the same terms for the same purposes. Except that the triumph of romantic primitivism in the West is now so complete that the term "civilization" is rarely heard in public discussion—and even more rarely without irony. But the real irony lies elsewhere. When Fèbvre notes that along with *civilité* and *politesse* was the word *police*, and says that this is an essential aspect of civilization, mental alarm bells should start ringing. In many places police actions are being undertaken by the United Nations against unruly, murderous, nationalistic cultures, each of them aggressively driven by the very best of cultural reasons (blood, soil, pride, dignity, national honor, historic duty to be avenged, and so forth), whether in the Balkans or the Horn of Africa or the Middle East. As we all know, the action being reluctantly taken in these situations, and largely paid for by the United States, is to impose standards of civilized behavior on tribalistic broils. Yet civilization must never be mentioned—it is the virtue which dare not speak its name.

Culture: The Anthropologists' Account

"What is culture? Even anthropologists struggle to define the word," *National Geographic* notes rhetorically, before offering the usual inventory definition in which "food, dress, tools, dwellings, laws, manners, art, myths," are all said to be culture indiscriminately, and in which picking the finest string quartet, picking tomatoes, and a politician caught thoughtfully picking his nose are all regarded as much the same thing. What middle-brow *National Geographic* does not seem to have caught up with yet is that some of the highest brows in the business are now disenchanted with both anthropology and its conception of culture, and are abandoning the discipline in droves. This is clear from a new 1999 book so heavy with foreboding that except for its author's intelligence, good humor, and light and readable style, one might easily take it for a funeral oration: it smells of mortality on many a page.

In this book Adam Kuper tries to assess what anthropology has done in the name of "culture" in our time. This means candidly recording many unhappy things. *Culture: The Anthropologists' Account* is also a calling of American anthropology to account, and it cannot be entirely accidental that on its opening page Matthew Arnold makes an appearance—and not for the last time—in this decidedly unfamiliar milieu. Kuper does his best to look on the bright side, to recognize achievement when recognition is due, but by the time he has worked his way through Geertz, Schneider, Sahlins et al., his final end-of-the millennium judgment on the anthropological use and abuse of the term "culture" is clearly negative. It also suggests that the hopes once built on it as the key to a "science of culture" were always chimerical.

He reminds us of the immodest ambitions voiced in years gone by. In 1917 Alfred Kroeber had published "On the Superorganic," a paper announcing how high we had soared above our biological nature; and by 1952, when Kroeber collaborated with Clyde Kluckhohn on a review of the meanings of the technical sense of "culture" in anthropology, the two men had convinced themselves that "In explanatory importance and in generality of application it is comparable to such categories as gravity in physics, disease in medicine, evolution in biology."[2] It is of course nothing of the sort and never was. Instead the anthropological concept of culture is far too general for its own good, a fact which makes its "explanatory importance" hard to evaluate—because it explains everything, it also tends to explain nothing, *explanans* and *explanandum* amounting to much the same thing.

Twenty years after Kroeber and Kluckhohn another anthropologist has his own try at defining "culture." Very little progress had been made—indeed, by 1973 things may have gone backwards. "Today we have culture just about digested—we seem to know what it 'is'" wrote Paul Bohannan. But what is this "just about digested," as if two more decades of academic chewing still hadn't been enough? And why was it that he only seemed to know what it is? If he and his colleagues still had a shaky grasp of their subject, how could their studies have been soundly based? Certainly, says Bohannan with anxious emphasis, culture is not to be confused with such vague notions as Emile Durkheim's *representation collective*—not at all:

The concept of culture is an important one because it gets us out of this particular kind of mysticism (not to say sentimentality). Indeed, that is the trouble. We switch uncomprehendingly from culture to 'a culture', get 'a culture' confused with ancestry, give the whole a mystical aura that is fundamentally narcissistic—and we are back in the racist ages that the idea of culture should have saved us from.[3]

Here he puts his finger on the dilemma facing the editors of *National Geographic*, who also "switched uncomprehendingly from culture to 'a culture'" last August. This remark by Bohannan shows that in 1973 the shift from the universal meaning to the romantic usages of the Culture Cult was well under way. As for that "mystical aura that is fundamentally narcissistic" it is hard to know what to say. Narcissism is of course exactly what grows out of flattering the proud ethnic particularity of cultures, and by neglecting the universal values of civilization. Overall this is a surprising statement. It expresses either sheer ignorance, or a determination to ignore the known facts about the historic origins of the term *kultur* in Germany, which were sentimental, mystical, "confused with ancestry," and ideological through and through. If today's Culture Cult is both romantic and mystical—and it is—then those origins ultimately tell us why. Bohannan is in a muddle, and is going around in circles, but he tells his fellow anthropologists that they must cling to that muddle and defend it and pretend it's The Way Ahead because if they don't they'll be overwhelmed by "racism"—and that would be worse.

Now another thirty years have passed, and Adam Kuper brings us the bad news. It seems that clinging to all the muddle didn't help. As more and more anthropologists came to realize this they bailed out and "switched their intellectual allegiance from the social sciences to the humanities, (where) they are likely to practice interpretation, even deconstruction, rather than sociological or psychological analysis."[4] In the deconstructed humanities confusion is par for the course, and no doubt they hoped it wouldn't be noticed there. Culture is also, observes Kuper—visibly distancing himself from this conception—a term now appropriated by social movements of one kind or another "based on nationalism, ethnic identity, or religion . . . in order to motivate political action" (in other words, it has reverted to what it was circa 1780), while the "pretensions" of cultural theories have never been matched by results.

Worse is to come. "At full strength, moreover," Kuper writes of these theories, "we may suspect that they are not good for the health. . . . Complex notions like culture, or discourse, inhibit an analysis of the relationships among the variables they pack together. . . . Religious beliefs, rituals, knowledge, moral values, the arts, rhetorical genres, and so on should be separated out from each other rather than bound together into a single bundle labeled culture, or collective consciousness, or superstructure, or discourse."[5] Instead of the old blooming buzzing confusion embraced by the founders of the discipline, Kuper has the nerve to suggest it might be better to study society institutionally, piece by piece. After which he raises the ante still further, and concludes his book by discussing the constraints on freedom and the deep ethical problems of "the cultural mode of thought" we have already seen in Herder and Berlin, and which those who are aware of the conflict between cultures and civilization cannot dismiss:

> Cultural identity can never provide an adequate guide for living. We all have multiple identities, and even if I accept that I have a primary identity, I may not want to conform to it. . . . If I am to regard myself only as a cultural being, I allow myself little room to maneuver, or to question the world in which I find myself. Finally, there is a moral objection to culture theory. It tends to draw attention away from what we have in common instead of encouraging us to communicate across national, ethnic, and religious boundaries, and to venture between them.[6]

In his opening sentence above, what Kuper means when he says that cultural identity "can never provide an adequate guide for living" is that *civilized life* requires the freedom to maneuver, to question, and to communicate—much more freedom and more room than most "cultures" allow, let alone primitive cultures. It needs the freedom of an open society and an extended economy, not the suffocation of closed cultures and autarchy. But Kuper is unable to say that directly, let alone use "civilization" as a positive alternative to the failings he so ably describes. Addressing himself to American liberals, he is trying in the politest way to help them see that in its renascent German Romantic form, "culture theory" is particularistic, chauvinistic, primitivistic, and deeply at odds with the analytic requirements of any social science worth the name.

Whatever the view from Peoria or Poughkeepsie, it is obvious that the leaky ark of old-style culture theory is sinking fast, and that it is now a case of *sauve qui peut*. One salvation strategy anthropology is being pressed to follow is the incorporation of cultural studies for its own survival—where they are still distinguishable, that is. As Gellner and others have shown (and Kuper effectively cites Gellner more than once), the discipline is behaving as if driven by a lust for self-immolation, and it is hardly surprising if academic obsequies are being prepared. But the supreme irony of the situation is one which, as an anthropologist, Kuper declines to comment on, even though he does mention Matthew Arnold now and then. Not only is cultural anthropology expiring as a serious discipline, but having seen its own relativism triumph within the humanities, it is dragging down everything else too.

The Habsburg Dilemma

Yet the humanities have no one to blame but themselves. Few intellectual misadventures in the twentieth century have been as consequential, or as damaging, as the eagerness of its most influential critics to adopt the anthropological meaning of "culture" to replace their own. T. S. Eliot was one who did this; and more deliberately and malignantly so did Raymond Williams. Both explicitly acknowledged the "anthropological conception" as their inspiration. Up until then culture as High Culture, as the best that had been said and done in literature and philosophy, or the fine or the performing arts, upheld the standards by which civilized artistic endeavor could be assayed. But the result of Eliot's somnambulistic ruminations, and Williams's knowing subversion, was the eventual death of a once serviceable term. Now it has been drag-dropped into the trash.

Just as intriguing is the way the communal mode of thought appealed as a refuge to intensely individualistic minds. Venturing too far into philosophical solitude, and finding the chill and isolation too much to bear, they then turned back to the groupish warmth and protection of the *Gemeinschaft* world. Ludwig Wittgenstein is the classic case, just as his birthplace, Vienna, is the location of the "Habsburg Dilemma."

Open society or closed culture? Individuality or collectivism? Universalism or ethnic particularity? Cosmopolitanism or nationalism?

Economic liberalism or socialism? Atomism or organicism? Knowledge as independently-arrived-at *truth*, to be experimentally confirmed or falsified, or knowledge as communally authorized *belief* forever beyond appraisal as true or false? Freely adaptable modern
mobility, interest in change and ability to handle it, openness to science and innovation—or roots fixed forever in unrelinquishable
blood-soaked tribal soil? In Austria, with the transformation of
Herder's cultural nationalism into nationalism per se, writes Ernest
Gellner, "The opposition between individualism and communalism,
between the appeal of *Gesellschaft* (society) and of *Gemeinschaft*
(community), a tension which pervades and torments most societies
disrupted by modernization, became closely linked to the hurly burly
of daily political life and pervaded the sensibility of everyone."[7] In
the terms employed in this book, for *Gesellschaft* read modern universal civilization and market economies; for *Gemeinschaft* read the
emotional complexes and intimidating coercive ties associated with
the waning communal world.

The decline of the communal is saturated in pathos. As Gellner
writes, "community is sung and praised by those who have lost it."
On this view its bards and celebrants nostalgically call to mind an
ideal that has gone, an innocence which is destroyed, and an idyll
which may in fact never have been. When it is alive, community is im-
perceptible, is hardly noticed, and provides a taken-for-granted matrix for events: "It is lived, it is danced, it is performed in ritual and
celebrated in legend, but it is hardly articulated in theory."[8] When it
is about to die the communal culture which has been unconsciously
accepted as an all-embracing *umwelt* now becomes consciously dwelt
on, theorized, idealized, mythicized, and may, in some cases, proceed
swiftly from the pathos of decline to the bathos of Disneyfication.
But as Gellner says, the central argument concerning cultural identity, vitality, and authenticity, everywhere makes similar claims:
"Roots are everything. Rootlessness is not just wicked but deeply
pathological and pathogenic."[9] Rootless cosmopolitanism is evil.

Along the path Gellner delineates lies the ominous marriage of cultural nationalism and political madness which, alas, anthropological
enthusiasm for the glories of human collectives has never been willing to confront: "The relatively gentle Herderian insistence on the
life-enhancing quality of a local communal culture was in due course
strengthened by a less benign element: Darwin mediated by Niet-

zsche. The vitality-conferring roots were to be not merely territorial-cultural, but also genetic. The legitimating community was not merely language-transmitting but also a gene-transmitting one. . . . The line of development towards extreme and racist nationalism was clear and plausible."[10]

Plausible it may be—but perhaps a little over-intellectualized in this account, for *pace* Gellner neither Darwin nor Nietzsche are needed to introduce biology. It is unlikely that the separatists in Chechenya today have been reading Darwin, and it is certain that Nietzsche is unknown in Tigray. But in each place the end result is the same. Like the antipodean thinking about nationalism which goes on in Aboriginal Australia, blood and territory and immemorial traditions, all bundled inseparably together as they were in Herder's day, are the legitimating foundations on which "cultural" identity supposedly rests. It was however in the heart of Europe, in Vienna, that the clash between the ideal of the "local communal culture" on the periphery, and the metropolitan civilization at the centre, split the social world philosophically, politically, and economically from top to bottom.

"Roughly speaking, the Habsburg Empire was torn between the cosmopolitan liberalism of the higher bourgeoisie, and the nationalist and socialist leaning of the ethnic groups, including the German speakers. The philosophical expression of the former interest was the ideal of an open society, individualist and cosmopolitan, an idea elaborated and made famous by Popper. The latter interest expressed itself largely in the romanticism of *Gemeinschaft*, of a closed community suffused by intimate affective relations, and delimited by an idiosyncratic culture which sustained those relations and endowed them with rich symbolic expression. It found its sacrament in the village green and the festival, not in the free market, whether of goods or ideas. Hayek and Popper, of course, voted for *Gesellschaft*, or the Open Society."[11]

In Austria-Hungary the conflict was paradigmatic. The division between the left-populist-peasantophile "cultural" side to which people like Karl Polanyi and his wife Ilona belonged, and the right-universalist-Jewish "civilization" side of the liberal trio of Popper, Hayek, and Mises, symbolized a general divide. That the formerly stigmatized Jews had come to constitute such a high proportion of the new professional and commercial bourgeoisie in Vienna, whose influence steadily grew at the expense of a decaying court and a declining clerisy, is something on which Gellner has many interesting things to say—including the oddity of the alliance they briefly formed. Highly successful, they "had every reason to be attracted to liberalism, to the cult of equal opportunity for all, and a free market in goods, ideas, and men—and they had every cause to combine this liberalism with a loyalty to the centre, whatever the past history and formal affiliations of that centre. An old and rigid dynasty, long linked with hierarchy, authoritarianism, and obscurantist dogmatism, did not exactly look like promising material for being the symbol of the Open Society. But, comic though it might be, the logic of the situation made it so."[12] In fact the old and rigid dynasty was not a symbol of the Open Society—and it is hard to believe that anyone thought it was. But at a turning point in history it provided a protective environment for the growth and development of Austrian liberalism. It did not succeed; but it was the best hope for civilization at the time.

Meanwhile cultural/national/socialist propaganda, from Germany to the Balkans in the east, took a turn for the worse. What had earlier begun in a Herderian vein as "a fairly timid and modest defence of peasant culture" against the condescension of the French, on the one hand, and British commercialism on the other, grew gradually into "an aggressive affirmation of the virtue of peasant roots. Roots were everything, and roots were to be found in the soil. Peasants were virtuous and they also made good soldiers. Cosmopolitanism was treacherous, alien, feeble and enervating."[13]

Suffusing this malevolently anti-metropolitan cast of mind were a number of features endemic in the emerging Culture Cult, especially a *Blut und Boden* slant the Nazis would find useful: "In this struggle nationalism employed the distinctive socio-metaphysic, or philosophical anthropology, provided by romanticism. . . . Those endowed with roots are healthy and vigorous, those devoid of them are pathological and indeed pathogenic. Man was true to himself when his specific, soil-bound or blood-bound culture spoke to him through spontaneous and powerful *feeling*; he was false to his true nature when he linked himself to some anaemic universalist humanitarian ideal. . . ."[14]

Under darkening skies, as the struggle deepened between the "arrested tribalism" of Hitler on the one hand, and the civilized ideals of Austrian liberalism on the other, Vienna's fugitives took flight before the storm. Hayek, Popper, and Michael Polanyi went first to England, to be followed later in 1939 by the thirteen-year-old Czech Ernest Gellner, while Mises moved in 1940 from Geneva to the USA.

Between them they comprised a talking compendium of healthy ideas vital to civilization. From Popper the legacy of the Open Society, something separated by a big ditch from more primitive social forms. From Mises the certainty that socialism "cannot achieve an efficient utilisation of resources" and would sooner or later be doomed.[15] From both Hayek and Polanyi, the concept of spontaneously self-adjusting economic order essential to modern market economies. And last, but not least, from Gellner a style of philosophical realism friendly to science and vigorously opposed to the decadent salon relativism and squalid astrologism of today. Those who died before escaping from Vienna should be remembered for what they endured. Those who escaped should be thanked for their contribution to the heritage of the West.

Romantic primitivism in Vienna was populistic and loved the idea of tightly-knit peasant households in the east. Its political outcome was, and shows every East European sign of continuing to be, extremely grim. Romantic primitivism in England on the other hand was somewhat hampered by the absence of peasants, though village smiths and wheelwrights made passable substitutes. In Gellner's interpretation, for F. R. Leavis the "organic community" of the country village stood in for the Carpathian commune; for Raymond Williams, who disparaged the organic community as passé, the solidarity of the working class and its institutions were more inspirational. Unlike the situation in Austria, English primitivism could not define its goals in opposition to a decadent Habsburg monarchy or to an officious bureaucratic center in Vienna; instead it took its stand against what it saw as the domestic evils of industrialization, science, and modern technique.

Politically the outcome in Britain was much less apocalyptic than in Austria, but it still cannot be considered a happy one for the fate of culture in the arts. It is after all to Raymond Williams that it owes its present fate, and the story of its degradation as it moved gradually downward to the awaiting nemesis of Cultural Studies is instructive in more ways than one.

Arnold: Civilization and Anarchy

But a discussion of these matters must begin at the beginning. And in England the beginning was Matthew Arnold's great sermon to his countrymen *Culture and Anarchy.* Since the framework of our discussion is the antipathy of civilization to the Culture Cult point of view—the downright hostile nature of their relationship—what needs to be said at the outset is that Arnold's book is not really about "culture" at all in the modern sense: it is about civilization. Ostensibly advocating for the nation's Populace, Philistines, and Barbarians (Arnold's terms for the working class, middle class, and aristocracy) a more educated acquaintance with the best that has been thought and said, it pays special attention to how these things are faring in Britain. But unlike those who work within the closed world of relativistic culture theory Arnold employs *universal* standards to judge this local state of affairs. The high exemplars which he invites his countrymen to consider, and to lift their game toward, are represented by the illustrious traditions of Hellenism, Hebraism, and Christianity, none of which are British, each of which represent superior historic measures for assaying British life, and all of which are integral to Western civilization as a whole.

In arguing that civilization, not culture, was Arnold's true concern, it is worth noting that in 1868 "culture" and "civilization" were often used synonymously, and in many places in his book are interchangeable. But the point is this: the British were not being told by Arnold, as Herder was so keen to tell the Germans a century before, and Hitler was to tell them sixty years hence, that their own national culture was as good as anyone's—if not better—and that they should therefore sit tight, raise their tankards, and look fierce. Calling on such foreign authorities as Lessing, Renan, and St. Beuve, Arnold invited his countrymen to turn their gaze upon classical Greece and Rome, reflect on the standards of truth and beauty Hellenism embodied, consider likewise the history of the Christian religion as a system of moral discipline, and ask themselves whether in 1868 John Bull's tight little island measured up.

Arnold's nineteenth-century English version of the term "culture" conveyed almost the opposite of German romantic usage. It did not glorify the prejudices of the small, closed, *gemütlich* communal mind, "rooted in the soil" as some would have it—instead it was a universal vision of human improvement. It may not be too much to claim that the meaning Arnold gave it in *Culture and Anarchy*—acquaintance with the best that has been thought and said—provided for many years the conceptual foundation of the old humanities, their very raison d'être. Arnold was not a romantic, unless it be romantic to have high ideals. Much less was he attracted to primitivism. In fact it was the complacent simplicity of his English contemporaries that he set himself to improve.

His language now seems almost unbearably archaic. What could a "counsel of perfection" possibly mean today? But for better or worse these were the words he used, and to understand the classical alternative to the degraded modern condition of the humanities it may still be worth listening to what he said. For this distinguished Victorian poet and social critic the term culture meant first of all a doctrine of personal improvement—something he urged his ignorant and self-satisfied countrymen to undertake by acquainting themselves with "the best that has been thought and said." Not anything that was thought and said, but the *best*. And not the best available locally, or in the High Street on Saturday morning, or in anyone's home town. The average Englishman, Arnold dryly observed, was not likely to find it in his daily paper. Nor was a satisfactory level of cultivation to be achieved by lazily accepting received ideas. What he recommended instead was the full and arduous development of the individual's tastes and talents, a goal which could only be won by

> turning a fresh stream of thought upon our stock notions and habits, which we now follow staunchly but mechanically, vainly imagining that there is a virtue in following them staunchly which makes up for the mischief of following them mechanically. . . . If a man without books or reading, or reading nothing but his letters and the newspapers, gets nevertheless a fresh and free play of the best thoughts upon his stock notions and habits, he has got culture. He has got that for which we prize and recommend culture; he has got that which at the present moment we seek culture that it may give us. This inward operation is the very life and essence of culture, as we conceive it.[16]

The common view that Arnold's thought was élitist is a misunderstanding. The attainment of culture was something open to all since he believed in a universal human nature. "Under all our class divisions," he wrote, "there is a common basis of human nature in every one of us. . . . (Therefore) there exist, sometimes only in germ and potentially, sometimes more or less developed, the same tendencies and passions . . ." Because he assumes a universal human nature, everyone, of whatever background or race or educational level, stands to gain by hearing, seeing, or reading the best which literature, philosophy, or art can offer, just as they stand to lose by being cut off from it.

His sometimes ironic critique of British life was aimed at every social class—at Barbarians, Philistines, and Populace together. By "Barbarians" he meant the aristocracy, wondering as he contemplated its deficiencies "whether upon the whole earth there is anything so unintelligent, so unapt to perceive how the world is really going, as an ordinary young Englishman of our upper class. Ideas he has not, and neither has he the seriousness of our middle class . . ."

The Philistines of the middle class had a superior seriousness, but they were too given to ardent nonconformist religion, business, and money-making; and like the more assertive of the Populace (the working class) the middle class was dangerously infatuated with "the cities it has built, the railroads it has made, the manufactures it has produced, the cargoes which freight the ships of the greatest mercantile navy the world has ever seen." Writing at a time of public riots his view of the working class was less than sanguine: "The sterner self of the Populace likes bawling, hustling, and smashing; the lighter self, beer." But the only way individual men and women of each and every class could progress was by cultivating "a curiosity about their best self," developing a bent for "seeing things as they are," and acquainting themselves as individuals with the best and avoiding the worst. For Arnold the credo of romantic primitivism—"Hold tight to your culture, however benighted, ridiculous, or debased, and be proud!"—doomed its believers to oblivion.

Now no one would pretend that Matthew Arnold's use of the term culture had much to recommend it for social science. I don't myself. But which conception of culture, Arnold's or anthropology's, more naturally belongs in the humanities? A universal project strenuously pursuing a wide acquaintance with the best that has been thought and said must surely win hands down. If your main goal is to keep alive the achievements of the past in the hope of achieving excellence in the future, honoring the Western tradition from the Greeks to the present day, then surely Arnold's is the sort of thing to aim at. Something that sets high standards, which challenges the reader's self-esteem and doesn't flatter it. Something that instead of appeasing the resentful and the envious, and adjusting standards downwards by accepting negligible work, selects the best without fear or favor.

Yet the paradox of the twentieth century is that by a strange and momentous twist some of the most influential commentators on culture in our time, when they turned to the wider issues of society, threw their weight behind the romantic primitivist point of view. Seemingly impressed by anthropology, they inflated the notion of culture toward a vapid normlessness on the one hand, while trying to accommodate the demands of communalism on the other.

Eliot and Anthropology

We have already seen this tendency at work in Isaiah Berlin. Earlier than Berlin—and in his reclusive fastidiousness a quite different personality—was T. S. Eliot, and it would be hard to find anyone whose work more clearly embodied the High Culture of the best that has been thought and said in contrast to the anthropological conception. But when after years in England working as a poet, critic, and editor, he turned his mind to general critical discussion, Eliot rejected Arnold in favor of the anthropological view:

> By 'culture,' then, I mean first of all what the anthropologists mean: the way of life of a particular people living together in one place. That culture is made visible in their arts, in their social system, in their habits and customs, in their religion. But these things added together do not constitute the culture, though we often speak for convenience as if they did. These things are simply the parts into which a culture can be anatomised, as a human body can. But just as a man is something more than an assemblage of the various constituent parts of his body, so a culture is more than the assemblage of its arts, customs, and religious beliefs. These things all act upon each other, and fully to understand one you have to understand all.[17]

This is of course the conception in which a nondescript assemblage of arts, customs, and religious beliefs are thrown together, and instead of being studied in their particularity and judged in terms of their value or lack of it, their artistry or crudity, their religious profundity or otherwise, are all welcomed in at the door. Eliot picks up and puts down the anthropological conception at various places in his discussion, the following example being the most revealing:

> The anthropologist may study the social system, the economics, the arts, and the religion of a particular tribe, he may even study their psychological peculiarities: but it is not merely by observing in detail all of

these manifestations, and grasping them together, that he will approach
to an understanding of the culture. For to understand the culture is to
understand the people, and this means an imaginative understanding.
Such understanding can never be complete: either it is abstract—and
the essence escapes—or else it is *lived*; and in so far as it is *lived*, the student will tend to identify himself so completely with the people whom
he studies, that he will lose the point of view from which one can be
conscious; one cannot be outside and inside at the same time. What we
ordinarily mean by understanding of another people, of course, is an
approximation towards understanding which stops short at the point at
which the student would begin to lose some essential of his own culture. The man who, in order to understand the inner world of a cannibal tribe, has partaken of the practice of cannibalism, has probably gone
too far: he can never quite be one of his own folk again.[18][emphasis in
original]

Having arrived more or less unconsciously at a the edge of a moral
cliff, Eliot draws back. It is as if he has been sleep-walking wherever
his thoughts led him until, arriving unexpectedly at their vertiginous
consequence, the practice of cannibalism, he hesitates, fearful both of
the relativizing of values and the "loss of something essential," which
the fullest possible "understanding" of an alien culture entailed.

He has good reason to hesitate: full understanding has consequences which are well known in the form *tout comprendre, c'est tout
pardonner*. And however humane a consideration this may be in particular cases, it is not a principle on which a new civilization can be
built. Eliot might well have paused to consider what exactly it was
that was going to be "lost" (was it the loss of one's moral bearings
perhaps?) and why that loss should be a concern. And he may also
have sensed that for the redemption of civilization—and even of the
sort of world in which serious poets have a respected place—"what
the anthropologists mean" is not nearly enough. But after footnoting
Conrad's *Heart of Darkness* his mind veers away in another direction
and the crisis passes. Here, and elsewhere in Eliot's book, one cannot
escape the irony of a man defending clearly established social classes
and élites, people of developed taste who can tell Haydn from Han-
del and Mozart from Mendelssohn, yet who does so by adopting an
idea of culture which would barbarize the very institutions where
alone his own art could be understood.

It is doubly ironic that this endorsement should come from a man whose poetry was enjoyed almost as much by educated men and women in Rome and Berlin, in New York and Chicago, in Delhi and Hong Kong and Sydney, as in Oxford or Cambridge—poetry which was read precisely because nothing could be further removed in form and meaning from the provincial conventionality of the closed communal world. *The Waste Land* begins with a dedication in mixed Latin and Greek, contains a line of German referring to both Russia and Lithuania in its opening stanza, invokes Tristan and Isolde over the page along with the Tarot-card-reading Madame Sosostris, a drowned Phoenician sailor, and the ships at Mylae, before passing on to contemplate a Shakespearean Cleopatra on her burnished throne.

And that is only the beginning. To complain about the poem's studied allusiveness and showy erudition would be absurd—form and manner were all of a piece. But it is not absurd to point out that in his lofty way Eliot-as-poet assumes an understanding of the history of the world and its literature which is completely at odds with anthropological provincialism. Neither Sweeney, nor Mrs. Porter, nor her daughter, would make any sense of it at all. So why was Eliot-as-critic drawn to "what the anthropologists mean"? Why did this polished and formal artist working in an essentially classical mode reach out toward an academic version of populist communalism for a political and aesthetic rationale?

Wittgenstein

Split minds mirror split countries of the mind. In both Berlin and Eliot divided allegiances were psychologically at work, leading them to sympathize with anthropological notions opposed at every point to their far too bookish lives.

But exemplary as these imported Anglophiles were in some respects, and revealing though their inner conflicts are, the twentieth century witnessed a still more dramatic example of the divided consciousness. This was Ludwig Wittgenstein, who grew up in Vienna at the very time when Habsburgia was falling down. As Gellner tells the story in *Language and Solitude,* the study of Vienna between the two world wars, which is our source, the Wittgenstein of the *Tractatus* (Wittgenstein Mark I) represented the dizzying extremity to which the cosmopolitan "culture-free" and "culture-denying" mind can go.

With awesome panache Gellner says that the whole of the *Tractatus* can be summed up in a single proposition: "There is no such thing as culture"—epistemologically anyway.[19] Instead of a cultural framework determining the relation of the knower and the known, "A single consciousness mirrored a single world and was coextensive with it. That is all."[20]

Fundamentally the *Tractatus* "is an attempt at giving an account of what the world looks like to a solitary individual, who is reflecting on the problem of how his mind, or language, can possibly 'mean', i.e. reflect that world . . ." If there are other people "they are irrelevant. Presumably they occupy their own private black holes . . ."[21]

In totally rejecting any cultural framework for thought the *Tractatus* went much too far: it was suicidally asocial and inhuman. It is not merely that peasants and village greens and jolly clog-dancing were excluded from Wittgenstein's rarefied philosophico-linguistic domain—everything else was too. T. S. Eliot's detachment, aloofness, and "cold-storage humanity" may have led to dangerously attenuated lines of communication. But the *Tractatus* went further than this, being a "poem to solitude," a work which "conveys the despair of a solitary and alienated individual" who had thought his way into a mental isolation cell where the limits of language shut off the mind and stifled utterance—hence the famous injunction, "whereof one cannot speak, thereof one must be silent."

The logical exercise of the *Tractatus* took Wittgenstein to the brink of madness; certainly to the muteness of the damned. But then he found a miraculous way out, the anthropological route which led to Wittgenstein Mark II. As in the case of other alienated minds he discovered the therapeutic values of groupthink, grouptalk, groupaction, all cozily packaged in a *Gemeinschaft* world.

This was immensely reassuring and must have been a great relief. Turning his back on the chilling conclusions of the *Tractatus* he now decided that the ordinary speech of the peasantry was a serviceable philosophical instrument after all—especially if you didn't worry about truth or logic. This conclusion was one anthropologists could only applaud. In his final notebooks he argues that however muddled it may be, what each community says is all that can be said, what each community knows and values is all that can be known or valued, human sociality is sufficient unto the day, and the rules it lives by are beyond any outsider's right to judge. Unlike Malinowski, the other main protagonist in Gellner's philosophical drama, Wittgenstein took the fateful step which "made it oh so easy to believe whatever he wishes: 'my cultural meanings right or wrong.'"

The lesson students were to learn from Wittgenstein Mark II at Cambridge was that "the cleverest philosophy has shown us . . . that culture is God and hermeneutics is its prophet."[22] In his esoteric but influential manner Wittgenstein Mark II pointed the way back to a closed society of the mind, a place where solipsistic primitivism holds sway.

Raymond Williams and *Ressentiment*

It's unclear whether the British writer Raymond Williams had ever heard of Wittgenstein—his biographer Fred Inglis is positive he had not.[23] Nevertheless, in his cunning and elephantine way Williams was plodding toward similar conclusions. He was born at Pandy in Wales in 1921, the son of a railway signalman. At Cambridge in 1939 young Raymond did the usual things a man on the Left did, and upon joining the Communist Party he let it be known that he wanted to be among "the reddest of the Red." Along with another communist student, the future historian Eric Hobsbawm, he was then directed by the Party to write a pamphlet defending Stalin's invasion of Finland in 1939–40. This they dutifully did—Stalin was a hero to both men—afterwards leading a campaign to "Stop the war against the USSR" (a war in which Finland was trying to defend itself against Soviet attack).[24]

Williams had a political temperament of "uncompromising radicalism" Inglis tells us—he was the sort of man for whom "it became all-important to stand up for the ideals of communism whatever communism did in practice . . ."[25] This is why, when millions were dying in the gulag, he could gleefully sing "Now's the time for a little liquidation"; why in 1966, when most people's eyes had been opened, he could still write a play honoring Stalin; why he thought the idea of the Chinese cultural revolution was rather splendid, and why, when the Cambodian townspeople were being driven into the countryside to die in hundreds of thousands, his heart went feelingly out to Pol Pot:[26]

Many people draw back at the spectacle of forceful repatriation to the countryside and the very brutal discipline employed to enforce it, although it could be argued that these were a consequence imposed by a revolutionary seizure of power in a situation made so exposed by a previous history. . . . The real tragedy occurs at those dreadful moments when the revolutionary movement has to impose the harshest discipline on itself and over relatively innocent people in order not to be broken down and defeated.[27]

About the political man this must suffice. Today Williams resembles one of those huge fallen statues of his hero Stalin, the legs broken and the head detached, with weeds growing out of its nostrils and mould mantling the lifeless eyes. It might well be asked what reason we have for discussing him at all. What could a man so morally corrupt possibly have to tell us about culture? His biographer Inglis tells us that Williams was without any feeling for painting or the pictorial arts, was blind to sculpture and architecture, and deaf to music of all kinds. How is it conceivable that anyone ever took seriously what he had to write about the best that mankind has thought and said and done?

But they did. And since he is the acknowledged father of cultural studies, we have a clinical obligation to inspect his mind. In *Keywords* in 1976 Williams noted with regret what he called "the hostility" toward the word culture "connected with uses involving claims to superior knowledge." Because he believed such claims were obviously baseless this hostility called for attention—the sort of attention anthropology could give. "It is interesting," he writes, "that the steadily extending *social and anthropological use* of **culture** and **cultural** and such formations as **sub-culture** has, except in certain areas, either bypassed or effectively diminished the hostility and its associated unease and embarrassment."[28]

Claims to superior knowledge or taste or artistry had to be knocked on the head. And why? Because they caused "unease and embarrassment," especially to Williams himself. If such claims were voiced by a particular class, that class might have to be removed—perhaps liquidated. People of Williams's delicate sensibilities had to be saved from the insulting effect of such claims, and the sheer scope of the anthropological definition was the way to do it. What could be more inclusive than "a whole way of life"? That's what the anthropologists said "culture" really meant, and if this weapon in the class war were to be wrested from those at Cambridge who had misappropriated it for their own exclusive uses, then he, Raymond Williams, felt free to push the extended meaning for all it was worth. Eliot had incautiously suggested that culture was eating Wensleydale cheese at Henley to the sound of Elgar. But this didn't go far enough. Why shouldn't culture also include "mixed farming, the Stock Exchange, coal-mining, the London Transport"? On anthropological grounds there could be no objection at all.

His extension of the term did not go unnoticed. The critic Ian Gregor drew attention to the oddity of regarding the British Trades Union Congress as something equivalent to a work of creative art, and was rebuked.[29] But in an interview published some time later Williams emerged from cover and candidly confessed his purposes. Asked what specific advantage he saw in the term "culture" for Marxist theory he replied:

> There are two answers to that. The single most shocking thesis to established liberal opinion in *Culture and Society*, including people who liked the book in other ways, was that I did not define working-class culture as a few proletarian novels . . . but as the institutions of the labour movement. That was the gain of talking about culture as a whole way of life.[30]

This explained the advantage of the all-inclusive anthropological conception. But even more dramatic revelations were to come. In *Marxism and Literature* he informed his readers that in the far-reaching cultural revolution he had in mind not only institutions would have to go—literature itself must go too. Some of his disciples might blench at this, might even draw back, but they would have to take their medicine. A now insatiable desire for "a whole way of life" purged of the last remnants of exclusiveness, privilege, and superiority had led destructively, step by step, to the declared belief that literature might have to be "cleared away." One of his followers, reviewing *Marxism and Literature* with quaking pen, wrote that "this annihilating insight (that some day there will be no literature) is extraordinarily difficult for a literary critic, even a Marxist literary critic, to come to terms with."[31]

No doubt it was. Yet what is poignant is that when T. S. Eliot gloomily foresaw an epoch so debased that it would be "possible to say that it will have *no* culture,"[32] Williams accused him of sliding

away from the anthropological conception. "No culture" anthropologically speaking would mean no life, no social forms, nothing at all,
and this was clearly absurd. But the prospect which he had denounced as an absurdity in Eliot's social thought was not so different
from what Williams was now proposing as the way ahead. As he
moved still further into an "ultra-Left radical phase" his interviewers
at the *New Left Review* voiced increasing anxiety and alarm. Was their
prophet of sound mind, they wondered?

> One theme of the work is a frontal attack on the very idea of literature
> as such. In effect, you denounce it as an élitist elevation of certain forms
> of writing to a special status—the 'literary', a category which you say
> possesses the same kind of reactionary spell today as that of the 'divine'
> in feudal society . . . (You argue that) since all forms of writing are by
> definition creative, it is reactionary and exclusivist to privilege some as
> literary, thereby tacitly or explicitly devaluing others . . . Doesn't your
> current position, if it were strictly maintained, lead to a complete rela
> tivism in which it becomes effectively impossible to discriminate be
> tween different forms of writing or types of work at all?
> *Williams:* Well, this is difficult. What I would hope will happen is that
> after the ground has been cleared of the received idea of literature, it
> will be possible to find certain new concepts which would call for spe
> cial emphases.[33]

So there it is. When the ground has been cleared of the received
idea of literature, in other words the entire tradition in England
from Chaucer on, certain new concepts will be found. Then we can
make a fresh start. First the revolutionary deluge . . . After that,
we'll see.

Williams and Cultural Studies

What in fact we see as the result of Raymond Williams's literary
cleansing is cultural studies, his legacy in contemporary academic life.
This not only "by-passes and effectively diminishes" culture as serious
art and literature, but, as Stefan Collini has observed, its animus appears to express a universal paranoia. Whether the subject is the arts,
the media, or the educational system, "The suspicion is that most
forms of cultural activity are essentially a disguise for the fact that

Somebody is Trying to Screw Somebody Else . . . hardly a page of this fat volume" (Grossberg, Nelson and Treichler's *Cultural Studies*, 1992) "goes by without our being told that somebody who possesses some kind of power . . . is trying to 'dominate,' 'suppress,' 'occlude,' 'mystify,' 'exploit,' 'marginalise'. . . someone else, and in response it is the duty of those engaged in cultural studies to 'subvert,' 'unmask,' 'contest,' 'de-legitimize,' 'intervene,' and 'struggle against.'"[34] Unmasking one thing may of course mean trying to cover up something else. This is a no-holds-barred struggle, and as Adam Kuper notes, if it should require the censorial silencing of reactionary hegemonic voices, there are plenty of academic enforcers to see it done.

What was there about Williams's state of mind that led to this? What was eating the man? And what was the role of *ressentiment*? We have already seen Isaiah Berlin refusing to make necessary hierarchical distinctions between "cultures," illogically arguing that because they all serve a common psychological purpose (providing a home for the mind) their virtues are much the same. Even more striking was the case of Herder, who Berlin described with insight and sympathy as a touchy provincial driven by a "mixture of envy, humiliation, admiration, resentment and defiant pride"; and along with Herder there was the entire German Culture Cult as a whole, humiliated and infuriated by the "high polish, great education, splendid prose style and generous and handsome outlook on life" to be found in Paris.

The portrait of Williams painted by his biographer, Inglis, is of a man similarly scarred, marked deeply by vengefulness, resentment, and an overweening conceit. He was impervious to others' opinions, and the loyal Inglis notes with regret his lifelong "determination to be in the right when obviously in the wrong."[35] Williams never stopped talking about the glories of class war—a war he was still prepared to justify in Cambodia's killing fields. Behind this, writes Inglis, "a momentous self-confidence and a muffled, obscure and fearful resentment settled themselves as deeply characteristic of Williams's disposition."[36] His insistence that no writing or painting or anything else called culture should be "privileged" seemingly derived from this deep resentment of elites.

Yet this was the man—blind to painting and architecture, deaf to music, hearing little but the echo of ideological voices inside his head—who reshaped the concept of culture for much of the English-speaking world. High culture was to be democratized in such a way

that nobody need be ashamed or embarrassed by their own inade-
quacies, and no class humbled by its shortcomings. That is why he
was "continually forced to extend" the meaning of the word until
nothing of ideological service was left out. That is why the British
Labour Party and the Trades Union Congress were wheeled in as
"creations" to be considered with as much respect as Restoration
drama or the paintings of Stubbs.[37] But what exactly was happening
in these ideological maneuvers? Was it the strategy of playing off A
against B?

In his examination of *ressentiment* Max Scheler writes that "the formal structure of ressentiment expression is always the same: A is affirmed, valued, and praised not for its own intrinsic quality, but with
the unverbalized intention of denying, devaluating, and denigrating
B. A is 'played off' against B."[38]

This psychological pattern is fundamental to the entire radical egalitarian impulse from Rousseau onwards. It aims to pull down and de-
value any linguistic terms and ideas and activities conferring distinction, eminence, and prestige. Natural man is affirmed, not because
Rousseau seriously believes him superior, but in order to subvert
Parisian self-esteem. Peasant dishes are affirmed, not for their intrinsic quality, but in order to reduce the status of "haute cuisine." The
curative claims of shamanism are idealized, not because people take
them seriously or intend to consult shamans rather than the nearest
qualified doctor, but to diminish the authority of medical science.
The "sophistication" and "richness" and "complexity" of the stone
age culture of the Bushmen of the Kalahari is romanticized by Professor Marshall Sahlins, not because anyone sincerely believes those
adjectives are applicable, but in order to attack civilization. And
though Max Scheler may perhaps go too far, the role of democratic
ressentiment which he identifies in these goings-on certainly deserves
consideration.

> Modern egalitarian doctrine generally—whether it takes the form of a
> statement of fact, a moral demand, or both of these things—is, how-
> ever, clearly the product of *resentment*. It is surely obvious that, without
> exception, the apparently innocuous demand for equality—of whatever
> kind, whether sexual, social, political, religious or material—in fact con-
> ceals only the desire for the *demotion*, in accordance with a selected
> scale of values, of those having more assets, and those who are in some

way *higher up*, to the level of those lower down. In any struggle for power, however great or petty, no one feels that the scales are weighted in his favour. Only the one who fears he *will lose*, demands it as a *universal principle*. The demand for equality is always a speculation on a falling market. For it is a law according to which people can only be equal in respect of those characteristics having the *least value*. 'Equality' as a purely rational idea can never stimulate desire, will or emotion. But resentment, in whose eyes the higher values never find favour, conceals its nature in the demand for 'equality.' In reality it wants nothing less than the destruction of all those who embody those higher values which arouse its anger.[39] [emphasis in original]

Those last two sentences are worth reading again. The destruction of those who so exasperatingly embody higher values accurately describes Raymond Williams's lifelong demand for "equality," and goes a long way to explain the determined effort of his disciples in cultural studies to drag-drop Shakespeare and company into the trash.

Appendix

The Four Stages of Noble Savagery

The impact of romantic primitivism on public life varies a good deal from place to place. In Europe it is less of a political issue than elsewhere. But in the old colonial worlds of the Americas, Australia, and New Zealand, it is widely and continuously felt. Here attitudes toward the Noble Savage have gone through a number of stages over the years—The Captain Cook Stage, War and Pacification, Transfiguration, and Disneyfication.

The Captain Cook Stage

In this era tribalism is as tribalism was, around 1750, when Rousseau first airs his fantasies. This is also before the pioneers go west of the Appalachians and before Australia and Polynesia are even mapped. On the frontier a clear line is drawn between savage and civilized behavior. When Cook and others meet the axe-and-club-wielding indigenes of the South Pacific, men are killed on both sides, but they are baked and eaten by one side only. There are misunderstandings, but there's no point in romanticizing an enemy who wants to split open your skull. Primitive culture is fought, not emulated. On the rare occasion when an explorer had the misfortune of prior exposure to Rousseau he lived to regret it. Julien Marie Crozet, an officer with Marion du Fresne in New Zealand, was particularly scathing about the Swiss romantic after losing his captain and fifteen men in a Maori attack.[1] Empirically, native customs are recorded matter-of-factly in journals; ethically, primitive culture is seen as leaving room for improvement; politically, the life of the stateless savage is seen as nasty, brutal, and short.

War and Pacification

European settlement brings war over land and the violent displacement of peoples. That is how nations were always made, and that is how they were made in North and South America, Australia, and New Zealand. At this stage the native is still the enemy, but settlers develop a healthy respect for his ability with spear or club, and a straightforward struggle takes place between the two. The outcome is heavily weighted against the indigenes, however many rifles they obtain, but growing out of antislavery agitation a movement is under way in the English-speaking world for the relief and protection of aborigines. This moderates the level of violence; valiant warriors appear as characters in fiction; scientific studies of native peoples begin. No colonial intelligentsia to speak of yet exists, but when it does it will pass a severe retrospective moral judgment on this period as a whole. Although they can hardly be expected to see this in the still distant future, by losing the material battle, Amerindians, Maoris, and Aborigines are well placed to win the moral war.

Transfiguration

In this stage the vanquished live in reserves and outskirts, demoralized, sullen, and often drunk. Efforts are made to assimilate them but these mostly fail. Using the resources of a growing world economy the settlers meanwhile apply themselves to agriculture, towns grow, and universities are built, while a critical intelligentsia emerges who read Rousseau and Marx and are much given to ruminating on things. And now comes a curious inversion. *By a process of moral reasoning the intellectuals use the degradation of the defeated as a motive for glorifying the culture they once had.* At the same time all knowledge of what was stagnant, miserable, cruel, and absurd about the old way of life is suppressed. Replacing it is a genteel upside down version of the past—a vision of native tradition which is domesticated and innocuous, where peace and smiling happiness prevail, where spirituality flourishes and the gods are kind. Unsurprisingly, the heirs of tribalism enthusiastically approve this new and academically authorized version of their lives.

Disneyfication

Sentimentalism begets puerility. The ruthless scalpers of yesterday become Loving Persons. One-time ferocious fighters are discovered to be Artists at

Heart. Hollywood becomes interested. Empirically, the children of the old-time tribesmen are now citizens like the rest of us who have needs like the rest of us—for housing, education, jobs. But their attempts to succeed are handicapped by the usual academic hostility to market society, and they are intimidated by a lot of newly invented "traditions" they are supposed to support. Combined with this a suffocating religiosity now descends on public discussion enforced by priests and judges, journalists and teachers, poets and politicians, all of whom claim that native culture possesses a "spirituality" found nowhere else. Soon the primitive is elevated above the civilized. In the words of one observer in New Zealand it is said that the whites "have lost the appreciation for magic and the capacity for wonder" while white culture, besides being "out of step with nature . . . pollutes the environment and lacks a close tie with the land."[2]

Few are unkind enough to note that "the imagined ancestors with whom the Pacific is being repopulated"—Wise Ecologists, Mystical Sages, and Pacifist Saints—"are in many ways creations of Western imagination."[3] The transfiguration of real-life tribal culture into the imaginary landscape of romantic primitivism is now complete. The defining texts of this last stage are two: *The Man-Eating Myth* by William Arens, an influential book denying that cannibalism ever existed; and the 1995 Disney epic *Pocahontas*.[4]

Notes

Introduction

1. Arthur O. Lovejoy and George Boas, *Primitivism and Related Ideas in Antiquity*, The Johns Hopkins University Press, Baltimore, 1935, p. 7.

2. See the appendix on page 179 for the four stages of transfiguration of the tribal world, from the Captain Cook stage to Disneyfication.

Chapter 1

1. L. R. Hiatt, "Mutant Message Down Under: A New Age for an Old People," *Quadrant*, June, 1997.

2. Ibid., p. 37. And not only American readers. In January 2000 I found a German-language edition of *Mutant Message* on the best-selling list of a bookshop in Vienna. (*Traumfänger*, Marlo Morgan, Wilhelm Goldmann Verlag, Munich, 1998.) It was accompanied by an attractively packaged pair of audiotapes, and placed two books away from a new edition of Arthur Schnitzler's *Traumnovelle*.

3. Brian D. Haley and Larry Wilcoxon, "Anthropology and the Making of Chumash Tradition," *Current Anthropology*, Vol. 38, No. 5, December 1997.

4. Ibid., 764.

5. Roger Keesing, "Creating the Past: Custom and Identity in the Contemporary Pacific," *The Contemporary Pacific*, Vol. 1, Nos. 1 & 2, 1989, p. 19.

6. Ibid., p. 22.

7. Ibid., p. 30.

8. Ibid., p. 30.

9. Chris Kenny, *It Would be Nice if There Were Some Women's Business: The Story Behind the Hindmarsh Island Affair*, Duffy and Snellgrove, Sydney, 1996, p. 36.

10. Ibid., p. 47.

11. Ibid., p. 51.

12. Ibid., p. 76.

13. Ibid., p. 229.

14. Ernest Gellner, *Plough, Sword, and Book*, CollinsHarvill, London, 1988, p. 61.

15. Ian Keen, "Aboriginal Beliefs vs. Mining at Coronation Hill: The Containing Force of Traditionalism," *Human Organization*, Vol. 52, No. 4, 1993, p. 353. (Emphasis added.)

16. Paper delivered at *Quadrant Magazine* seminar on Aboriginal affairs, Gazebo Hotel, Sydney, August 22, 1999. The authorities who control the college in Darwin intervened to stop publication of their principal's paper.

17. Bettina Arndt, "The Stolen Education," *Sydney Morning Herald*, Spectrum, June 12, 1999, p. 6s.

18. Ibid. Collins is married to an Aborigine and is well informed about the situation he describes.

19. John Stuart Mill, *Autobiography*, Penguin Books, 1989 (1873), pp. 28–30.

20. Ibid., p. 30.

21. David S. Landes, *The Wealth and Poverty of Nations*, Little, Brown & Co., Boston, 1998, p. 178. Emphasis in original.

22. Ernest Gellner, *Spectacles and Predicaments*, Cambridge University Press, England, 1979, p. 273. Bilingual education has severely handicapped thousands of Aborigines. Australia is still a long way from recognizing the need for California's Proposition 227, a measure replacing bilingual education with crash courses in English.

Chapter 2

1. Arthur E. Bestor, *Backwoods Utopias*, Ibid., p. 117.

2. Aristotle, *Politics*, full reference in "Aristotle and Primitivistic Ideas," A. O. Lovejoy and George Boas, *Primitivism and Related Ideas in Antiquity*, The Johns Hopkins University Press, Baltimore, 1935, pp. 184–85.

3. Maren L. Carden, *Oneida: Utopian Community to Modern Corporation*, The Johns Hopkins University Press, 1969, pp. 1–2.

4. Ibid., pp. 53, 100.

5. Lawrence Foster, *Religion and Sexuality*, Oxford University Press, New York, 1981, p. 77.

6. Ibid., p. 78.

7. A contents list drawn from two of Noyes's early and fundamental writings, *The Berean* and *Bible Communism*, and which helpfully provides an outline of his religious and social ideas, is included in his 1870 book, *History of American Socialisms*. This appears at the end of the book in his account of the Oneida Community. Under chapter II propositions 5 and 6, he provides the biblical references and justifications for his ideal of "complex marriage."

8. John Humphrey Noyes, *History of American Socialisms*, New York, 1870, p. 628.

9. Maren L. Carden, *Oneida: Utopian Community to Modern Corporation*, p. 53.

10. Foster, *Religion and Sexuality*, p. 94.

11. Pierrepont Noyes, *My Father's House*, Farrar and Rinehart, New York, 1937, p. 158.

12. Pierre L. van den Berghe, *Human Family Systems: An Evolutionary View*, New York, Elsevier, 1979, p. 59.

13. Carl Nicolai Starcke, *The Primitive Family in Its Origin and Development*, University of Chicago Press, 1976 (1889), p. 124.

14. Pierrepont Noyes, *My Father's House*, Farrar and Rinehart, New York, 1937, p. 10.

15. Laura Betzig, *Human Nature, a Critical Reader*, Oxford University Press, New York, 1997, p. 375.

16. Friedrich Engels, *The Origin of the Family, Private Property, and the State*. New York, New World Paperbacks, 1972, p. 97.

17. Ibid., p. 259n.

18. Rebecca West, *Black Lamb and Grey Falcon*, Macmillan & Co., London, 1943, Vol. 1, p. 502. Anyone interested in realistic accounts of the *zadruga* should read the essays by Hammel and Halpern in Peter Laslett's 1972 *Household and Family in Past Time*.

19. Joseph Bussell, in Henry Near, *The Kibbutz Movement, a History*, Oxford University Press, 1992, Vol. 1, p. 50.

20. Pierre L. van den Berghe, *Human Family Systems: An Evolutionary View*, pp. 72–73.

21. Noyes, *My Father's House*, p. 65.

22. Lionel Tiger and Joseph Shepher, *Women in the Kibbutz*, Harcourt Brace Jovanovich, New York, 1975, p. 226.

23. Eleanor Leacock, ed., Introduction to Friedrich Engels, *The Origin of the Family, Private Property, and the State*, New York, New World Paperbacks, 1972, p. 44; Eva Figes, *Patriarchal Attitudes*, Greenwich, Conn., Fawcett Books, 1971, p. 181.

24. Laurence Vesey, *The Communal Experience*, University of Chicago Press, 1978, p. 186.

25. Ibid., p. 186.

26. Ibid., p. 187.

27. Rousseau fathered five babies born to his mistress Thérèse Levasseur, each of which was promptly left unidentified at a foundling hospital. In the middle of the eighteenth century only five percent of such infants survived to adulthood, most becoming beggars and vagabonds.

28. Compare Adam Ferguson's eighteenth-century account of the social role of the family. Making due allowance for his rhetoric, and for the period

in which he wrote, which makes more sense? "Families may be considered as the elementary forms of society, or establishments the most indispensably necessary to the existence and preservation of mankind . . . They are the nurseries of men; the basis of empires, as well as of nations and tribes; and the compartments of which the greatest fabrics of political establishment are composed . . ." Adam Ferguson, *Principles of Moral and Political Science*, Edinburgh, 1792, Vol. 1, p. 27.

29. Ibid., p. 188. On the subject of the extended family Jack Goody's verdict is as follows: "I have tried to establish that it is not only for England that we need to abandon the myth of the 'extended family' . . . Whatever the shape of the kin groups of earlier societies, none were undifferentiated communes of the kind beloved by nineteenth century theorists, Marxist and non-Marxist alike. Units of production were everywhere relatively small, kin-based units; differences in size and context are important in the comparative study of the family, but they should never obscure the basic similarities in the way that domestic groups are organized throughout the whole range of human societies." "Evolution of the Family," in *Household and Family in Past Time*, Peter Laslett and Richard Wall, eds., Cambridge University Press, London, 1972, p. 124.

30. Vesey, *The Communal Experience*, p. 383.

31. Montesquieu, *Spirit of the Laws*, Book XI. It must be conceded that one of the freest nations, England, has lacked a formal separation of powers at the highest level. The nearest thing the country has to a Supreme Court are the Law Lords. They are simultaneously members of the legislature.

32. Rosabeth M. Kanter, *Commitment and Community*, Harvard University Press, Cambridge, Mass., 1972, p. 105.

33. Vesey, *The Communal Experience*, p. 303.

Chapter 3

1. Jean-Jacques Rousseau, *Lettres à Malesherbes*, No. 1. I am indebted for sundry references here and elsewhere to Paul Johnson's essay on Rousseau in his *Intellectuals*, London, Weidenfeld and Nicolson Ltd., 1988.

2. Kingsley Widmer, "The Diogenes Style," in César Graña and Marigay Graña, eds., *On Bohemia: The Code of the Self-Exiled*, p. 119.

3. George S. Snyderman and William Josephs, "Bohemia, the Underworld of Art," in César Graña and Marigay Graña, eds., *On Bohemia: The Code of the Self-Exiled*, p. 92.

4. Jean-Jacques Rousseau, *A Discourse on Inequality*, Penguin Books, 1984 (1755), p. 44.

5. Rousseau, *A Discourse on Inequality*, p. 68.

6. Claude Lévi-Strauss, *Tristes Tropiques*, Hutchinson, London, 1961, 388–89.

7. See note 1 above.

8. Rousseau, *A Discourse on Inequality*, p. 109.

9. Adam Ferguson, *An Essay on the History of Civil Society*, London, 1773, p. 205. [Facsimile reprint by Gregg International Publishers, 1969.]

10. Ronald L. Meek, *Social Science and the Ignoble Savage*, Cambridge University Press, 1976, p. 155, n104.

11. Daniel Bell, *The Cultural Contradictions of Capitalism*, Basic Books, New York, 1976, p. 58.

12. I ignore the anthropological ideas contained in the French *un*romantic or *anti*-romantic Enlightenment tradition here (Montesquieu, Turgot, Voltaire, Helvetius, Quesnay). Firstly because they did not continue through to the 20th-century romantic-Rousseau nexus respectfully noted by Lévi-Strauss; secondly because the best representative of that particular style of thought may have been Millar: "In Millar's books and lectures . . . the new social science of the Enlightenment comes of age . . . Millar's great achievement was to transform the four stages theory (hunting, pastoralism, agriculture, commerce) into a true *philosophy of history*, of the kind which Voltaire wrote about but never himself wrote." Ronald L. Meek, *Social Science and the Ignoble Savage*, Cambridge University Press, 1976, p. 161.

13. Maurice Cranstone, in Rousseau, *A Discourse on Inequality*, p. 29.

14. Voltaire, Letter to J.-J. Rousseau from Delices, August 30, 1755.

15. Frank E. Manuel and Fritzie P. Manuel, *Utopian Thought in the Western World*, Basil Blackwell, Oxford, 1979, p. 562.

16. Manuel and Manuel, *Utopian Thought in the Western World*, p. 559.

17. George W. Stocking Jr., *Victorian Anthropology*, The Free Press, New York, 1987, p. 33.

18. César Graña, *Bohemian Versus Bourgeois*, Basic Books, New York, 1964, p. 93.

19. Graña, *Bohemian Versus Bourgeois*, p. 145.

20. Graña, *Bohemian Versus Bourgeois*, pp. 132–33.

21. Graña, *Bohemian Versus Bourgeois*, p. 133.

22. Graña, *Bohemian Versus Bourgeois*, p. 135.

Chapter 4

1. George W. Stocking Jr., *Romantic Motives: Essays on Anthropological Sensibility*, University of Wisconsin Press, Madison, 1989, p. 215.

2. George W. Stocking Jr., *Romantic Motives: Essays on Anthropological Sensibility*, p. 223.

3. Regna Darnell, *Edward Sapir*, University of California Press, Berkeley, 1990, p. 171–72.

4. Margaret Mead, *Blackberry Winter*, New York, 1965, p. 90.

5. Malcolm Cowley, *Exile's Return*, Viking Press, New York, 1968, p. 69.

6. Jane Howard, *Margaret Mead: A Life*, Simon & Schuster, New York, 1984, p. 119.

7. Margaret M. Caffrey, *Ruth Benedict, Stranger in This Land*, University of Texas Press, Austin, 1989, chap. 7, "The Personal Vision."

8. Margaret Mead, *Blackberry Winter*, p. 106.

9. Regna Darnell, *Edward Sapir*, p. 172.

10. Stocking, *Romantic Motives*, p. 226, n6.

11. Stocking, *Romantic Motives*, p. 227.

12. Ibid., p. 227.

13. Ibid., pp. 227–28.

14. Douglas Preston, "Cannibals of the Canyon," *New Yorker*, 30 November 1998. Anasazi cannibalism is confirmed by Marlar et al., *Nature* 407 (July 9, 2000), pp. 74–78.

15. D. H. Lawrence in George W. Stocking Jr., *Romantic Motives*, p. 220.

16. Derek Freeman, *The Fateful Hoaxing of Margaret Mead*, Westview Press, Boulder, Colo., 1999, p. 74.

17. Freeman, *The Fateful Hoaxing of Margaret Mead*, p. 153.

18. Freeman, *The Fateful Hoaxing of Margaret Mead*, p. 145.

19. Stocking, *Romantic Motives*, p. 244.

20. Ibid., p. 244.

21. Margaret Mead, *Coming of Age in Samoa*, Penguin Books, 1966 (1928), p. 19.

22. Keith Melville, *Communes in the Counter Culture*, William Morrow & Co., New York, 1972, p. 12.

23. Melville, *Communes in the Counter Culture*, p. 13.

24. Melville, *Communes in the Counter Culture*, pp. 127–29.

25. The essay was not typed. In some places in Australia handwritten student work is still accepted.

26. Melville, *Communes in the Counter Culture*, p. 69.

27. Ernest Gellner, *Postmodernism, Reason, and Religion*, Routledge, London, 1992, p. 23.

Chapter 5

1. "Nigeria in civvy street," *The Economist*, June 19, 1999.

2. John Maynard Keynes, *General Theory of Employment, Interest and Money*, 1936.

3. Transcript: "Clinton Charts New U.S.-Africa Course in Ghana Speech," *USIS Washington File*, 23 March 1998.

4. Transcript: "Clinton Charts New U.S.-Africa Course in Ghana Speech." Someone might have alerted the president to an old seafarer's warning: "Sailor beware of the Bight of Benin, where one man comes out for every two that go in."

5. Karl Polanyi, *Dahomey and the Slave Trade*, University of Washington Press, Seattle, 1996, p. xxi.

6. Peter F. Drucker, *Adventures of a Bystander*, Harper & Row, New York, 1979, p. 128.

7. Ibid., p. 127.

8. Paul Ignotus, "The Hungary of Michael Polanyi," in *The Logic of Personal Knowledge: Essays Presented to Michael Polanyi on His Seventieth Birthday, 11th March 1961*, Routledge and Kegan Paul, London, 1961, p. 11.

9. Lee Congdon, "Polanyi in Hungary, 1900–1919," *Journal of Contemporary History*, Vol. 11 (1976), p. 173.

10. Karl Polanyi, *The Livelihood of Man*, Academic Press, New York, 1977, p. xiv.

11. Ian Buruma, "Divine Killer," *The New York Review of Books*, February 24, 2000, p. 20. Review of *Mao: A Life*, by Philip Short.

12. Richard Pipes, *Property and Freedom*, The Harvill Press, London, 1999, 212. Richard Pipes, *Russia Under the Bolshevik Regime, 1919–1924*, HarperCollins, London, 1994, p. 371.

13. Raimondo Cubeddu, *The Philosophy of the Austrian School*, Routledge, London, 1993, p. 113. The original title of Mises's paper was "Die Wirtschaftsrechnung im sozialistischen Gemeinwesen," in the *Archiv für Sozialwissenschaften*, Vol. 47, 1920, pp. 86–121. See F. A. Hayek, *The Collected Works of F. A. Hayek*, Vol. IV, *The Fortunes of Liberalism*, The University of Chicago Press, 1992, p. 132, n18.

14. Raimondo Cubeddu, *The Philosophy of the Austrian School*, Routledge, London, 1993, pp. 113–14.

15. Karl Polanyi, "Sozialistische Rechnungslegung," *Archiv fur Socialwissenschaft und Sozialpolitik*, Vol. 49 [1922] pp. 377–420.

16. J. R. Stanfield, *The Economic Thought of Karl Polanyi*, Macmillan, London, 1986, p. 5.

17. Ilona Duczynska, *Workers in Arms: The Austrian Schutzbund and the Civil War of 1934*, Monthly Review Press, New York and London, 1978, p. 94.

18. Paul Bohannan and George Dalton, "Karl Polanyi, 1886–1964" [obituary], *American Anthropologist*, Vol. 67, 1965, 1508–11.

19. Signs of mental stress are reported in other sources as well. Noting a relation between ideas of suicide and of "therapeutic nihilism" in this period, William Johnson cites Karl Polanyi's article on *Hamlet*. [*Yale Review*, Vol. 43, 1954, p. 339] as an example. "The brother of Michael Polanyi recounted that while serving in the Austro-Hungarian cavalry during World War One he read that play twenty times. In the figure of Hamlet he saw epitomized an attitude that afflicted many of his contemporaries; like the Prince of Denmark they could not decide to live. If challenged to choose between life and death, he [Hamlet or the Austrian] would be undone, since

he cannot deliberately choose life." William M. Johnston, *The Austrian Mind*, University of California Press, Berkeley, 1972, p. 180.

20. Drucker, *Adventures of a Bystander*, p. 126.

21. Karl Polanyi, *The Livelihood of Man*, Academic Press, New York, 1977, p. xvi.

22. Michael Polanyi, *The Contempt of Freedom: The Russian Experiment and After*, Watts & Co., London, 1940, pp. 42–43.

23. Ibid., p. 47.

24. Ibid., p. 47.

25. Drucker, *Adventures of a Bystander*, pp. 133–34.

26. Karl Polanyi, *Primitive, Archaic, and Modern Economies. Essays of Karl Polanyi*, Doubleday and Company, New York, 1968, p. 253. It is these incredible claims that Hayek is referring to, without identifying the source, in an entertaining dismissal of Polanyi in chapter three, "The Evolution of the Market: Trade and Civilisation," of *The Fatal Conceit: The Errors of Socialism*, University of Chicago Press, 1988, p. 44.

27. Ibid., p. 255. A convincing refutation of fourteen main points in Polanyi's claims about ancient Near Eastern economies is provided in Morris Silver, "Karl Polanyi and Markets in the Ancient Near East: the Challenge of the Evidence," *The Journal of Economic History*, Vol. XLIII, No. 4, December 1983.

28. Karl Polanyi, *Primitive, Archaic, and Modern Economies*, pp. 81–82.

29. Michael Polanyi, *The Logic of Liberty: Reflections and Rejoinders*, Routledge and Kegan Paul, London, 1951, p. 159.

30. Ibid., p. 123.

31. Ibid., p. 126.

32. Ibid., p. 111. For a full discussion see three related essays in *The Logic of Liberty*: "The Span of Central Direction," "Profits and Polycentricity," and "Manageability of Social Tasks."

33. Ilona Duczynska, in Karl Polanyi, *The Livelihood of Man*, p. xvii.

34. Karl Polanyi, *Dahomey and the Slave Trade: An Analysis of an Archaic Economy*, University of Washington Press, Seattle and London, 1966, p. xviii.

35. Ibid., pp. 38–39.

36. Ibid., p. 46.

37. Ibid., p. 51.

38. W. J. Argyle, *The Fon of Dahomey*, Oxford, Clarendon Press, 1966, p. 94. A somewhat fuller description of the census tallies, and of the circumstances in which Herskovits got his data, may be found in Roger Sandall, "Herskovits' Last Day in Dahomey," *Anthropology Today*, Vol. 15, No. 6, December 1999, pp. 18–20.

39. Drucker, *Adventures of a Bystander*, p. 138.

40. Polanyi, *Dahomey and the Slave Trade: An Analysis of an Archaic Economy*, p. 9.

41. In West Africa scarcely imaginable brutalities were routine. Visiting Benin in the 1860s, Sir Richard Burton saw a slave lashed to a keg of dynamite and blown up. "'When he descended,' Burton wrote, 'his brains were beaten out with clubs and sticks, even the women and children joining in the pastime gleefully, as boys killing a rat.'" In Mary S. Lovell, *A Rage to Live: A Biography of Richard and Isabel Burton*, Little, Brown & Company, Boston, 1998, p. 389.

Chapter 6

1. Michael Ignatieff, *Isaiah Berlin: A Life*, Chatto & Windus, London, 1998, pp. 3, 18.
2. Ibid., p. 7.
3. Ibid., p. 11.
4. Ibid., p. 13.
5. Ibid., p. 15.
6. Ibid., pp. 11, 13, 15, 21.
7. Karl R. Popper, *Unended Quest*, Routledge, London, 1992, p. 105.
8. Michael Ignatieff, *Isaiah Berlin: A Life*, p. 289.
9. Ibid., p. 34.
10. Ibid., pp. 34–35.
11. Ibid., pp. 246–47.
12. Isaiah Berlin, *Vico and Herder: Two Studies in the History of Ideas*, Hogarth Press, London, 1976, pp. 145–47.
13. Isaiah Berlin and Ramin Jahanbegloo, *Conversations with Isaiah Berlin*, Charles Scribner's Sons, New York, 1991, p. 70.
14. Ignatieff, *Isaiah Berlin*, pp. 250, 257.
15. Isaiah Berlin, *The Roots of Romanticism*, Chatto & Windus, London, 1999, p. 140.
16. Isaiah Berlin, *Vico and Herder: Two Studies in the History of Ideas*, p. 205, n1.
17. Ibid., p. 180.
18. It might be noted that a "universal human nature" was exactly what romanticism was strongly inclined to deny. Humanity was supposed to be infinitely variable; there were no universals; each culture had its own moral scheme and the Nazis presumably had theirs too.
19. Originally written for *Foreign Affairs* not long before the final version of his essay on Herder appeared, the first in 1972, the second in 1976. A still later and much changed version appeared in *The Crooked Timber of Humanity* in 1990.
20. Isaiah Berlin, *Against the Current: Essays in the History of Ideas*, Hogarth Press, London, 1979, p. 346.
21. Ibid., p. 350.

22. Ibid., p. 339.

23. Gellner, *Nationalism*, Weidenfeld, London, 1997, p. 4.

24. Berlin, *Vico and Herder*, p. 184.

25. Berlin, *Vico and Herder*, p. 155. [My emphasis.]

26. Ignatieff, *Isaiah Berlin*, p. 95.

27. Ibid., p. 96.

28. Ibid., p. 98.

29. Ibid., p. 95.

30. Ibid., p. 93.

31. Ibid., p. 101.

32. Ibid., p. 106.

33. Johann Gottfried von Herder, *Reflections on the Philosophy of the History of Mankind*, University of Chicago Press, 1968, p. 58.

34. Berlin, *Vico and Herder*, p. 164.

35. Ibid., pp. 190–91.

36. Robert B. Edgerton, *Sick Societies*, The Free Press, New York, p. 1.

37. Ibid., p. 140.

38. Berlin, *Vico and Herder*, p. 182.

39. Isaiah Berlin and Ramin Jahanbegloo, *Conversations with Isaiah Berlin*, pp. 63–65.

40. Berlin, *Vico and Herder*, p. 190.

41. Napoleon Chagnon, *Yanomamo: The Fierce People*, Holt, Rinehart & Winston, New York, 1968, pp. 126–27.

42. For the Bolshevik poster see the opening scenes of Russian filmmaker Marina Goldavskaya's remarkable 1988 *The Power of Solovki*, a documentary about the Special Purpose Solovetski Camp established on the Solovetski Islands in the White Sea in 1923. This labor camp became the model for the entire gulag in the decades to come.

43. Isaiah Berlin, *Vico and Herder*, p. 210.

44. Ibid., p. 184.

45. Ibid., pp. 182, 188, 191.

46. Ibid., pp. 139–40.

47. Berlin, *The Crooked Timber of Humanity*, p. 38.

Chapter 7

1. Richard Pipes, *Property and Freedom*, The Harvill Press, London, 1999, p. 96.

2. Until recently it had been thought that moa extinction was a gradual process which took place over several centuries. Not anymore. An authoritative report in *Science* for March 24, 2000 ("Rapid extinction of the moas—Aves: dinornithiforms—model, test, and implications," by R. N.

Holdaway and C. Jacomb) concludes that they were all killed in well under one hundred years: "The elimination of the moa by Polynesians was the fastest recorded megafaunal extinction, matched only by the predictions of the 'Blitzkrieg' model for North American late Pleistocene extinctions."

3. "A Forceful Impact: the East Polynesians' Effect on Fauna and Flora," Plate 12 in the *Bateman New Zealand Historical Atlas*, Department of Internal Affairs, New Zealand Government Publications, 1997.

4. Bruce Biggs, "In the Beginning," in Keith Sinclair, ed., *The Oxford Illustrated History of New Zealand*, out-of-print, 1996 (2nd edition), pp. 17–18.

5. Tim Flannery, *The Future Eaters*, Reed Books, Melbourne, 1995, p. 248.

6. Karl Popper, *Unended Quest*, Routledge, London, 1992, p. 222, n165.

7. F. E. Maning, *Old New Zealand*, Golden Press, Auckland, 1973 (1887), pp. 107–8.

8. Ibid., p. 108.

9. Ibid., p. 122. Hayek in *The Fatal Conceit* (p. 157) notes that in Sir James Frazer's 1909 *Psyche's Task*, *tapu* is identified as "a powerful instrument for strengthening the ties, perhaps our socialist friends would say riveting the chains, of private property."

10. Popper, *The Open Society and Its Enemies*, Vol. 1, p. 182.

11. Ibid., p. 182.

12. Ibid., p. 172.

13. Ibid., p. 172. A more sympathetic account of taboo is given by Hayek in his "Notes on the Evolution of Systems of Rules of Conduct." See F. A. Hayek, *Studies in Philosophy, Politics and Economics*, London, Routledge & Kegan Paul, 1967, pp. 79–81. Hayek's book is dedicated to Popper.

14. Popper, *The Open Society and Its Enemies*, Vol. 1, p. 173.

15. James Belich, *Making Peoples: A History of the New Zealanders*, Allen Lane, the Penguin Press, Auckland, 1996, p. 201. Belich gives a wide range of sources for these arrangements under footnote 62.

16. Ibid., p. 201.

17. Ibid., p. 201.

18. Ibid., p. 259.

19. "The superior virtue of the oppressed" is the title of one of Bertrand Russell's "unpopular" essays.

20. Ivan Sutherland, "The Maori Situation," in I. L. G. Sutherland, *The Maori People Today*, p. 410.

21. Tim Flannery, *The Future Eaters*, p. 245. Anyone interested in pursuing these matters further should consult chapter 23 of Flannery's *The Future Eaters* and follow up the sources he himself has used.

22. Whatever truth there is in the hypothesis relating "the strain of civilization" to its manifold discontents, "the strain of primitive life" may well

have been even greater. It would surely have been more stressful being a Maori in 1750 than in 1950.

23. Sigmund Freud, *Civilization and Its Discontents*, The Hogarth Press, London, 1951, p. 44.

24. Ibid., p. 45.

25. Ibid., p. 46.

26. Popper, *The Open Society and Its Enemies*, 2 volumes, Routledge & Kegan Paul, London, Fifth Edition (revised), 1966, p. 98.

27. For information about Popper and the spying accusation I am indebted to conversations with the late Colin Simkin. An account of Popper's days in New Zealand may be found in Colin Simkin, "The Birth of the Open Society," *Quadrant*, December 1990.

28. Popper, *The Open Society and Its Enemies*, Vol. 1, p. 175.

29. A. E. C. and R. E. C., "I. L. G. Sutherland, 1897–1952" (obituary) *Journal of the Polynesian Society*, Vol. 61 (1952), p. 126.

30. Ibid., p. 126.

31. Charles Waldegrave, "Enemies, Friends or Partners?," in *1840—1990: A Long White Cloud?* Graphic Publications in association with Citizens Association for Racial Equality, Auckland, 1989, pp. 48–49.

32. Garfield Johnson, "The Young Shoots of the Flax," in *1840—1990: A Long White Cloud?* Graphic Publications in association with Citizens Association for Racial Equality, Auckland, 1989, pp. 105–6.

Chapter 8

1. For the Ice Man see Konrad Spindler, *The Man in the Ice*, Orion Books, 1995. Re metallurgy: "Rather than searching blindly for a base alloy with the ideal set of intrinsic properties, materials designers will use computers to calculate the charge densities of candidate base alloys. . . . For the first time, a new alloy will be designed beginning with its electronic structure." Mark E. Eberhart, "Why Things Break," *Scientific American*, October 1999.

2. John P. Powelson, *Centuries of Economic Endeavor*, The University of Michigan Press, Ann Arbor, 1994, p. 42.

3. David Landes, *The Wealth and Poverty of Nations*, Little, Brown & Company, Boston, 1998, p. 45.

4. Ibid., p. 46.

5. Ibid., p. 46.

6. Carlo M. Cipolla, *Clocks and Culture, 1300–1700*, Collins, London, 1967, p. 39.

7. David Landes, *The Wealth and Poverty of Nations*, p. 50.

8. Powelson, *Centuries of Economic Endeavor*, p. 172.

9. David Landes, *The Wealth and Poverty of Nations.*, pp. 46–47.

10. Ibid., p. 51, n8.

11. Ibid., p. 52. For the Chinese case see Mark Elvin's various writings, including "China as a Counterfactual," chapter 5 in *Europe and the Rise of Capitalism*, edited by Jean Baechler, John A. Hall, and Michael Mann, Basil Blackwell, Oxford, 1988. In the 1998 edition of John K. Fairbank and Merle Goldman's *China: A New History* (Harvard University Press), Fairbank raises the question of footbinding and the subjection of women as having direct "psychic, social, and economic costs," pp. 173–76.

12. Fairbank and Goldman, *China: A New History*, enlarged edition, Harvard University Press, 1998, p. 181.

13. Ibid., p. 182.

14. Peter L. Bernstein, *Against the Gods: The Remarkable Story of Risk*, John Wiley & Sons, New York, 1998, p. 42.

15. Landes, *The Wealth and Poverty of Nations*, pp. 58–59.

16. The quotation used for the epigraph is from a letter by Malthus to Ricardo in 1817.

17. Landes, *The Wealth and Poverty of Nations*, Powelson, *Centuries of Economic Endeavor*; Ernest Gellner, *Plough, Sword and Book: The Structure of Human History*, Collins Harvill, London, 1988; E. A. Wrigley, *People, Cities and Wealth: The Transformation of Traditional Society*, Basil Blackwell, 1987; Alan Macfarlane, *The Origins of English Individualism: The Family, Property, and Social Transition*, Basil Blackwell, 1978; John A. Hall, *Powers and Liberties: The Causes and Consequences of the Rise of the West*, Basil Blackwell, London, 1985.

18. Gellner, *Conditions of Liberty: Civil Society and Its Rivals*, p. 7.

19. Macfarlane, *The Origins of English Individualism*, 1978.

20. Ibid., pp. 3–4. Shakespeare's father was a glove-maker and wool-dealer by trade. Around 1570 the family home in Stratford was a large and substantial house with two storeys and many rooms. A comparable residence for a man comparably employed in Nepal today might be one half or one quarter the size.

21. Ibid., p. 199.

22. Ibid.

23. Adam Smith, *The Wealth of Nations*, Penguin Books, 1997 (1776), p. 117.

24. Richard Pipes, *Property and Freedom*, The Harvill Press, London, 1999, p. 127.

25. Ibid., pp. 123, 127.

26. Ibid., p. 166. The historian referred to by Pipes is Aleksandr Lakier. Further east in China, a century or so before Ghengis Khan, even more totalitarian ideas were common. The famous Song Dynasty reformer Wang Anshi "tried to knock out the private sector, as we would now call it, by strictly limiting land-holding and private wealth, and by organizing the populace into mutual-responsibility groups for the purpose of controlling it. He

would not tolerate opposition, which he considered immoral; in a properly unified state and society all men would have the same values, all people would function at their level in the hierarchy, and none would have independent means to support others and so possibly support dissent . . . all people would depend entirely on the government." J. K. Fairbank and M. Goldman, *China: A New History*, Harvard University Press, Cambridge, Mass., 1998, p. 97.

27. Pipes, op. cit., p. 185. It is worth bearing this in mind in connection with the control of Russian emigration. It is true that the Communists forbade emigration. But there was nothing unusual about this—it was in keeping with a long tradition which regarded the Russian people as the property of the Czar.

28. Pipes, *Property and Freedom*, p. 186.

29. Ibid., p. 188.

30. Landes, *The Wealth and Poverty of Nations*, p. 221.

31. It is appropriate to add, and to remember, that millions also starved to death in the artificial famine Stalin's laws induced.

32. Hedrick Smith, *The Russians*, Sphere Books, 1972, p. 132.

33. Can there now be anything described as normality in Russia? Two views in April 2000: "'If you are in the Government and you don't take a bribe now, people don't look at you as honest. They look at you as stupid. It means we have a huge moral crisis—people don't have values of what is good and bad.' It also means a permanent economic crisis. A privatised Russian state cannot act as a normal state—adjudicating disputes, protecting private property and the sanctity of contracts or harnessing the energy of the nation so that Russia can create new wealth . . . " Thomas L. Friedman quoting Russian political analyst Sergei Markov in *The New York Times*. "Modern Russia rests on the moral and intellectual foundations of feudalism and communism, which are antithetical both to democracy and to a properly functioning economy: 'a thousand years of negative selection', as one Moscow-based American financier puts it." *The Economist*, April 1, 2000.

34. H. Smith, *The Russians*, p. 131. [My emphasis.]

35. Mario Vargas Llosa, "Foreword," in Hernando de Soto, *The Other Path: The Invisible Revolution in the Third World*, Harper & Row, New York, 1989, p. xiv. [My emphasis.]

36. Hernando de Soto, *The Other Path*.

37. Tom Bethell, *The Noblest Triumph*, St. Martin's Press, New York, 1998, p. 196.

38. Tom Bethell, op. cit., p. 197.

39. Ibid.

40. Ibid.

41. De Soto, *The Other Path*, p. 139.

42. Keith B. Richburg, *Out of America: A Black Man Confronts Africa*, Harcourt Brace & Company, New York, 1998, p. 170.

43. Ibid., pp. 170–71.

44. Powelson, *Centuries of Economic Endeavor*, p. 98.

45. Ibid., p. 101. It should not go unnoticed that many things specified by Powelson are the very attributes which Karl Polanyi *admired*.

46. Ibid., p. 103.

47. Adda B. Bozeman, *Conflict in Africa: Concepts and Realities*, Princeton University Press, Princeton, N.J., 1976, p. 124. In Powelson, p. 108.

48. Powelson, *Centuries of Economic Endeavor*, p. 108.

49. Thomas Sowell, *Conquests and Cultures*, Basic Books, 1998, p. 349.

50. Ibid., p. 349.

51. Ibid., pp. 350–51.

52. Paul Johnson, *Modern Times*, p. 531. At the time of writing Kérékou once again held power.

53. *SBS World Guide*, 6th Edition, Hardie Grant Publishing, Melbourne, 1998, pp. 77–79. [This is a version of the ITN Factbook.]

54. Landes, *The Wealth and Poverty of Nations*, pp. 505–6.

55. Richburg, *Out of America*, p. 173.

56. These and other aspects of Ferguson's thought are discussed in Ernest Gellner's *Conditions of Liberty: Civil Society and Its Rivals*, Penguin Books, 1997.

57. John P. Powelson, *Centuries of Economic Endeavor*, p. 103.

58. Ernest Gellner, *Conditions of Liberty: Civil Society and Its Rivals*, pp. 71–72. [Emphasis added.]

59. Ibid., p. 8.

60. Ibid., p. 12.

Chapter 9

1. Adam Kuper, *Culture: The Anthropologists' Account*, Harvard University Press, Cambridge, Mass., 1999, pp. 25, 29.

2. A. L. Kroeber and Clyde Kluckhohn, *Culture: A Critical Review of Concepts and Definitions*, Random House, New York, (nd), p. 1. Originally published in 1952 as Vol. XLVII, No. 1 of the Papers of the Peabody Museum of American Archaeology and Ethnology, Harvard University. Notice that it is the old singular meaning of the term as a universal process which Kroeber and Kluckhohn are using here.

3. Paul J. Bohannan, *High Points in Anthropology*, Alfred A. Knopf, New York, 1973, p. xvi.

4. Adam Kuper, *Culture, The Anthropologists' Account*, Harvard University Press, 1999, p. 10.

5. Ibid., p. 245.

6. Ibid., p. 247.

7. Ernest Gellner, *Language and Solitude: Wittgenstein, Malinowski and the Habsburg Dilemma*, Cambridge University Press, 1998, p. 12.

8. Ernest Gellner, *Language and Solitude: Wittgenstein, Malinowski and the Habsburg Dilemma*, p. 21. Cf. "The principle that a culture is most stridently defended when it is irretrievably lost applies beyond issues of ethnicity. In the United States, it was the generation of Southerners born after the demise of the Confederacy who glorified the lost cause of the Civil War era and its aftermath, as in the motion picture classic, *Birth of a Nation* . . . and the grandest glorification of all, the novel and movie *Gone With the Wind*." Thomas Sowell, *Race and Culture: A World View*, BasicBooks, 1994, p. 29.

9. Ernest Gellner, *Language and Solitude*, p. 24.

10. Ibid., pp. 24–25.

11. Gellner, *Anthropology and Politics*, Blackwell, Oxford, 1995, p. 13.

12. Gellner, *Language and Solitude*, p. 33.

13. Ibid., p. 32.

14. Ibid., p. 37.

15. F. A. Hayek, "Ludwig von Mises (1881–1973)," *The Fortunes of Liberalism: Essays on Austrian Economics and the Ideal of Freedom*, Vol. IV of *The Collected Works of F. A. Hayek*, The University of Chicago Press, Chicago, 1992, p. 127.

16. Matthew Arnold, *Culture and Anarchy*, Cambridge University Press, 1963 (1868), pp. 6–7.

17. T. S. Eliot, *Notes Toward a Definition of Culture*, Faber & Faber, London, 1948, p. 120.

18. Ibid., p. 41.

19. Gellner, *Language and Solitude*, p. 68.

20. Ibid., p. 63.

21. Ibid., pp. 63–64.

22. Ibid., p. 153.

23. Fred Inglis, *Raymond Williams*, Routledge, London, 1995, p. 220.

24. Ibid., p. 84.

25. Ibid., p. 107.

26. Ibid., pp. 84, 182, 194, 227. The line about "liquidation" was from a left-wing pantomime. The Pol Pot statement can be found in Raymond Williams, *Politics and Letters: Interviews with* New Left Review, New Left Books, London, 1979, p. 395. Not surprisingly his biographer, Fred Inglis, loses all patience here: "Yes, many people do indeed draw back," he writes. "This is language filthy with dishonest use . . . It is not just culpable ignorance at work here, it is venal self-deception . . . [which disfigures] the best face of the Left's intelligentsia, the man who could be depended on to judge the events of the day justly." If Williams is what Inglis calls the best face of

NOTES

the Left-intelligentsia, one wonders uneasily what its worst face might have looked like in those times.

27. Ibid., p. 227.

28. Raymond Williams, *Keywords*, Fontana, London, 1976, p. 82.

29. Ian Gregor, comments in *Essays in Criticism*, Vol. IX, No. 4, pp. 425–30.

30. Raymond Williams, *Politics and Letters: Interviews with* New Left Review, NLB and Verso, London, 1981, p. 155.

31. John Sutherland, review of *Marxism and Literature*, by Raymond Williams, *New Statesman*, 19 August 1977.

32. Eliot, *Notes Toward a Definition of Culture*, p. 19.

33. Williams, *Politics and Letters*, p. 325.

34. Stefan Collini, "Badly Connected: The Passionate Intensity of Cultural Studies," *Victorian Studies* (Summer 1993), p. 457. Excerpted in Adam Kuper, *Culture, the Anthropologists' Account*, p. 230.

35. Inglis, *Raymond Williams*, p. 83.

36. Ibid., p. 50.

37. Achievements both of them are—political achievements—and both in their day have contributed to British life. It is the motive behind their reclassification which concerns us here.

38. Max Scheler, *Ressentiment*, Schocken Books, New York, 1972, p. 68.

39. Max Scheler, 'Das Ressentiment im Aufbau der Moralen,' *Gesammelte Werke*, Vol. 3, p. 121. Excerpted in Helmut Schoeck, *Envy: A Theory of Social Behaviour*, Liberty Fund, Indianapolis, 1987 (1966), p. 282.

Appendix

1. So was one of the first Englishmen to describe Aboriginal life in Australia, Captain Watkin Tench. "Several times in his narrative he alluded to Rousseau's views in order to repudiate them." L. R. Hiatt, *Arguments About Aborigines*, Cambridge University Press, 1996, p. 80.

2. Allan Hanson, "The Making of the Maori: Culture Invention and Its Logic," *American Anthropologist*, Vol. 91 (1989), p. 894. Regarding religiosity, ninety percent of those producing it are renegade Christians or Jews. Spurning their own religion, they incorporate a dimly perceived primaeval hodgepodge into their romantic fantasies.

3. Roger M. Keesing, "Creating the Past: Custom and Identity in the Contemporary Pacific," *The Contemporary Pacific*, Vol. 1, Nos. 1 & 2, Spring & Fall, 1989, p. 29.

4. William Arens, *The Man-Eating Myth: Anthropology & Anthropophagy*, Oxford University Press, New York, 1979; *Pocahontas*, Buena Vista/Walt Disney, animated feature film directed by Mike Gabriel and Eric Goldberg, 1995.

Bibliography

Arens, William. *The Man-Eating Myth: Anthropology & Anthropophagy*, Oxford University Press, New York, 1979.

Argyle, W. J. *The Fon of Dahomey*, Clarendon Press, Oxford, 1966.

Arndt, Bettina. "The Stolen Education," *The Sydney Morning Herald*, Spectrum, June 12, 1999.

Arnold, Matthew. *Culture and Anarchy*, Cambridge University Press, 1963 (1868).

Beaglehole, J. C. "I. L. G. Sutherland, 1897–1952," (obituary) *Journal of the Polynesian Society*, Vol. 61 (1952), 120–21.

Belich, James. *Making Peoples: A History of the New Zealanders*, Penguin Books, New Zealand, 1996.

Bell, Daniel. *The Cultural Contradictions of Capitalism*, BasicBooks, New York, 1976.

Berghe, Pierre L. van den. *Human Family Systems: An Evolutionary View*, Elsevier, 1979.

Berlin, Isaiah. *Four Essays on Liberty*, Oxford University Press, London, 1969.

Berlin, Isaiah. *Vico and Herder: Two Studies in the History of Ideas*, The Hogarth Press, London, 1976.

Berlin, Isaiah. *Concepts and Categories: Philosophical Essays*, The Hogarth Press, London, 1978.

Berlin, Isaiah. *Against the Current: Essays in the History of Ideas*, The Hogarth Press, London, 1979.

Berlin, Isaiah. *The Crooked Timber of Humanity*, John Murray, London, 1990.

Berlin, Isaiah. *The Roots of Romanticism*, Chatto & Windus, London, 1999.

Berlin, Isaiah, with Ramin Jahanbegloo. *Conversations with Isaiah Berlin*, Charles Scribner's Sons, New York, 1991.

Bernstein, Peter L. *Against the Gods: The Remarkable Story of Risk*, John Wiley & Sons, New York, 1998.

Best, Elsdon. *The Maori as He Was*, Dominion Museum, Wellington, 1934.

Bestor, Arthur E. *Backwoods Utopias*, University of Pennsylvania Press, Philadelphia, 1950.

Bethell, Tom. *The Noblest Triumph*, St. Martin's Press, New York, 1998.

Betzig, Laura. *Human Nature: A Critical Reader*, Oxford University Press, New York, 1997.

Biggs, Bruce. "In the Beginning," in Keith Sinclair, ed., *The Oxford Illustrated History of New Zealand*, Oxford University Press, New Zealand, 1996 (2d edition).

Bohannan, Paul J. *High Points in Anthropology*, Alfred A. Knopf, New York, 1973.

Bohannan, Paul, and George Dalton. "Karl Polanyi, 1886–1964," *American Anthropologist*, Vol. 67, 1965, 1508–1511.

Bozeman, Adda B. *Conflict in Africa: Concepts and Realities*, Princeton University Press, Princeton, New Jersey, 1976.

Buck, Peter. "Introduction," in Sutherland, I. L. G. (ed.), *The Maori People Today*.

Burton, R. F. *A Mission to Gelele, King of Dahomey*, 2 Vols. London, 1893 (1864).

Buruma, Ian. "Divine Killer," *The New York Review of Books*, February 24, 2000.

C., A. E. and R. M. C., "I. L. G. Sutherland, 1897–1952," (obituary) *Journal of the Polynesian Society*, Vol. 61 (1952) 121–127.

Caffrey, Margaret M. *Ruth Benedict, Stranger in This Land*, University of Texas Press, Austin, 1989.

Carden, Maren L. *Oneida: Utopian Community to Modern Corporation*, The Johns Hopkins Press, Baltimore, 1969.

Carsten, F. L. *The First Austrian Republic, 1918–1938*, Gower/Maurice Temple Smith, Cambridge, England, 1986.

Chagnon, Napoleon. *Yanomamo: The Fierce People*, Holt, Rinehart, & Winston, New York, 1968.

Cipolla, Carlo M. *Clocks and Culture, 1300–1700*, Collins, London, 1967.

Collini, Stefan. "Badly Connected: The Passionate Intensity of Cultural Studies," *Victorian Studies* (Summer 1993).

Congdon, Lee. "Polanyi in Hungary, 1900–1919," *Journal of Contemporary History*, Vol. 11 (1976).

Cowley, Malcolm. *Exile's Return*, Viking, New York, 1968 (1934).

Crocker, Lester G. *Jean-Jacques Rousseau: The Quest (1712–1758)*, Macmillan, New York, 1968.

Cubeddu, Raimondo. *The Philosophy of the Austrian School*, Routledge, London, 1993.

Darnell, Regna. *Edward Sapir*, University of California Press, Berkeley, 1990.

Dawkins, Richard. *River Out of Eden*, Weidenfeld and Nicolson, London, 1995.

de Soto, Hernando. *The Other Path: The Invisible Revolution in the Third World*, Harper & Row, New York, 1989.

Drucker, Peter F. *Adventures of a Bystander*, Harper & Row, New York, 1979.

Duczynska, Ilona. *Workers in Arms: The Austrian Schutzbund and the Civil War of 1934*, Monthly Review Press, New York and London, 1978.

Eberhart, Mark E. "Why Things Break," *Scientific American*, October 1999.

Edgerton, Robert B. *Sick Societies*, The Free Press, New York, 1992.

Eliot, T. S. *Notes Toward a Definition of Culture*, Faber & Faber, London, 1948.

Elvin, Mark. "China as a Counterfactual," in *Europe and the Rise of Capitalism*, edited by Jean Baechler, John A. Hall, and Michael Mann, Basil Blackwell, Oxford, England, 1988.

Engels, Friedrich. *The Origin of the Family, Private Property, and the State*, New World Paperbacks, New York, 1972.

Ergang, Robert. *Herder and the Foundations of German Nationalism*, 1976 [1931].

Fairbank, John K., and Merle Goldman. *China: A New History*, Harvard University Press, Cambridge, Mass., 1998.

Ferguson, Adam. *An Essay on the History of Civil Society*, London, 1773, p. 205 [Facsimile reprint by Gregg International Publishers, 1969].

Ferguson, Adam. *Principles of Moral and Political Science*, printed for A. Strahan and T. Cadell, London, and W. Creech, Edinburgh, 1792, Vol 1.

Figes, Eva. *Patriarchal Atttitudes*, Fawcett, Greenwich, Conn., 1971.

Flannery, Tim. *The Future Eaters*, Reed Books, Melbourne, Australia, 1995.

Foster, Lawrence. *Religion and Sexuality*, Oxford University Press, New York, 1981.

Franklin, Benjamin. *A Benjamin Franklin Reader*, edited by Nathan G. Goodman, Thomas Y. Crowell Company, New York, 1945.

Freeman, Derek. *The Fateful Hoaxing of Margaret Mead*, Westview Press, Boulder, Colo., 1999.

Freud, S. *Civilization and Its Discontents*, The Hogarth Press Ltd, London, 1951.

Gellner, Ernest. *Spectacles and Predicaments*, Cambridge University Press, Cambridge, U.K., 1979.

Gellner, Ernest. *Plough, Sword and Book: The Structure of Human History*, Collins Harvill, London, 1988.

Gellner, Ernest. *Postmodernism, Reason, and Religion*, Routledge, London, 1992.

Gellner, Ernest. *Nationalism*, Weidenfeld, London, 1997.

Gellner, Ernest. *Conditions of Liberty: Civil Society and Its Rivals*, Penguin Books, London, 1997.

Gellner, Ernest. *Language and Solitude: Wittgenstein, Malinowski and the Habsburg Dilemma*, Cambridge University Press, Cambridge, U.K., 1998.

Graña, César, and Marigay Graña, eds. *On Bohemia: the Code of the Self-Exiled*, Transaction Publishers, New Jersey, 1990.

Graña, César. *Bohemian Versus Bourgeois*. BasicBooks, New York, 1964.

Gregor, Ian. *Essays in Criticism*, Vol. 9, No 4.

Haley, Brian D., and Larry Wilcoxon, "Anthropology and the Making of Chumash Tradition," *Current Anthropology*, Vol. 38, No. 5, December 1997.

Hall, John A. *Powers and Liberties: The Causes and Consequences of the Rise of the West*, Basil Blackwell, London, 1985.

Hanson, Allan. "The Making of the Maori: Culture Invention and Its Logic," *American Anthropologist*, Vol. 91 (1989).

Harris, Marvin. *The Rise of Anthropological Theory*, Columbia University Press, New York, 1968.

Hayek, F. A. *The Three Sources of Human Values*, The London School of Economics and Political Science, London, 1978.

Hayek, F. A. *Knowledge, Evolution, and Society*, Adam Smith Institute, London, 1983.

Hayek, F. A. *The Fatal Conceit: The Errors of Socialism*, University of Chicago Press, Chicago, 1988.

Hayek, F. A. "Ludwig von Mises (1881–1973)," *The Fortunes of Liberalism: Essays on Austrian Economics and the Ideal of Freedom*, Vol. IV of The Collected Works of F. A. Hayek, The University of Chicago Press, Chicago, 1992, p. 127.

Herskovits, Melville. *Dahomey: An Ancient West African Kingdom*, 2 Vols. J. J. Augustin, New York, 1938.

Hiatt, L. R. "Mutant Message Down Under: A New Age for an Old People," *Quadrant*, June, 1997.

Hiatt, L. R. *Arguments About Aborigines*, Cambridge University Press, Cambridge, U.K., 1996.

Hildebrandt, George H. "Economic Systems: Post-War Planning" (Review of *The Great Transformation*), *The American Economic Review*, June 1946.

Howard, Jane. *Margaret Mead: A Life*, Simon & Schuster, New York, 1984.

Humphreys, S. C. "History, Economics, and Anthropology: The Work of Karl Polanyi," *History and Theory*, Vol. 8, No. 2, (1969), pp. 165–212.

Ignatieff, Michael. *Isaiah Berlin: A Life*, Chatto & Windus, London, 1998.

Ignotus, Paul. "The Hungary of Michael Polanyi," in *The Logic of Personal Knowledge: Essays Presented to Michael Polanyi on his Seventieth Birthday, 11th March 1961*, Routledge and Kegan Paul, London, 1961.

Inglis, Fred. *Raymond Williams*, Routledge, London, 1995.

Johnson, Garfield. "The Young Shoots of the Flax," in *1840–1990: A Long White Cloud?*, Citizens Association for Racial Equality, Auckland, 1989.

Johnson, Paul. *Modern Times*, Harper & Row, New York, 1983.

Johnson, Paul. *Intellectuals*, Weidenfeld & Nicolson, London, 1988.

Johnston, William M. *The Austrian Mind*, University of California Press, Berkeley, 1972.

Kanter, Rosabeth M. *Commitment and Community*, Harvard University Press, Cambridge, Mass., 1972.

Keen, Ian. "Aboriginal Beliefs vs. Mining at Coronation Hill: The Containing Force of Traditionalism," *Human Organization*, Vol. 52, No. 4, 1993.

Keesing, Roger M. "Creating the Past: Custom and Identity in the Contemporary Pacific," *The Contemporary Pacific*, Vol. 1, Nos. 1 & 2, Spring & Fall, 1989.

Kenny, Chris. *It would be nice if there were some women's business: The story behind the Hindmarsh Island Affair*, Duffy & Snellgrove, Sydney, 1996.

Keynes, John Maynard. *General Theory of Employment, Interest and Money*, London, 1936.

Koepke, Wulf, ed. *Johann Gottfried Herder: Language, History, and the Enlightenment*, Camden House, South Carolina, 1990.

Kroeber, A. L., and Clyde Kluckhohn, *Culture: A Critical Review of Concepts and Definitions*, Random House, New York, (nd), p. 1. Originally published in 1952 as Vol. XLVII, No. 1 of the Papers of the Peabody Museum of American Archaeology and Ethnology, Harvard University.

Kuper, Adam. *Culture: The Anthropologists' Account*, Harvard University Press, Cambridge, Mass., 1999.

Landes, David. *The Wealth and Poverty of Nations*, Little, Brown and Company, Boston, 1998.

Laslett, Peter, and Richard Wall, eds. *Household and Family in Past Time*, Cambridge University Press, London, 1972.

Law, R. *The Slave Coast of Africa, 1550–1750*, Oxford University Press, Oxford, U.K., 1991.

Leacock, Eleanor. Introduction to Friedrich Engels, *The Origin of the Family, Private Property, and the State*, New York, New World Paperbacks, 1972.

Lévi-Strauss, Claude. *Tristes Tropiques*, Hutchinson, London, 1961.

Lovejoy, Arthur O., and George Boas. *Primitivism and Related ideas in Antiquity*, The Johns Hopkins University Press, Baltimore, 1935.

Lovell, Mary S. *A Rage to Live: A Biography of Richard and Isabel Burton*, Little, Brown and Company, Boston, 1998.

Macfarlane, Alan. *The Origins of English Individualism: The Family, Property, and Social Transition*, Basil Blackwell, London, 1978.

Maning, F. E. *Old New Zealand*, Golden Press, Auckland, 1973 (1887).

Manuel, Frank E., and Fritzie P. Manuel. *Utopian Thought in the Western World*, Basil Blackwell, Oxford, 1979.

Mead, Margaret. *Coming of Age in Samoa*, Penguin Books, 1966 (1928).

Mead, Margaret. *Blackberry Winter: My Earlier Years*, Morrow, New York, 1972.

Meek, Ronald L. *Social Science and the Ignoble Savage*, Cambridge University Press, 1976.

Melville, Keith. *Communes in the Counter Culture*. William Morrow & Co., New York, 1972.

Mill, John Stuart. *Principles of Political Economy*, Longmans, Green. (6th Edition), 1865.

Mill, John Stuart. *Autobiography*, Penguin Classics, 1973.

Minogue, Kenneth. *Waitangi, Morality and Reality*, New Zealand Round Table, Wellington, New Zealand, 1998.

Montesquieu, *Spirit of the Laws*, Book XI.

Mosse, G. L. *The Crisis of German Ideology*, H. Fertig, New York, 1981.

Near, Henry. *The Kibbutz Movement, a History*, Oxford University Press, Oxford, 1992, Vol. 1.

Ngata, Apirana. "Maori Land Settlement," in Sutherland, I. L. G., ed. *The Maori People Today*.

North, Douglass C., and Robert Paul Thomas. *The Rise of the Western World: A New Economic History*, Cambridge University Press, New York, 1973.

Noyes, John Humphrey. *History of American Socialisms*, J. B. Lippincott & Co., Philadelphia, 1870.

Noyes, Pierrepont. *My Father's House*, Farrar and Rinehart, New York, 1937.

Pipes, Richard. *Property and Freedom*, The Harvill Press, London, 1999.

Pocahontas, Buena Vista/Walt Disney, animated feature film directed by Mike Gabriel and Eric Goldberg, 1995.

Polanyi, Karl. *The Great Transformation*, Rinehart & Company, New York, 1944.

Polanyi, Karl. *Dahomey and the Slave Trade: An Analysis of an Archaic Economy*, University of Washington Press, Seattle and London, 1966.

Polanyi, Karl. *Primitive, Archaic, and Modern Economies. Essays of Karl Polanyi*, edited by George Dalton, Doubleday and Company, New York, 1968.

Polanyi, Karl. *The Livelihood of Man*, edited by Harry W. Pearson, Academic Press, New York, 1977.

Polanyi, Michael. "The Growth of Thought in Society," *Economica*, 8 (1941).

Polanyi, Michael. "The Span of Central Direction," in *The Logic of Liberty: Reflections and Rejoinders*, Routledge and Kegan Paul, London, 1951.

Polanyi, Michael. *The Logic of Liberty: Reflections and Rejoinders*, Routledge and Kegan Paul, London, 1951.

Popper, K. R. *The Open Society and Its Enemies*, 2 volumes. Routledge & Kegan Paul, London, Fifth Edition (revised), 1966.

Popper, K. R. *Unended Quest: An Intellectual Autobiography*. Routledge, London, 1992.

Powelson, John P. *Centuries of Economic Endeavor*, The University of Michigan Press, Ann Arbor, 1994.

Preston, Douglas. "Cannibals of the Canyon," *New Yorker*, Nov. 30, 1998, 76–89.

Richburg, Keith B. *Out of America: A Black Man Confronts Africa*, BasicBooks, New York, 1997.

Rousseau, Jean-Jacques. *A Discourse on Inequality* (translated and with an Introduction by Maurice Cranston), Penguin Books, 1984.

Rousseau, Jean-Jacques. *Lettres à Malesherbes*, No 1.

Russell, Bertrand. *History of Western Philosophy*, George Allen & Unwin, 1961 (1946).

Sandall, Roger. "Herskovits' Last Day in Dahomey," *Anthropology Today*, Vol. 15, No. 6, December 1999.

Scheler, Max. "Das Ressentiment im Aufbau der Moralen," *Gesammelte Werke*, Vol 3.

Scheler, Max. *Ressentiment*, Schocken Books, New York, 1972.

Schoeck, Helmut *Envy: A Theory of Social Behaviour*, Liberty Fund, Indianapolis, 1987 (1966).

Shaw, T. et al., eds. *The Archaeology of Africa*. Routledge, 1995 (1st printing 1993).

Simkin, Colin. "The Birth of *The Open Society*, a Personal Reminiscence," *Quadrant*, December, 1990.

Sinclair, Keith. *A History of New Zealand*. Penguin Books, 1959.

Smith, Adam. *The Wealth of Nations*, Penguin Books 1997 (1776).

Smith, Hedrick. *The Russians*, Sphere Books, London, 1972.

Snyderman, George S., and William Josephs, "Bohemia, the Underworld of Art," in César Graña and Marigay Graña, eds. *On Bohemia: The Code of the Self-Exiled*.

Sowell, Thomas. *Race and Culture: A World View*, BasicBooks, New York, 1994.

Sowell, Thomas. *Conquests and Cultures*, BasicBooks, New York, 1998.

Spindler, Konrad. *The Man in the Ice*, Orion Books, New York, 1995.

Stanfield, J. R. *The Economic Thought of Karl Polanyi*, Macmillan, London, 1986.

Starcke, Carl Nicolai. *The Primitive Family in Its Origin and Development*, University of Chicago Press, Chicago, 1976 (1889).

Stocking, George W., Jr., ed. *Malinowski, Rivers, Benedict and Others: Essays on Culture and Personality* (History of Anthropology, Vol. 4), University of Wisconsin Press, Madison, 1986.

Stocking, George W., Jr., ed. *Romantic Motives: Essays on Anthropological Sensibility*, (History of Anthropology, Vol. 6) University of Wisconsin Press, Madison, 1989.

Stocking, George W. Jr. *Victorian Anthropology*, The Free Press, New York, 1987.

Sutherland, I. L. G., "The Maori Situation," in I. L. G. Sutherland, *The Maori People Today*.

Sutherland, I. L. G., ed., *The Maori People Today*, Oxford University Press, London, 1940.

Sutherland, John. Review of *Marxism and Literature*, by Raymond Williams, *New Statesman*, August 19, 1977.

Tiger, Lionel, and Joseph Shepher. *Women in the Kibbutz*, Harcourt Brace Jovanovich, New York, 1975.

Vargas Llosa, Mario. "Foreword," in Hernando de Soto, *The Other Path: The Invisible Revolution in the Third World*, Harper & Row, New York, 1989.

Veblen, Thorstein. *The Theory of the Leisure Class*, George Allen & Unwin, London, 1949 (1899).

Vesey, Laurence. *The Communal Experience*, University of Chicago Press, Chicago, 1978.

Waldegrave, Charles. "Enemies or Partners?" in *1840–1990: A Long White Cloud?*, Citizens Association for Racial Equality, Auckland, 1989.

West, Rebecca. *Black Lamb and Grey Falcon*, Vol. 1, Macmillan & Co., London, 1943.

Widmer, Kingsley. "The Diogenes Style," in César Graña and Marigay Graña, eds., *On Bohemia: The Code of the Self-Exiled*.

Williams, Raymond. *Keywords*, Fontana, London, 1976.

Williams, Raymond. *Politics and Letters: Interviews with* New Left Review, NLB *and* Verso, London, 1981.

Wrigley, E. A. *People, Cities and Wealth: The Transformation of Traditional Society*, Basil Blackwell, London, 1987.

Index